First published in Great Britain as a soft back, 2024.

Typeset in Baskerville Old Face (Body), Generic Teenager (Titles), Arial Regular (back cover). and Impact (spine).

Editing, design, typesetting & publishing by Garter Press

ISBN: 978-1-7395571-0-2

Cover images by © Daniel Inman

www.danielinmanauthor.com

For my mother

ACKNOWLEDGEMENTS

I am grateful to His Majesty, King Charles III who, in 1984, while Prince of Wales, described the extension to the National Gallery in London as, "a monstrous carbuncle on a well-loved face."

My thanks also go to many people without whose guidance, support and advice this book would not have been possible.

I am indebted in particular to, Donna Bruce, Bob Wilde, Suzannah Brissenden, Maria Jones, Suzanne Lane, Carole Lattin, Leila Reid, Storm Johnson, Margaret Armstrong, and last, but by no means least, Michael K Foster.

I met a traveller from an antique land,
Who said—"Two vast and trunkless legs of stone
Stand in the desert. . . . Near them, on the sand,
Half sunk a shattered visage lies, whose frown,
And wrinkled lip, and sneer of cold command,
Tell that its sculptor well those passions read
Which yet survive, stamped on these lifeless things,
The hand that mocked them, and the heart that fed;
And on the pedestal, these words appear:
My name is Ozymandias, King of Kings;
Look on my Works, ye Mighty, and despair!
Nothing beside remains. Round the decay
Of that colossal Wreck, boundless and bare
The lone and level sands stretch far away."

- Percy Bysshe Shelley

One

Witton-le-Cone
September 2013

Laurence Boyle always allowed the telephone on his desk to ring at least six times before picking it up. Keeping others on the hop was something he relished.

As the principal of Titas College, he presided over an institution that merged both the Durham and West Durham colleges of further education. Nicknamed, "The Cathedral", it had been built only a couple of years before on the site of Witton-le-Cone's demolished, glass civic centre, consuming also the local police station, a neighbouring supermarket and, against much local protest, many adjacent allotment gardens. The main building featured a central tower with something resembling a short spire in the middle of its roof, and on the four sides of the tower were enormous clock faces.

After the seventh ring, Boyle had picked up and was being made rapidly aware of a pressing concern. Sitting behind his enormous desk, his uppermost chin pegged his jowls into place, and the receiver pinned to his ear by a shoulder.

'I need a risk assessment on the safety of everything at the top of the tower, and I need it today,' he barked down the line. 'There's bound to be an inquest and some termite will probably come poking around...

'...If there is anything, and I mean *anything,* wanting, it needs to be corrected tomorrow morning, or in the next few days at the most. And another thing, I'm relying on you to get it done as quickly and as quietly as possible. You catch my drift?'

'...*Of course* the door to the viewing platform should be locked. The scene will need to be uncontaminated in case of an investigation by the coroner, police, or some other nosy bastard.'

What he heard next caused him to simmer. 'If it was supposed to have been locked before the "accident", how the hell did Villiers get up there in the first place?'

More excuses followed from the other end.

'...You don't know because your department doesn't have the keys! Passing the buck, eh? In that case, who could've got hold of keys to the roof?'

'...Was the access to the keys risk assessed?' A hint of sarcasm began to taint Boyle's delivery.

The reply caused a small sigh of relief. '...Good, well, in that case the fault lies squarely with whoever left the door to the roof unlocked. Even so, you must keep the assessment unavailable to anybody. And I mean *anybody.*'

Boyle placed his hands on his desk and leant back in his seat, the receiver still wedged against his ear. He usually avoided using the device's conference facility as one never knew what termites could be listening in. '... Irregular or not, I am The Maestro. I want you to take the existing risk assessment out of the files and destroy it. Wipe it clean from all the systems that could hold it. If there is a hard copy, shred it. The prying eyes of the Inquest must never see it, is that clear?'

He sighed at the reply. 'Just do it. Get a new handrail put in, TOMORROW. Then carry out a new risk assessment when it complies. It's vital we don't get taken to the cleaners for negligence, especially with certain outsiders likely to be sniffing around. And by the way...?

'...I don't need your conscience. When I tell you to do something, I do not expect an inertia-reeled heart string. Remember, if any vice-principal places herself - or himself - as an outsider, I will have absolutely no compunction getting rid. Is that clear?'

Hanging up the receiver, he sniffed dismissively.

The things I have to think of.

TWO

After a hard day's grind at the college, Margaret Bulmer, known as "Grit", stood at home preparing dinner for herself and her nine year old son, George, in the back room of their terraced house.

'What's this?' asked George in a surly fashion, as he sat before the place she had just set at the table.

'Spanakotyropita.'

He looked baffled.

'Little pies with cheese and spinach,' she explained. "They're delicious. Really!' Grit was trying to sound enthusiastic about the food she had prepared and frozen at the weekend, and warmed up in the microwave.

George stabbed his fork into one of them and lifted it up, regarding it with deep suspicion. 'It looks like seaweed with snot in it,' he observed with a grimace.

'Do try it, darling. What did you have for lunch?'

'Chicken nuggets and chips.'

Grit sighed as she picked up the salad bowl, 'Would you like some salad?'

'No.'

'No what?'

'No, I don't want any salad.'

Grit let the wooden salad bowl drop to the table with a bang. 'George, darling, you are really starting to try my patience.'

'How?'

Her annoyance rising, she changed the subject. The events of the past week had left her tetchy as well, 'How was kick-boxing?'

'Good. I managed to kick the teacher in the ribs. And the boy I was practising with, Thomas, well I flattened him four times.' George reluctantly picked up one of the spanakotyropita again and began gnawing at the pastry.

'How many times did he flatten you?'

'Only three, so I won.'

'You're enjoying it, then?'

'Yeah, it's good.' Little enthusiasm accompanied the lowering of the pie-on-his-fork before George picked off a bit of pastry containing a small amount of the snotty seaweed filling, putting it into his mouth. 'Yuck!'

'Do you want to stop going?'

'No, I'll keep going. You're my single mother and I have to be able to protect you.'

'I do know how to look after myself, George.'

He shrugged and dropped the fork on his plate.

'Are you going to eat that?'

George shook his head and Grit sighed again. 'So what would you like to have?'

'Burger and chips.'

'Not burger and chips again! Honestly, I'm doing my best not to raise a philistine, but my seeds fall on stony ground. Alas.'

'What's a philipstine?'

'Someone who isn't interested in trying or learning about new things.'

'You mean not interested in trying spankycrapita?'

Having gone to the lengths of preparing something new which included *a vegetable*, Grit realised she had perhaps bitten off more than she could chew. 'I mean new things generally.'

'I'm not a philipstine. I like trying new computer games.'

'That's *wonderful,* darling.'

Leaving her dinner half-eaten, Grit had got up, retrieved a burger and plastic bag of frozen chips from the freezer, putting the former on the griddle and emptying the contents of the latter sardonically onto a metal tray.

Her thoughts turned to the main event of the day, Horace Villiers falling to his death from the main tower at the college. She couldn't stand the man, but as the one and only staff governor at Titas College, this was definitely something that should concern her, she thought. But how could she approach the subject with the board?

'Why don't you make the dinner when I come in from work, George?' she asked, back in the moment.

'I wouldn't know how. Anyway, that's your job, isn't it?'

Grit was about to make the comparison between the relative division of labour between this one-parent family and the one she had grown up in, but remembered how she hated it when adults - especially several teachers when she was at school - suggested her generation had it easy compared with those that had gone before.

She had often thought, but hardly ever articulated, *you seriously think my life is a walk in the park?* In spite of this she was about to do the same inter-generational thing. "Kids are spoilt nowadays." On the other hand, it was probably a gender issue. Men always got the lion's share, didn't they?

Grit stopped herself just in time, but the thought vexed her nonetheless. 'Why should it be my job?'

'I dry the dishes after, don't I?' Answering one question with another was a ploy he often employed.

'Yes darling and it *is* a big help.'

On the back of this praise, he changed the subject to something he wanted, 'There's this computer game I've got to have for my GammaTerminus.'

'What's that?'

'Zombie Expunger Two.'

'I thought you wanted "Build a Torture Chamber".'

'Yeah, well I'd like that, but I had a go on Brandon's Zombie Expunger. It's awesome. Your missions are to find zombies and exterminate them.'

'Charming. How do you do that?'

'Do what?'

'Exterminate them.'

'You have to knock a wooden stake right between their eyes. It can be tricky 'cos they are moving all the time.' He picked up his knife and pointed it downwards, patting the end of the handle.

'Don't do that, darling, you'll mark the table. How long have you been playing this game for?'

'Two weeks. It's Brandon's and he won't let me play it much.'

'Why not?'

'He's only on Level Four and I'd be on Level Five before him if he gave me the mission time.'

'I think I'd better have a word with Brandon's mam. Does she know he plays this game?'

'Dunno. Probablys.'

Having eaten her dinner, Grit had moved her chair next to a slightly open casement window, lit a cigarette and held it in the gap. 'George, darling, if you think this will help your case then you might be disappointed.'

Grit took a hard draw on the cigarette and blew it out in the general direction of the window, but the smoke was wafted back indoors by a sudden malty draft coming from the direction of Richards's brewery.

He folded his arms and pushed out his bottom lip, 'Brandon's got it and he's three days younger than I am.'

Grit picked up an ashtray with a long, thin arm, and flicked the ash from her tab into it, 'That doesn't mean you should have it as well.'

'Phwoah, it costs less than a week's worth of your cancer sticks.' He flapped his hands in front of his face as the now nicotine-tainted malty draught reached him.

She twirled a dark gel-sharpened side-burn in front of her ear and looked down at the lighted tab. 'I need these. I'm an addict, and I've got a lot to put up with.'

George had been down this route with his mother many times, so returned undeterred to his new pet subject. 'I like the school Zombie Expunger, 'cos you can kill teachers who've turned into zombies.'

'They aren't letting you play it in school are they?' Grit was dismayed but not at all surprised.

'Nooo, on the game, one of your theatres of expunging is a school. One of the zombies looks like Miss Roberts. You should see how the brains explode out of her. The noise she makes is wicked. Take that, mega-bitch!' George had picked up the salad bowl and whacked the handle end of his knife with its base, causing a slight indentation on the wooden table top.

'What the hell are you doing?' exclaimed Grit, shocked by this action.

'Expunging Miss Roberts,' replied George as though he were talking about tying his shoelaces.

'You've marked the table now! What have I told you about playing with knives?'

* * *

'Can I have Zombie Expunger Two for Christmas, then?' repeated George again on his way to bed.

'I said I'll have to look into it. Do you know what the recommended age is?'

'No. So I might get it?'

'I don't want to get your hopes up.'

'So you will, then!'

'I didn't say that. Goodnight, darling.'

'Night Mam.'

The topic of Zombie Expunger lead seamlessly back to the matter that had been troubling Grit for the past week. Who were the zombies on the board of governors at Titas College? Could they all be zombies in fact, working together or placed there by some higher power to ensure total domination by the Principal? The thought of Boyle as the Zombie Master made Grit shudder: there was to be a governors' meeting tomorrow for which, given Villiers's death, she felt less well-prepared than ever.

* * *

The local English department was the first to be hit by new contracts. Grit thought she ought to stay on top of the game by applying as soon as possible. She had completed her application that evening. This meant agreeing to greater duties, unspecified working hours, a twenty percent pay cut, and also to teaching something she had avoided hitherto like the plague called "Basic Skills". It galled her that she had been unable to do anything about these changes. But what could she do against The Maestro?

Grit had not finished her marking until after midnight, but her mind kept pulling back to Villiers's death. Could Maestro or his coterie have had anything to do with it? Was she just being paranoid? Either way, this was still a matter that demanded what little attention she had to spare.

Getting into bed, Grit suddenly remembered some enigmatic words said by a tall stranger she had met in the college's smokers' corner that morning: *Villiers had a good case.* It had gone over her head at the time. Did this mean the man was some sort of a lawyer? What did he mean by it? How exactly was he looking forward to helping Villiers? If so, what on earth was the man doing at the college?

'Maybe I'll find out. If I see him again I should probably ask... ask.' With that she finally fell asleep.

Three

The next morning, Grit had woken with a dull ache in her stomach. After dropping George off at school, she headed to work. Listening Tom Petty, playing on the car stereo, "I won't back down", she began to think George's aspersions about the spanakotyropita well founded.

Arriving at her "workspace", Grit searched in her drawer and took a couple of peptic pills, but it made no difference at all, niggling her throughout the GCSE English Literature class. By lunch time she could just about eat, but wasn't hungry, so had only half a sandwich. Then it occurred to her that this was no tummy bug. Rather, it might have been caused by the stress of having to face the dreaded Board of Governors' meeting that afternoon.

* * *

Still nursing these thoughts, she waited for the meeting to start. The board room was large but claustrophobic. Slithers of light were given permission to enter by two tall but very narrow windows at one end. The ceiling seemed an infinite distance away behind a large circle of LED lights suspended somewhere between board members and vice-principals which surrounded them. If George wanted to build a torture chamber, she thought, he could do worse than visit this place for ideas.

Grey, thick-pile carpets adorned the floor and walls, deadening, but not preventing, an echo from above of all that was said - or whispered. Board members, including

Grit, were treated to luxurious, reclining leather chairs, which incorporated small desks, integral lamps, and microphones that could be turned on or off by the occupant of the seat. There were also flashing red lights, rather like those on self-service checkouts at supermarkets, intended to gain the attention of the chair.

As the backs of board members were effectively lit by the circle of lights, the size of their chairs afforded some protection against any of Titas College's twenty three blood-thirsty vice-principals seated behind, gnashing at the bit, restrained only by the principal's invisible reins. These predators had to make do with ordinary office chairs, poised to make a lightning attack on any duck occupying a recliner in front.

The sense that anything she wanted to say would have its blood sucked out of it by the consensus of zombies left Grit feeling overwhelmed even before the meeting opened... Or was it only vampires that sucked blood? George probably knew.

Sitting there, she did her best to observe those that had already arrived. She switched her desk lamp off temporarily. It took several seconds adapting to the dimness to see well enough for her comparison between board members, and George's description of the game he wanted, to be confirmed with startling accuracy.

As Grit struggled to find a collective noun with which to describe them, the chairperson, Councillor Mrs Phyllis Roberts, known behind her back as "Mrs Propalot", took her place on what looked like an elevated lavatory, before Boyle's voice sounded through the chamber, silencing the room.

He was in conversation with Alison Morrell, one of his closest allies. 'I ABSOLUTELY HATE BLOWN-AIR HAND DRYERS,' he barked. 'Did you know that they circulate tiny bits of poo around the room?'

'I heard Engineering had a brief from Richards's brewery to develop one that doesn't do that.'

'Always keen, as I am, to encourage College to work with local enterprise, I'll be sticking with towels, thank you,' he said as he took his place next to the lavatory.

'Very good, Maestro,' said Morrell, heading to her own seat.

Grit pressed a button on her console, causing her red lamp to flash on and off. The words, *please wait; someone is coming to help you,* recited themselves several times in her head.

'Excuse me, Chair?' she called out, eventually, 'I wondered where in the meeting I could raise the matter of Horace Villiers's death.'

'There isn't anywhere, Miss Bulmer,' the words emerged sourly from the relative darkness, 'Please will you turn your flashing light off?'

'I thought meetings normally had a section at the end called *Any Other Business*.'

'We don't do that any more. It isn't best practice. Members have to be inflamed of any derision to be taken at the meeting at least three days before.'

'Isn't that at your discretion, Chair?'

The gloaming produced a long sigh. 'Only if there is an insurgency.'

'Surely it is very insurgent, urgent I mean, if one of our colleagues has just died on the premises in uncertain circumstances.' Had Grit been able to see the chairperson clearly, she would have noticed the expression of suspicion bearing down upon her.

'What decisions would you like the board to take going forward, Miss Bulmer?'

Grit resisted the urge to shut up, as her gut was telling her. 'There are a few questions I would like to ask. What actually caused Dr Villiers to fall from the tower? Could he have been pushed? Might it have been an accident? If so, was College's health and safety up to scratch? If it was suicide, could it have been because of the pressures of his work here? Could other members of staff be under similar pressures? If so, what can we do about it?' If she couldn't do anything about the new contracts, at least the event had given her a chance to imply their folly.

Given that one of his band members had stepped forward to play a solo in the wrong key, Boyle/the principal/The Maestro replied, 'I agree with Margaret that the death of a member of staff this way is a *tragedy*.' His vowels were long-drawn out as he did his best to make his adenoidal voice sound sympathetic. 'I understand the police are investigating, but until the inquest has been completed...' He shot an unseen warning glance towards Grit, but the sinister note in his voice was all too clear, '... it would be *very* dangerous to start talking about it based on hearsay.'

'That's all very well,' said Grit.

'I think that settees the matter for now, Miss Bulmer.'

'I was just going to say that I think we should send our condolences to his family – as representatives of Titas College.'

'That's a very good idea,' said Boyle, 'Of course we can do this as a board of governors. I have already sent my – personal – condolences to his family.'

Boyle appeared sincere, but Grit didn't believe it. In fact she had impressed herself by her manoeuvre. Disagreeing with her sentiments surely risked embarrassment.

'Also,' Grit added, 'I think we as a board should be doing all we can to get to the bottom of it, police or no police, to make sure this doesn't happen again.'

The meeting stiffened.

'But we must WAIT FOR THE FINDINGS OF THE INQUEST.' insisted Boyle.

Grit knew this was correct, but felt herself resisting a zombie-like desire to sweep the matter under the carpet. 'Surely we have a duty of care, and we need to be concerned.'

Boyle looked at his watch. 'Can I move progress, Chair?'

'Yes, of course. First on the agenda is the new vision statement for College.'

'I have had a meeting with the public relations focus group.' Boyle turned on a sixpence from sinister consolation to abundant enthusiasm. 'We are very excited about this. Our new vision statement will be "SHINE". This is the acronym of the five words which best encompass Titas College going forward.' He pressed a button, sparking up a projected PowerPoint next to the front desk and the word appeared in neon colours. 'These words are-

'"Support" because we have a particularly supportive environment here at Titas. If anybody wishes to voice an alternative opinion, I expect them to refrain from doing so...

'...Oh yes, "Humility" is something we should all aim for in all our dealings with everyone, staff, students... inspectors!' A weak laugh followed.

'"Inclusion", because Titas is an inclusive college. I don't think anyone could disagree with that, although if they do, then I'll see to it that he or she is not included, if you follow me...'

'I think we all understand that, Maestro,' the Chair interjected.

'I would hope you do... "Nurture" is something Titas College does very well. That is particularly important, because it shows the *caring* side of Titas, especially for students embarking on their learning journey, perhaps after having a bad start at school...

'...Finally, "Embolden" is something we do with our students, giving them the confidence to go out into the world and tackle it head on.

'Very oppressive indeed!' said the Chair, clearly impressed.

'As you see,' Boyle continued, 'these words encapsulate the learning experience at Titas from start to finish.'

'Can I make a proposal, Chair?' asked Grit.

Boyle and the Chair sighed in sync. 'Please make it brief, Miss Bulmer. We are pressed for time'.

'Replace the word, "nurture" with "thrive". I think nurture a slightly pretentious word, but equally we want our students to thrive, both while they are here and after they have left the college.'

'The suppository vision statement has already been passed by PR, Miss Bulmer,' said the Chair. 'I'm not sure it would be in order to accept atonements to it at this stage.'

'Couldn't we send it back to the PR committee for its thoughts?' asked Grit, trying to sound as innocent as she could.

'The vision statement should be agreed at this meeting ready for its launch in the new year,' said Boyle.

Chuckling, the elderly Cyril Richards spoke out, 'We've a couple more meetings before then when we can agree it. And I actually prefer, "Thrive". "Nurture" makes me think of plants. This is a college, not a bloomin' garden centre.'

The Chair sighed again, 'It looks as if we have a proposer and a seconder.' She looked at Boyle, dazzling him with her laser glasses, asking hopefully, 'Is there any reason we can recluse this motion, Maestro?'

Before he could reply, Alison Morrell's voice echoed from the eaves. 'I've just realised something, Maestro.'

'What, Alison?'

'Do you realise what changing "Nurture" to "Thrive" will do to the acronym?'

'The what?'

'"Shine" becomes...'

As Grit let out a titter, Mount Boyle began rumbling ready to erupt.

Four

Wesley Johnson arrived at Student Services waving his latest bank statement in a state of agitation. A tall man in his forties emerged from the cubby hole behind, 'What seems to be the problem?'

'I got a grant from the Students' Benevolent Fund and it hasn't been paid into my account.'

The man groaned. He had lost count of the number of similar complaints he'd had from students already that term, 'Mr...Johnson, isn't it?'

'Yeah.'

'And how much was the grant for?'

'Three hundred pounds. It was towards a new laptop-'

'-I don't need to know what it was for. I'll go and check on the computer... Again.' He disappeared back into his cubby hole and pressed a few buttons on a keyboard before re-emerging. 'Grant was paid on the seventh of September.'

'No it wasn't. That's what my letter from the Students' Benevolent Fund said. I was overdrawn on my account, so I ordered a bank statement. It hasn't been paid in.' He waved the statement under the man's nose.

'I'm telling you, it's been paid! Why don't you give it a few more days? I'm sure it'll show up in your next statement.'

'I'm not happy about this,' said Wesley. 'I'm going to miss my football practice now 'cos I've come here. You tell me everything's cool, but I'm going to have to pay a fine to my bank because this letter told me the money was there.'

* * *

After soccer practice, Wesley's friend, Terry, asked him why he had turned up late.

'It's the fucking college pissing me about, man. I haven't got my grant for my laptop, but they say I have. Went to Student Services to tell them. The dickhead there just told me to wait longer. Now I've bought it. My fucking bank has charged me for being over-drawn.'

'You aren't the only one. I put in for a new football strip and it didn't come through. I was lucky I got some bread off my Nan.'

'That doesn't make it any easier, does it? I'm telling them I want compensating. And so should you. I'm well pissed off with this place, man.'

'Have you seen this?' Terry got his phone out. It showed a shaky image of Villiers falling from the tower and landing on a car, crumpling its roof right down, apparently filmed from one of the language labs.

'What the fuck? Is that here?'

'Yeah. I'll send you the link.'

'Is that why the police were here yesterday?

'I guess.'

'Who was it?'

'Some dude called Horace Villiers. Suzy who does engineering told me.'

Wesley was shocked. 'No way, man. I knew him. He was alright. Let's see it again.'

Having watched the clip once more, Wesley could just about recognise the plunging figure, 'Jesus! Why would he do that?'

'How would you know him? You're not engineering.'

'Sometimes I just go into classes to see what they're like.'

'What for?'

Wesley frowned. He had never really thought about why he did this, but the question forced him to.

'Just curiosity.' Yes, that was probably what it was. 'Most of the lecturers won't let you sit in unless you're enrolled. He was like, "Hey, come and see what we're doing." They were working on a hand dryer which was mega-powerful. It was supposed to burn up all the poo that got sucked into it. Did he top himself?'

'I couldn't see anyone else up there. Maybe it was an accident.'

'I heard say he might have had like mental health issues.'

'Caused by this place, probably.'

'You reckon?'

And so the process of rumour-spreading began.

Five

Grit was smarting at having been expelled from the meeting. Tracing over what had happened, she remembered the chairperson becoming irate and rolling up her sleeves, which fell back down almost immediately. Roberts had taken a few puffs on her inhaler before telling Grit she was "naming and shaming" her.

What precisely was it she had done to evince this performance from Councillor Mrs Roberts? The lead balloon of a proposed change to the vision statement might have caused an outburst from the principal, but it undoubtedly put Roberts on edge in anticipation of anything else Grit said.

Stupid vision statement, she thought. *It means the sum total of nothing anyway.*

On reflection, Grit remembered that, when Boyle had told the meeting a new facial recognition system had been installed without consultation but wasn't operational, Grit had called it, 'a fart that doesn't function.'

Had she refrained from this comment, Grit would probably not have missed a subsequent vote in favour of extending the college's foray into offender learning even further, or the vote of thanks for the donation of half a million pounds from Cyril Richards, the aged member of the board who owned the local brewery, towards the Students' Benevolent Fund.

* * *

Grit was also unaware that, after the meeting, Boyle had taken aside Alison Morrell, the vice principal in charge of Human Resources (V-P HR).

He was not a tall man, standing eyeball-to-eyeball with Morrell, he looked over his left shoulder and then directly, piercingly, at her. 'I want her off my board.' he said.

'It would be easier for us to get through business without Margaret Bulmer there. Shall I mention her misconduct to Phyllis?'

'No. There's a reason why I'm talking to you about it.'

'What do you mean, Maestro?'

'If I thought her conduct on the board would be the best way to get her off it, our lady chairman, Councillor Mrs Propalot would be the one I'd talk to.'

'Well, Miss Bulmer is the *staff* governor. A staff governor has to resign if they are no longer a member of staff.' Morrell had produced what Boyle was looking for. 'But they can of course continue in a different role... If the board believes it appropriate'

'I thought that'd be the case.' The outer points of his mouth twitched slightly upward.

'What do you want me to do?'

Boyle made a slicing gesture across his throats with his right hand, his gold watch strap dangling in front of his cuffs.

'I see,' Morrell said with a mild smirk.

'There's the next stage of the staff reorganisation coming, isn't there?'

'But we don't have enough English teachers.'

'She's a trouble maker. If we don't make an example of her, the other termites will be walking all over us.'

'We could give her even worse conditions, and hope she leaves.'

'Bugger that. Just find someone else to do her job.'

'Oh, you mean like we did with...' Feeling some shame about the situation, Morrell had mouthed the words, '...Horace Villiers. Are you sure it'd be wise to do that again, so soon after...?'

'Just do what you can.' Boyle patted the small of Morrell's back. 'I do trust you, you know that?'

Morrell chuckled, coquettishly, 'I know you do, Maestro. That's what worries me.'

'Come on, you don't have to be frightened of Old Laurence.' Boyle pressed on, 'The locusts here do, not you.' He was then struck by a disturbing thought.

Morrell smiled.

Six

Grit's day at work was drawing to a close. It was almost time to go and pick up George from Brandon's house. She wondered if it would be a good idea to go to the doctor's about her anxiety, if it was that. But what would be the point? She had a fair idea of the cause. It was something about death. Only recently had she become aware that death, either accidental or suicide, had haunted her through her life.

Grit's father died after having been made redundant as a miner. She was five at the time. He had been at odds with the consensus in his community, choosing to support the government in the early days on the grounds that the strike was not democratic. This entailed going to work against being called "scab", avoiding some projectiles, and being ignored in his local working men's club. Later, he had come to support Scargill and the striking miners on reflection of the way the government had behaved. Grit hadn't understood how her dad had come to be deceased, not least because nobody had told her.

Only on her recent consideration of events had the likely cause of his departure occurred to her. The fact that a week before he was found dead he had crashed his car into a large oak tree at high speed, but escaped with only minor injuries and a written-off Mk2 Ford Escort indicated to her his probable intention. But the tree had been hollow and rotting inside, collapsing fortuitously away from his body.

When he did come to die by a different means a few weeks later, Grit had coped with what happened by pretending it wasn't real, while her mother managed her own grief by promptly having a breakdown. This was when an anarchic Polish widow, Rivka Robson, had taken her in hand. Mrs Robson lived over the road. Sometimes Grit got back from school and her mother, who had found a job, had not returned home. Mrs Robson would take her in and fed her *bigos* or *flaki* with bagels.

Mrs Robson was a highly cultured woman who taught piano. It was not at school where Grit gained her love of literature, it was at Mrs Robson's. 'Your schools don't teach you your own classics,' she complained. 'The English language has so many great writers and what of them are they teaching you at school? Sod all! You should learn these. I will help you.'

By the time she was twelve, Grit had ploughed her way through *Little Women*, *Jane Eyre*, and had more than a slight acquaintance with the works of Shakespeare, Dickens and also Karl Marx, giving her a love of reading she had taken with her to university and beyond. Mrs Robson had also tried her on an English translation of a novel called *The Doll*. This had proved too much for Grit at the time, although she had come to read it later.

When Grit was twenty five, just after George was born, Mrs Robson died. Even worse was the manner of her death. At the age of ninety, she had developed breast cancer, but survived it. The very afternoon Mrs Robson had been given the all-clear, a lollipop lady (school crossing patrol) yelled at her not to step out onto the road. Mrs Robson replied, 'I will not follow the orders of a government apparatchik.'

Taking hold of her arm, the lollipop lady said bemusedly, 'I am employed by the county council!'

'Central or local government apparatchik. It makes no difference to me!' replied Mrs Robson, shaking free of the woman's hold before stepping straight into the path of a speeding articulated lorry.

Grit felt as if she had lost her father and her mother even though Evelyn, her own mother, was still very much alive, but as bad-tempered and dismissive as always. Grit saw her mother as little as possible. She hated having her visit at Christmas.

A year later, when George was a toddler and Grit's maternity leave was over, she realised there was no affordable nursery provision locally. This would not do. True to character, she set about starting a nursery at West Durham College, where she worked at the time. This was when Grit first came across her then principal, Joan Fisher. Dr Fisher had found a suitable place in the building for a nursery, and given her time off work to enable her to set things going. Whenever Grit had had a problem, Dr Fisher had always been there to lend an ear and give her advice, some of which was difficult to swallow, but always well-meant and nearly always appreciated. This had carried on for the first term at Titas, but now Dr Fisher had taken early retirement. Grit was older and more independent, but still felt a painful gap. As a less involved, but deeply supportive vessel, Dr Fisher had served unwittingly as a maternal figure towards Grit.

But now, with the culture that was prevalent at the college, especially on the board, Grit felt depressed enough. However, this was before she was to become aware of the plans afoot to dispense with her services.

Seven

During one of his free periods, the next day, Wesley Johnson had found his way to a botany lab, with a second, glass door into a sort of greenhouse. He saw what looked like a lecturer in there. At least that was what he took the bespectacled man with a receding hairline and wearing a white coat to be, although he could just as easily have been a technician. Wesley waved and the man noticed him, gesturing for him to enter.

As soon as he opened the second door, a stench blasted out. He closed it again and pulled his shirt up over his nose before going in.

'What can we do for you, sir?' asked the man.

'I was just looking around.'

'Are you a student here?'

'Yeah, but I'm just doing GCSEs and a BTEC in sports. I like finding out what other classes are up to.'

'I see. I don't think you're supposed to be here, but since you are, would you like to give me a hand?'

Wesley waved a hand in front of his face. 'No offence, sir, but it smells like something crawled up your arse and died.'

'That's our friend here, *Bulbophyllum phalacnopsis.* I'm going to propagate her, so if you can help me?'

'How?' asked Wesley through his tracksuit, which he had now zipped up over his nose.

'Do you see those bulbs growing on the plant?'

'Yeah.'

'Cut them off. Here's a knife and then we can get started...'

'Alright, but might have to go outside in a minute.'

'That's understood. It isn't a very pleasant smell, but like all anathemata you get used to it up to a point. Besides, given the general direction of Titas College, I can't see such miasmatic educational aids being supported for much longer!' The man tilted his head back to look at Wesley through his spectacles.

'Really, Sir?' Wesley had barely the faintest idea of what the man was talking about.

He went on to assist for about twenty minutes before the smell became too much for him to bear. Wesley didn't know it at the time, but he would come to have a use for this foul-smelling orchid.

Eight

The following day, Grit had given some further thought to her ache, and decided there was only one thing for it, subsequently finding herself dialling Dr Fisher's number. Dr Fisher seemed pleased to hear from her, but something seemed to make her more reserved than when they last spoke. 'Had you heard about Horace Villiers from engineering?'

'Yes I had Very sad, dear. I know it seems callous, but I'm glad it isn't my concern anymore.'

'Why?'

'Because if I'd still been there I would have wanted to know what happened. If it was caused in any way by conditions at the college I'd have gone my ends. To be honest, dear, I don't know if I've still the strength for all that. And Boyle is such an odious... Stop it, Joan!'

'Not at all. I'd be the first to say that Boyle was odious.'

'He reminds me of someone I was at college with...' Dr Fisher's voice trailed away.

'Anyway, about Horace. The funny thing is...' This time it was Grit trailing.

'What, dear?'

'Well, the thing is I've had a pain in my gut since I heard about Horace doing what he did.'

'Have you dear? I didn't think you liked him.'

'I didn't. That's what makes it strange.'

Dr Fisher spoke in a low and enquiring voice, 'How did you say your father died?'

'He was hit by a train near the Plawsworth viaduct.'

'Exactly.'

'But what does that have to do with Horace?'

'I apologise deeply if I am speaking out of turn, dear, but the instance of one possible suicide could well provoke the memory of a, if you will forgive me for saying, likely suicide.'

Grit felt herself becoming angry. 'The coroner concluded my dad died by misadventure. And we don't know why Horace fell.'

'I'm sorry dear. It isn't for me to tell you what has happened. I remember your telling me about your father, but you didn't say much more. Have you ever talked about what happened to anyone?'

Crash!

'School referred me to a psychologist. He just seemed to think I was coping very well. And Mrs Robson, actually she didn't really talk to me about it.'

'Nor you to her?'

'I don't think so.'

'So you haven't addressed how you felt about your father for a long time, if ever. And then Horace Villiers, a man I know you'd had sharp words with, *might* have killed himself. Without wanting to presume too much, dear, I suspect you are suffering from guilt. You shouldn't, you know, but it could be useful to talk it through with someone, a counsellor perhaps?'

* * *

Was Dr Fisher right? Could Grit have had childhood anguish resurrected by what Villiers had done? The way she was coming to see it, she owed it to Villiers to find out what she could about his death. Could her harsh words toward him possibly have pushed Villiers over the edge? If they did, at least she would know, but if they didn't, as she hoped, it might set her mind - and her stomach - at rest.

* * *

Unable to articulate exactly what all this amounted to, Grit found herself making her way to the place which held information about her and, she supposed, also about Villiers. Having gained the attention of the woman behind the counter at HR, she handed her the job application she had completed two nights before, twitching involuntarily.

'Was there something else?' the woman asked.

'Yes.' Grit told her she had also come to view her Employee's Record.

'Of course, what's the name, please?' said the clerk with a friendly, albeit wooden, smile.

'Margaret Bulmer.'

'I see, and it's on your badge, lovely.' Tracy Millicent spoke in a sing-song voice as she bent forward and peered closely at the lanyard hanging over Grit's slim midriff. 'Yes, lovely, I'll just go and get it for you.'

Grit observed Miss Millicent make her way over to an unlit part of the room, where there was what appeared to be a large bank of filing cabinets. She opened one of them, searched through some files in the cabinet and removed one, taking it to somewhere with more light and studying it for a few moments.

Not wanting to be seen to follow what Miss Millicent was doing too closely, Grit looked down onto the far side of the counter and noticed something. It was a memorandum entitled “Staff Training”, which detailed two half-days for personnel staff on 25th September. There were further details, but as she was reading upside down and they were in very small print, Grit wasn’t able to determine them.

Miss Millicent returned to the counter, still smiling, but it had become awkward, somehow. ‘I’m sorry,’ she said. ‘We need to have a written request for staff to view their files.’

‘I see,’ said Grit, suspicious. ‘How long have you worked here?’

‘Since it opened. I was at Durham College for nearly three years before.’

‘Three years. And you just happened to remember this?’

‘It’s a new thing. All I know is those are the rules.’

‘So if I were to write a formal letter here, now, requesting my record, could you bring me the file?’

‘No, I’m sorry.’ Miss Millicent shook her head apologetically, ‘All requests for staff employment records have to go through Alison Morrell.’

‘So I should address any such request to her, then?’

‘That’s right.’

‘Well that’s a faff, isn’t it? After all, it’s *my* employment record!’

‘I know, I know. Sorry. I don’t make the rules.’

‘I’m not blaming you. Christ, I know what it’s like having to serve our masters.’

* * *

That Tracy Millicent seemed happy to dig out Grit's file for her, but uneasy on her return, indicated she may have read something to be kept hidden. What could it have been?

Then something occurred to Grit. What if the staff training day meant that HR would be empty that afternoon? She surmised that going through the proper channels could mean that, when she finally did get to see her employment record, crucial parts of it would be absent. The germ of an impetuous idea began taking root in her head.

Grit may have been a bit of a rebel, but that rebellion tended to amount to speaking out against, authority when she believed strongly enough that it was in the wrong, not to mention poking fun at it from time to time. The sort of thing, in fact, that could get you kicked out of meetings. But a covert plan to access personnel records, even her own, made her deeply uneasy. Could her parting remark to Miss Millicent about Serving our Masters have been ill-advised should she choose to execute such a plan?

Grit had managed to glean from the memorandum that at least one of the training sessions was to take place when she did not have a class. Might she be able to find her way to look at her own, and perhaps even Villiers's, files on the off chance? Would the door to the offices behind the HR counter be locked? Sometimes it was open, but needed a combination, and if nobody was there, the chance of the department being left open was small.

As Grit turned to leave, a man walked to the dividing door between the reception area and the office space. She looked closely as he typed a number into the combination lock keypad: Two. Three. Seven. Four. This had to be serendipity. Grit typed the number into her phone and stored it under "MI5".

Sneaking into Human Resources and looking at files, what the hell was Grit thinking of? But recent experience had shown the proper channels let those pulling the strings play you like a puppet. Something had to be done.

* * *

Searching for an alternative plan she hoped might render the risky visit unnecessary, it occurred to Grit that she should talk to someone close to Villiers. Did he have children? A wife? Having known and scorned the man for all of two terms, she knew nothing at all about his private life. And while it might provide useful information about him, she didn't want to interrogate bereaved relatives.

Perhaps she could ask at his funeral. Perhaps that would be a callous thing to do. Would it be appropriate to go? Would its time and location be made available, even? Grit became aware that the ache, which had subsided while she entertained notions of sedition, began returning to a new nadir, or should that be zenith, strictly, she wondered? Whatever it was called, it was worse than it had been before.

Then a light bulb went on in her head. What about the stranger who said Villiers had a good case? Maybe he was just the person to contact. The trouble was, she had not seen him since that day, and had no idea how to get in touch with him.

Getting out of her rusty Suzuki Baleno on arrival at home that evening, she received a text from her colleague Bill Ogle, *'Horace's funeral to be at 12.30pm on Tues, 22nd Sept in St. Cuthbert's Church, Lariat Lane. Family would like everyone 2 attend and I'm going, please come if u can.'*

Nine

22nd September, 2013

St. Cuthbert's church had a delightful exterior. Art-Deco mixed with Neo-Gothic. Indeed, it could have been an architectural expression of Villiers's personality.

The stout figure of Father Aloysius O'Hanlon entered the much plainer interior in his cassock and surplice. Jarred by the rickrolling rhythm of 'Never Gonna Give You Up' on the organ, his wispy, grey hair seemed to fly around his head with the vibrations.

'Excuse me, sir?' He called out, unable to compete with the giant speakers of the Viscount digital organ, which had replaced the old pipe organ some years previously. Slightly unsteady on his feet, but aware of the funeral being due to start in about twenty minutes, the priest was concerned that early comers might be distressed further by such demonic music emanating from the building, so he climbed the flight of stairs to the balcony and across to the consul.

A portly, bald man in his fifties sat at the manuals, his surplice barely covering his suit, 'Er, excuse me?' said the father, but the organist appeared not to hear, so he waved in the man's line of sight. The man, still playing, glanced across briefly, scowled, lifted his left hand from the keyboard and pointed towards the priest. Having played for about another minute, he turned towards Father O'Hanlon, exclaiming, 'I just love that, don't you?' with unexpected enthusiasm.

'It's well... it's certainly a change from what we're used to hearing in church. You're the stand-in organist, I presume?'

'I am.'

'You've been provided by the undertakers?'

'That's right.'

Well, sir, it's good to have you among us. You're playing for this afternoon's funeral service I understand?'

'Er... yes, Father.'

'I was just wondering about the programme. There isn't anything of that sort in the Order of Service is there?'

'No, I was just playing. Introductory music, you know.'

'Are you sure that's entirely appropriate for a funeral service?'

'Any man who's tired of Stock Aitken Waterman's tired of life!'

At this last utterance by the organist, the priest felt as if he had just experienced a body blow. 'I don't doubt it, sir. Do you have the hymns and the Order of Service?'

'Right here.' The man picked up the A5 booklet that had been sitting on the bench the other side of him, waving it casually around.

'That's good. By the way, I wondered if you wouldn't mind playing something a bit more, er, suited to the occasion. It's a particularly sad occasion you know. Mrs Paterson, our usual organist, couldn't bring herself to...'

'About it being a possible suicide?'

'Yes. But of course we can't be certain of that, can we?'

'No fears about that, Father. I'm not Roman Catholic.'

'Oh, well, I expect the mourners will begin arriving shortly.'

'Alright, Father; you're the boss,' said the man, muttering afterwards, 'in here, anyway.'

'I most certainly am not the boss in here!' In spite of his age, the priest's hearing was as sharp as ever. 'Our Lord is, as you would put it, "the boss" in here, as he is in all places.'

'Of course,' said Mr Stand-In. 'I wasn't meaning to imply -'

'-That's quite alright,' Father O' Hanlon smiled, 'Just as long as we both remember that. There are times I can get above myself as well.'

'He's not the boss in my college,' mumbled the organist as O' Hanlon departed. The priest heard that too, but as he did not know the organist's day job, he thought it best to let it go. Besides, he was still smarting at the man's reference to being "tired of life" and wanted to ensure he was sufficiently composed to lead the service. Time was perhaps running a little short to give the man another dressing down.

The organist began to play the tune "Austria" more quietly than before, but still at a slightly higher volume than would perhaps have been ideal.

* * *

Given that she couldn't stand Villiers when he had been alive, Grit was still a little uncomfortable about attending the funeral. It could have been out of her sense of guilt for all the times she had given him an earful. But there might also have been a forlorn hope of finding something out about his circumstances. Besides, she knew Ogle was going to be there, so was less ill-at-ease about going to pay her respects to the man she had called "Horrors".

It was a crisp, sunny, autumn day and, as the mourners gathered outside the church, Grit waited for Ogle. When he arrived, the tall man with the flared trousers from smokers' corner the previous week was with him: the one who had told her about Villiers's suicide. Remembering immediately the comment he had made two weeks before, she wondered how the man had been looking forward to helping Villiers.

'I don't know if you've met Bob Smith.' Ogle said as the man extended a hand to her.

'Yes, we have met.' she replied, taking it, but things took a moment to dawn. 'You aren't Robert Smith, by any chance?'

'For my sins.'

'The Robert Smith with the column in the Draguian Educational Journal?'

'None other.'

In that case I need to talk to you. Later, of course.'

He frowned wryly, 'I see. That sounds ominous.'

'Your reputation docs precede you,' said Ogle.

Smith shrugged, 'That's just the price you have to pay for fame, I gucss.'

'Or infamy perhaps?' joked Grit.

'Sadly not much fortune in my case, but infamy, indeed!'

As Smith played affronted, the hearse pulled up and the pallbearers emerged to carry the coffin.

The majority of mourners had been colleagues. Some were from Titas College, like Grit and Smith, but a far greater number were employees and ex-employees of his previous place of work, Cholmondeleys Engineering. Grit was made aware of this by the mention of it in the eulogy, given by a young man she did not recognise. It was also mentioned that, having gained a first in engineering from Liverpool, he eventually became a director and Head of Product Development at the company. The hymns, *All is well with my soul* and *How great thou art* were unduly rushed, as the stand-in organist left all but the most proficient singers in his wake.

* * *

Grit noted the apparent absence of the principal, Laurence Boyle, at the service, and commented to Smith and Ogle in a loose assembly of mourners afterwards that he probably had a hand in Villiers's demise, so wouldn't dare to turn up. Unconvinced, Smith asked her why.

'Being new here, you, well perhaps you are unfamiliar with his management style, if not his delightful personality,' she replied as she realised that, from what she had read in his column, Smith knew The Maestro's management style only too well. 'I doubt he cares about anyone except himself. You could imagine him saying, "*I've got more important things to do with my time than indulging in going to staff's funerals. I'll need to get myself a new car for a start!*" This led to an ill-placed snigger among the company, as Grit did her best to imitate the uneven, gargly sound of Boyle's voice.

'I wonder whose picture he has on his dartboard at the moment,' mused Ogle, pleased at an opportunity to impart this piece of gossip.

'He has a dartboard he puts pictures on, does he? How do you know?'

'My lips are sealed.'

'I'd have guessed Joan Fisher, or Horace, but now she's retired and he's passed on, I would say probably that I'm next. Or Bob if Boyle knows he's here.'

'But that doesn't mean he had anything to do with Villiers, you know, doing what he did.'

'Doesn't it? That's just what I'm trying to find out.'

Smith got his diary out. 'He sounds like a par for the course principal in my experience. How about Thursday lunch?'

This proposal struck Grit in the gut. It was after Thursday lunch she was planning her covert excursion to Human Resources. 'I can't then. I'm a bit tied up, I'm afraid.'

'Oh, well actually I'm going to be free tomorrow lunch time. Any good?'

'Lunch time – where?'

'We could try the college canteen.'

'That's bloody expensive!'

'I thought that. We could get a coffee and, well I usually bring sandwiches.'

'So do I. And a flask, but I can probably run to coffee... just -especially if I'm being advised by such an *infamous* expert.'

'Of course I'd like to help, but don't hang too much on what I can say... or do,' said Smith, 'I'll see you, what time?'

'About one o'clock.'

'Okay. See you Bill.' Smith then swept away. The urbanity of his thick, flowing salt-and-pepper hair and wool overcoat were undermined by the flopping motion of his salmon-pink, flared trousers. Grit looked in his wake, unaware of the effect he was having on her.

'Can I have a lift back to college, please Grit?' asked Ogle, 'GRIT?'

'What?'

'You said you would give me a lift back. Would that still be okay?'

'I'm meeting him at one o'clock tomorrow.'

'I can get the bus if it's a problem.'

'If what's a problem?'

'Your taking me back in time for my class.'

'Oh, did I offer to?'

'You did, but it doesn't matter-'

'-Did I? What time is it?'

'Quarter past one.'

'Fine, fine. I think I need to speak to Horrors's wife before we go, though.'

'Do you know her?'

'I didn't know he had one till the priest mentioned her in the service.' As she spoke, Grit had noticed the short, plump, red-faced woman of roughly Villiers's age who had sat at the front.

'That's her,' said Ogle.

Grit rummaged in her handbag and took out a pen and pad, wrote down her contact details, before approaching Mrs Villiers, who was surrounded by several people, 'Hello, Excuse me?' she waved, struggling to get her attention.

Mrs Villiers eventually looked bemusedly in Grit's direction. 'I'm very sorry to intrude and about what has happened.' Grit had the sense of gate-crashing a collective, private grief as she held the piece of paper between the heads of the two people who were between her and Mrs Villiers, 'I'm a governor at Titas College. If there is anything you would like to talk about at any time, please call me. No rush and I do mean anything, okay?'

Taking several seconds to register what was going on, Mrs Villiers asked, 'Who did you say you were?'

'I'm a governor at the college. And I work there.'

To Grit's dismay, Mrs Villiers's face showed a small spark of anger amid its hitherto benign expression. Taking the piece of paper, she thanked Grit in rather bitter sounding tones. Grit departed expecting nothing to come of it.

Un-noticed, the stand-in organist looked down on the proceedings from the organ loft at the back of the church.

Ten

Boyle was secretly delighted that Villiers was dead. During his time in accounting, he had come across a letter he had kept. Its contents had made Villiers his target for some years. With Villiers now committed to the thereafter, however, Boyle felt that now was the time to dispose of the letter.

He knew Alison Morrell had the job of foisting the new contracts of employment onto the lecturing staff. This should subdue troublemakers while saving a few bob, he thought. He was also aware it might not be a job she would relish. But as a man who demanded total loyalty from his lieutenants, Morrell's finer feelings did not concern him.

Poring over a paper about a new government grant available to pay for sixteen to twenty four year olds to do "Functional Skills", Boyle heard a knock at the door.

It's probably Alison trying to cover her back again.

'YES,' he shouted.

The door opened slowly. Sure enough, Morrell's head appeared around it. 'It's me, Maestro. I don't know where your secretary is.'

'She had to go over to Student Services. Come in.'

She entered, shutting the door behind her.

Looking at some papers on the desk, he passed them to her, smiling, 'Have you seen this, Alison?'

'No, Maestro. What is it?'

'It's a new government funding stream to support students with special educational needs on vocational courses.'

'Sounds a good idea. Are we the right college to do this, though?'

He looked at her as though she were a misguided child. 'Of course it is. What we do is build up the post-sixteen department and have them all doing Basic Skills.'

'But what about them learning a trade?'

'Few, if any, will progress to bricklaying, hairdressing or motor mechanics. If we require them to get to Level Two English and Maths, they'll be stuck here in perpetuity.' Boyle smirked aslant.

'Do we want that? I mean, I doubt we have enough English and Maths teachers to cover them?'

'We'll find them somewhere, especially when we take over Gutside and Ouseburn Colleges, but with the extra money to support SEN students and vocational courses we really are on to a winner. Kerching!' Boyle clenched his fist and pulled it back towards his shoulder, flashing his gold watch strap.

'Well, Maestro that's um... well, it's very perspicacious thinking... But is it fair on the students?'

'Most of them are losers who'll never succeed in life. Better that we collect funding for them instead of the Jobcentre or some tin pot agency. Seriously, it's a win-win.'

Morrell's re-appearance reminded Boyle of the thing that troubled him before she had left him earlier: the fact that his credit card had been charged six pounds twenty for "Internet Services". While the amount was quite small, Boyle was someone who liked to know where every penny of his money sat, but no matter how much he had interrogated his wife on the subject, he was none the wiser.

He noted her demeanour even more sheepish than he would have expected. 'What do you want?'

'I don't know if you'd heard about, er...'

'About what? Come on, spit it out!'

'It seems we have a new member of staff in the Centre for Employees' Education.'

'We have several new members of staff. Much as I'd like to, I haven't the time to vet them all personally.'

'I know,' Morrell swallowed. 'That's why we've got this one.'

Boyle sighed, 'Alright then, who is it?'

'Bob Smith.'

He looked at her in disbelief.

'I know it isn't exactly your favoured reading, Maestro, but you must glance at the Draguian Educational Journal sometimes?'

'Occasionally: it helps to know what the termites are up to, but I wouldn't waste my time reading it every week.'

'Smith has a regular column in that publication.'

The warm feeling Boyle had been harbouring from the prospect of new funding evaporated. 'You mean the corybantic commie that propagates leftist crap about employment cases? I'm sure you're wrong there, Alison. He's one of the bastards I keep an eye on, maybe not a close eye, but I do watch him. He lives in London; works at Charlton College.'

'Not - any - more.' Morrell quivered as she spaced out the words of her answer.

Boyle began looking down over the papers on his desk as if the meeting was over, so she turned to leave the room.

There's no way it could be that termite!

Then the penny dropped. 'Tall man, dresses like some kind of popinjay?'

Morrell stopped in her tracks and pursed her lips, 'That could be one way to describe him.'

'Yeah, now I know who it was I saw talking to the Bulmer girl.' Boyle looked down and stabbed his dagger-shaped paper knife into a small brown envelope on the desk, his face darkening, 'Who was responsible for making the appointment?'

He glared straight towards her, noticing the question seemed to have shaken Morrell even more than he thought it would.

'Well the panel had three people on it.'

'Yes?' Boyle took the letter out of its envelope, glanced at it briefly and grimaced, before crumpling them both into a tight ball and throwing them into the wastepaper basket.

That's the termite Villiers disposed of!

He then looked directly at Morrell, holding the letter-opener as if it was a hammer, his face now a darker shade of puce. He raised his thin eyebrows. 'Go on.'

'A young man called Stephen Wilson, from my department. Then there was John Robley, who works in the Centre for Employment Education. Then... you know it's thought good practice to have a vice-principal on appointment panels... well quite a few didn't - couldn't - do it, so...'

'So what? Come on, Alison; I haven't got all day.' Boyle leant back in his chair, shaking the letter-opener tremulously.

'So Joan Fisher chaired the panel.'

As Morrell said this, she released the breath she had been holding suddenly, losing her voice at the end of the sentence.

Though he had never met Smith in person, Boyle's view was that, with the possible exception of the late Horace Villiers, there was nobody viler. 'Jesus Christ, Alison. You know vice-principals are there to do my bidding. And what have you done here, eh? Only gone and put on the panel the only vice-principal I wouldn't have trusted with the wife's goldfish, let alone my vision for College.'

'But it went out to all vice-principals. She was the only one to volunteer.'

'But what the hell were you doing sending it to Old Vinegar Tits in the first place? Good God, Alison. You see what happens when you take your eye off the ball. I bet Smith wouldn't have got that job if Fisher hadn't been on the panel.'

'At least Dr Fisher has gone now.'

Boyle was clearly beginning to sweat now, as if his collar was suddenly tighter around his neck than before. He started fingering it. 'She's gone, but my God she managed to appoint her successor first.'

'Not really. I mean he's only a lecturer.'

'With a bastard like that, it'll hardly matter. He's here now.' As Boyle fulminated towards a state of frenzy, Morrell froze. 'Were you born stupid?' He heaved himself up out of his chair, his small, dark eyes looking as though they were about to pop out of his head.

Walking over to the door, he turned to face Morrell. 'Now I've got another fuck up on my plate. Cheers Alison!'

Boyle then turned on his heels once more, leaving the office.

Stupid Cow! Why am I surrounded by incompetence?

* * *

Morrell stood shaking in her sensible shoes, which still added a good few inches to her height, inhaling the aura of cologne mixed with a greater dose of sweat than usual left behind by Boyle, competing successfully even with her perfume. She felt deeply vulnerable. Perhaps out of a vain search for something to defend herself with, Morrell became curious about whatever documents Maestro had just crumpled and thrown away. Retrieving the ball from the wastepaper basket and separating the letter from the envelope, she put it in her pocket and left his office, closing the door behind her.

Back in her own office, she flattened it out as best she could and read its contents.

Suddenly Morrell found herself with tears streaming down her face. She had always done her best to support The Maestro and thought he recognised this. After all, when she had started at Durham College, she had been a secretary in Personnel and worked her way up, but the final promotion to V-P (HR) had been at his behest.

She placed the flattened the letter out as best she could, noticing its title "RE: WILFRED GARNIER". Morrell then took the letter to a photocopier and pressed the button. At that moment she didn't know exactly how, but was sure its contents would be of use should the knives come out.

Eleven

Grit had rushed from her mid-day finish, only to find Smith had not turned up yet. The canteen was a moderately large area, with glass windows all the way up its great height. It was filling up fast, and things were getting very loud indeed.

She trusted Ogle as much as anyone in the place, but this would always be marred by some degree of doubt. Grit knew Smith by reputation, but had met him only twice. Her instincts told her to trust him, but then she didn't always trust those. And if she didn't trust her instincts, then surely this meant she should refrain from anything as audacious as sneaking into HR to look at files without permission, didn't it?

Something didn't quite add up about Bob Smith either. Whatever it was, she couldn't quite put her finger on. As a regular reader of the Draguian Education Journal, Grit now remembered that Smith had written more than one article which made specific criticism, not only about the employment practices of Titas College, but Durham College as well. The management of Titas must have known this so why, or how, was he engaged by the college?

While Grit sat immersed in these thoughts and, increasingly, the noise surrounding her, Wesley Johnson brought up a tray, and sat down opposite. This she could have done without. Compounding it was that he was clearly unhappy about something.

'I'm glad I've caught you, Miss. My money still hasn't been paid.'

Grit had no idea what he was talking about. 'Sorry. What money?'

'Money for a new laptop. My mam's on benefits so I applied to the Students' Benevolent Fund. They said they paid three hundred quid into my bank account last Wednesday, but the bank said nothing was paid in.'

Grit had informed her students about the existence of the fund several times since the meeting when the matter was first discussed, but so far no student had approached her about it. 'Have you gone back to Student Services? After all, they are the ones you make the application through.'

'I just told you, they say it's been paid.'

'I'm afraid I don't know what I can do. Have they shown you any records to support this?'

Wesley showed Grit the print out from Student Services indicating that three hundred pounds had been paid into a bank account on the fifteenth of September. He then pulled out his corresponding bank statement and showed it to her, managing to drag one corner into the dollop of tomato sauce on his plate. Grit could see no payment was recorded. As she double-checked the account details all matched, she became aware of a slight draft and, merging with the smell of commercial catering, a waft of an aftershave she remembered from when she was a girl left the ache in her belly competing with a tingling of excitement. 'Well, Wesley. I'm stumped,' she shouted above the din.

'So you're not going to do nothing, then?'

'I didn't mean that, but I am trying to have my lunch and I'm supposed to be having a meeting. When do I see you next?'

'English Language. Thursday morning.'

'Come and see me after and we'll see what we can do.'

'It might be too late then.' Wesley griped,

'Oh, I'm sure it won't!' Grit smiled at him, trying to look reassuring. Wesley returned a most cynical glance as she turned to Ogle and Smith.

'Where have you two been?'

'Yes, er, sorry we're late, Grit. I bumped into Bob and we both went to HR I had to update my DBS and Bob had to hand in his P45. As it was, though...' Ogle adjusted his glasses, '...it seemed like a good opportunity to, er, case the joint.' He began to sound very excited, 'Bob's going to advise us on his plans.'

Grit wondered for a second whether they could have been planning anything as intrepid as she was. Doubting this, she looked at Smith, 'Bob's got plans, has he? Well this is hardly the place to talk about them.'

'I think you'll find that in places like this, with so much noise everywhere at the moment,' Smith bellowed above the din, 'it's one of the safest locations for a confidential discussion.'

'A confidential discussion about breaking into HR? Hey, you can count me in, Miss!' Chatting with a couple of his mates, Wesley had turned around suddenly.

Grit was mortified to have been reminded of the action she had been planning to take by two different sources, 'Nobody's breaking into anywhere!' she snapped. 'Even if they were it wouldn't be any of your business.'

Wesley smiled. 'I won't tell on you. Not if you help get the money I'm due.'

'Oh, so it's blackmail now, is it?' Grit pursed her lips as she turned back to Smith and Ogle, 'Come on, I need to get out of here.'

As they began making their way out of the canteen, Wesley called after them, 'Good luck, and don't worry. Your secret's safe with me!' was half-heard only too clearly.

'I could kill that boy,' she seethed into the relief of quietude.

'Where shall we go?' asked Ogle.

'We could go to Smokers' Corner.' said Grit. 'The weather's not great, though.'

'Why don't we go to my house?' suggested Smith. 'It's in Durham Road, just at the far end of the front street.'

Twelve

Smith telephoned ahead to tell his wife they were coming. When they arrived at what looked to Grit as though it should have been a block of Victorian flats, an Amazonian, red haired woman of about forty answered the door. The sounds of children echoed around the big house, exacerbated by its bare floors. Grit looked up the stairwell which, having turned back on itself countless times appeared to have a roof light as its final destination. Smith introduced the woman as Helen, before disappearing up a couple of the flights of stairs.

As Helen invited them through to the kitchen, strong, spicy smells enveloped Grit's nostrils. This was very agreeable, but not quite what she had expected. Neither was the level of untidiness, which was far greater than she would have thought normal in such a household.

'Do come through to the kitchen. It's along here,' said Helen, gesturing with her right hand. 'Bob should be down in a minute. Would you like some coffee?'

'Oh, yes please, that would be lovely.'

The kitchen was an enormous room at the back of the house. It appeared to take up two full floors and must have been about thirty feet long. As Grit and Ogle sat on one of the stools around a large deal table, Helen started busying around with a bag of roasted beans and a hand grinder which was clamped onto the edge of the table, making it look more like a woodworking bench.

'I've told Bill already, I'm never quite sure what's expected of me with people from Bob's work. You see there are all different sorts, union people, lecturers, journalists. Bob says to me, just be yourself, it's fine. But I don't think it is, so I work on the principle of least said soonest mended.'

These last words hit Grit like a bolt from the blue. Did this refer to the various disputes she understood Smith had been mixed up in? Or might it possibly mean that he was capable of being up to more than she would have imagined? Grit made a note to herself to keep close tabs on the feelings she was beginning to realise she had for him.

Helen stopped grinding the coffee.

'Shall I put the kettle on?' Grit asked.

'No, it's fine.'

'Really, I'd like to help.'

'Oh, alright, then.'

Grit looked for an electric kettle, but there was none. On seeing what she was trying to do, Ogle made his way over to the Aga and moved a tin kettle from the edge of one of the hotplates to the middle. He then looked at Grit in a knowing way.

'I'll whap you in a minute,' she said.

He smiled, 'We used to have one of these when I was little.'

Grit thought that everyone around her was just too posh to comprehend, but said nothing for fear of offending Helen.

'We weren't posh.' said Ogle, as if reading Grit's thoughts. 'Ours ran on coal and we didn't have central heating. The Aga heated the water, and you'd struggle to cook a rice pudding if someone was having a bath.'

'We don't have an electric kettle, I'm afraid, but this does fine,' said Helen, opening a cupboard next to the

Aga and getting out a large cafetière. Have you had lunch yet?'

'You really don't have to go to all this trouble,' said Grit, 'I'd have been quite happy with instant.' This was a fib. Grit liked her coffee freshly ground and strong, even though she didn't usually have the energy or inclination to make "proper" coffee at home. The stronger the better and her mouth watered at the thought of whatever was making all the spicy smells.

'Don't worry about feeding us. We've brought our sandwiches.'

'Well if you're sure.'

Grit remembered why something seemed not quite right about Smith. She just had to ask about it. 'The first time I met Bob, he said you both moved up here from London because of your job.'

'Did he, really?' Helen's inflection and raised eyebrows suggested this wasn't a notion she agreed with. Having apparently landed Bob in it with this, Grit thought it best to ignore this reaction and continue, but Helen pre-empted her. 'It is true I got a job here before we moved, but it's part-time. I got it because we both planned to move up.'

'What is your job?'

'I'm a peripatetic violin teacher.'

'Oh, I'm sorry if I've put my foot in it there... Why did you move up, then?'

'Several reasons, really. The main one was just that it's so expensive and polluted in London and we can live far more comfortably. But that could've been in a lot of places. The reason we chose here was because of Bob's job.'

'So Bob got the job first?'

'I don't know, actually. When I applied it was a punt really, and as a peripatetic I'm not tied to one place. I could be anywhere in County Durham.

So far, so opaque. Helen pushed the plunger down on the cafetière slowly, but with indomitable force. Grit felt fear at being the object of her ire, 'Was there something about Titas College which made Bob want to be involved there?'

'I don't honestly know. I'll ask him. Or you could if you wanted to.'

Ogle smiled again and looked at Helen, 'I'm sure there was. Had to be.'

Helen got three enormous earthenware mugs out of a cupboard and began pouring the coffee into them.

'Milk?' asked Helen.

'I like mine black, thanks.'

'Yes please,' said Ogle.

Helen got a bottle of unpasteurised, full fat milk out of the fridge and poured.

'Say when?'

'When,' said Ogle.

'I was wondering. Why do you put it in after?' asked Grit.

'Dunno. Doesn't everyone?'

'I never have.'

'Oh, how odd!'

It was strange how the question of when milk was added to coffee seemed to lead to what Grit thought was a real sense of unease between herself and Helen.

The sound of the children, which had been distant ever since they had gone into the kitchen, suddenly seemed very loud and a small boy ran into the room.

'Mummy, daddy's being nasty to me.'

'Really, darling? What's he done now?'

'He said he would take one of his dirty old socks and shove it in my mouth.'

Smith appeared in the kitchen doorway.

'Toby, you know fine well Daddy didn't mean he was actually going to do that.'

'He did. I know he did.'

Smith looked at Toby and bit the air.

'Bob, I told you to stop provoking him.'

'What have I got to do to make the little devil be quiet, then?'

'Don't call me a little devil, you great big pajero,' said Toby, rocking from one foot to the other on straightened legs.

'You can both stop this now!' shouted Helen. 'Bob, darling, Grit and Bill are here, now sit. Toby, daaarling, leave the kitchen at once!'

'What's a pajero?' Grit queried.

'You don't want to know,' said Helen. Smith laughed embarrassedly.

Toby went off, apparently to join the other children, singing, 'Daddy's a pajero; daddy's a pajero' in a high, choirboy voice.'

'You would have to have Toby and his friends home *this* lunch time,' grumped Smith.

'Oh, I'm sooo sorry I didn't have a crystal ball to tell me My Lord and Master would be coming home for lunch today.' She turned to face Grit and Ogle. 'Your being here is no problem but, like Bob, you have to take us as you find us.' Grit nodded earnestly at the woman whose husband she was growing to fantasise of cuckqueaning.

'Isn't it time you got them back to school?' asked Smith, 'Anyway, after all that, what was it you wanted to pick my brains about?'

Helen disappeared on a mission.

'I've already explained to Bob that you're the staff governor and worried about how Horace died.' Ogle interjected.

'Oh yes? I still don't know how you two know each other.' Grit shot into the blue.

'Bob tracked me down because I'm a union rep.'

She turned to Smith, 'Now why would you want to track down the union rep?'

'That should be self-explanatory. I am a member of the FUCA union and have a column in a national supplement which reports on disputes between colleges and unions.'

This reference to the *Draguian Educational Journal* brought out what was troubling Grit. 'I would've thought that, having written about Titas College, the last thing you would do was apply for a job here. And how you actually came to be appointed is beyond me.'

'We wanted to move out of London and the job was going. It's quite a specialised area I teach. Not many colleges do it.'

'So how did you actually get the job after you'd written such forceful criticism of the college?'

'I don't know exactly. It might have had something to do with who was on the panel.'

'Who was?'

'One of the vice principals. I believe she was turned down for Boyle's job.'

'Joan Fisher.'

'Yes.'

While Grit could see quite well how this enabled Smith to be offered his position at the college, it still seemed to her that he was avoiding discussing his reasons for moving to Witton-le-Cone. She wasn't to be deterred. 'What did you mean when you said you were looking forward to helping Horrors?'

Smith became irritated, 'Now you're putting words in my mouth.'

'No, I'm not. You definitely said it the first time I met you when we were outside in Smokers' Corner.'

'Did I really? All I can say then is it's confidential; I shouldn't have done. You were a stranger then. Never talk to strangers!'

Helen breezed conspicuously in front of Smith, plonking what looked like a timetable in front of him, 'Oh look, darling,' she said, feigning surprise as she pointed to it, 'You don't have another lesson until three o'clock. How about you take Toby and his friends back to school, hm?'

'I would, darling but, as I told you, this is a meeting.'

'And all the world stops turning so Bob can have his meetings. Next week *you're* bringing Toby home for lunch. I don't care what you have on.'

'You'll have to remind me.'

'Don't worry, I will.' With that, Helen picked a waxed jacket from a coat hook and went to chaperone the children.

Smith sighed, 'Where were we?'

'Doesn't the fact that Horace is dead make any difference to that?' asked Ogle, 'I mean, if he isn't here, are you still breaking a confidence?'

'I think I would need to discuss it with his wife before I told anyone else.'

'But surely if Grit is trying to find out what happened about Horace, wouldn't it be relevant?'

'Perhaps, but I don't think it would make much difference anyway. Changing the subject, can we get to the more immediate matter of what the junta are up to and possible industrial action?'

Grit was irritated at having her worries brushed aside on the basis of confidentiality. On the other hand, she did appreciate having to be back at work that afternoon, even if nobody else did. 'If you can't tell us about that, at least explain about what we can do to stop the new contracts and the fart system.'

'The what?'

'The facial recognition system. In a governors' meeting, I called it a fart, and the chairwoman threw me out.'

Smith laughed, 'Did she indeed?'

Smith went on to explain that the new contracts did not specify working hours because it made it harder for staff to claim they were working to their contracts if all the work didn't get done. But there were other ways to bargain. One of these would be to accept the fart system on condition Boyle stopped pursuing the new contracts of employment. However, Smith thought Boyle unlikely to let this stop him, claiming it would take mass industrial action and as many employment tribunals as possible to make him back down.

Grit and Ogle were happy for this advice, but she was still in the dark about how Smith was supposedly about to help Villiers before the final plummet. And she couldn't deny a slight feeling that Smith's explanation as to why he had moved to Witton-le-Cone had a cozen quality to it. Regrettably perhaps, this did not detract from the excitement she now felt whenever he was nearby.

Thirteen

Wednesday, 25th September

Grit had barely slept. Today was the day of staff training for the HR department. Today was supposed to be the day when she would commit dastardly acts that could lead to no end of trouble. Today could be the day she would be spotted and given the Grand Order of the Boot.

In her panic Grit encountered a last minute doubts. Would anyone be left behind in the department? Might she be seen by cameras she didn't know about? The real sticking point was whether the cabinets were locked and how she could get into them. She had not discussed her plan with anybody and thought that was how it should be. Smith or Ogle could easily have talked her out of it, and a careless word by anyone could lead to disaster for her career, such as it was. No, she concluded. It was better to tell *nobody*.

There would be other staff training days, wouldn't there, other opportunities to look in those cabinets? But could Grit possibly be better-informed than she was already?

If it wasn't to be now, would there ever be another time she might pluck up the courage? No, she needed to try to find out what she could *now*. Grit *was* going to HR, but would play it by ear. If she could get to her file that was one thing, but she would look for Villiers's file only if she was sure there was no chance of being caught.

That was the plan, at least.

* * *

After lunch, Grit made her way along to HR. Her legs were like jelly. Entering the reception area, the place seemed deserted. Then she realised that, if someone did appear, she had no explanation for being there. She hadn't even brought her formal request to see her records to provide a cover for her presence.

Bugger!

It would only take about ten minutes to write one out and put it in an envelope. There was plenty of time for that wasn't there?

Grit made her way back to her workspace. Finding her hands were shaking too much for her to write legibly, she typed the letter on the computer, printed it, bunged it into an envelope and addressed it to Alison Morrell. Her writing on the envelope was still very shaky, but she didn't know exactly how to set the printer up for envelopes and working it out would take precious time. Then it struck her: could this shakiness betray her seditious intentions to Morrell? Too late to worry about that. Grit headed back to HR with the request.

On the way, she felt even worse than before. An overbearing nervousness had become an underlying sense of dread. Arriving back, Grit checked her phone for the time: What on earth was the worry? There should be three hours to play with and she had taken only about twenty minutes. A degree of relief that had begun to sink in was blown away by voices, and a rustling sound, as two members of staff emerged from behind the secure door.

'There's nobody here now.' the first said when she saw Grit.

'That's alright; I'm just dropping this off.'

'You can give it to me; I'll take it in.'

'Okay,' Grit noticed how the envelope was quivering visibly in her hand as she gave it to the woman, who took it inside behind the door. Surely the woman must have noticed this.

'Thank you,' said Grit. She took her phone out, and tried to pretend she was texting, hoping that they wouldn't expect her to leave the reception area while they were still there.

'Come on, we're late already,' said the second woman. They rushed off, evidently more concerned about other matters.

On reflecting she may just have averted a catastrophe, Grit looked around for security cameras. There was one overlooking the desk. She looked through and around the area, half pretending to look for leaflets, and picked one up, entitled, *Bullying in the Workplace*. She then stood in silence for a while in case anyone came back. It was a relief to have been told nobody was there. This gave her the courage to go ahead with her plan. Grit looked up "MI5" on her phone.

Here goes, she thought as she entered the number 2374 into the key pad half expecting it not to work, but the door opened obediently - almost too obediently - as if it were inviting her inside.

* * *

Remembering where the filing cabinet Tracey Millicent had looked in was, she moved quickly to the unlit area. Her breathing became very rushed. Grit could just make out the letters "A-J" on a cabinet which looked in the right place and tried the drawer, but it wouldn't open, leading to a moment of blind panic. She stopped, looked round, and started to head back out to the public area. Then she noticed a small bunch of keys on a desk. No, they were too big, but she scanned a couple more desks for keys. Grit had always thought of herself as streetwise, but was coming to realise just what a novice she was at anything like this.

Then she noticed that on top of the very cabinet she had tried to open. Marked "Staff, A-J" was a single key. It wasn't easy to make out in the relative dark, so it wasn't surprising she'd missed it before. It fitted, and turned, but the drawer wouldn't open.

Bloody thing!

She turned and pulled, turned and pushed and then, as a final attempt before bottling out, turned and pushed, but held the key, turned it and let go of the drawer. The cabinet opened.

'Now, B, B, Bulmer.' Grit found her file straight away, removed it from the cabinet and took it to a desk where there was enough light to read it by. Staring aghast at the cover, she read the words "DO NOT RE-EMPLOY" scrawled in felt tip. Grit tempered the shock at seeing this with reason: *So this was what bothered Miss Millicent when she went to get the file!*

Annoyed at the effort she had put into re-applying for the job, Grit wondered what on earth there was in the file to justify such a direction. With great trepidation, she opened it, but didn't really know what she was looking for, so scanned over it all as best she could.

Some of the records seemed a little negatively worded, but there was nothing to worry about as far as she could tell at a glance. Then she found a statement by Phyllis Roberts, and another by Alison Morrell. These both seemed to be reporting how Grit had misbehaved in the recent governors' meeting.

Roberts had written, '*Miss Bulmer spoke in an abusive tone to the principal*'.

Morrell claimed that *'It was impossible to make progress in the meeting with Miss Bulmer's repeated and vexatious interruptions.'*

She took out her phone and photographed these statements, and the cover of the folder.

Surely they don't want to get rid of me because of what I say in governors' meetings!

After reading through her files in detail, she returned them to the cabinet and locked it, Grit checked the time. It was now a quarter to four. She had apparently been alone in silence since about half past two. How much longer could her luck hold, she wondered? A renewed urge to leave and not bother to look for Villiers's file was countered: *If they are getting rid of me anyway, could I really be in any more trouble by rummaging through a lot of other confidential documents?*

In answer to this, Grit made her way along to the cabinet marked "T-Z" and began trying the bunch of keys in the lock. None of them fitted. She then looked around for another errant key, but there was none. As a last gambit, the single key found on top of the 'A-J' cabinet was tried. It fitted like a glove and turned rather more easily. Grit wondered if all the cabinets could be opened by this key, but wasn't going to waste time finding out. The Rubicon had certainly been crossed now.

She searched up and down the cabinet, front and back, and through the 'V's several times, just to be certain that there was no file for Horace Villiers. Why was this? What happened to the files of deceased members of staff? Wasn't it usual to retain them for a period? If so, how long was this period?

Then she heard a door open.

Fourteen

Boyle had been chewing over what he had done with the passbook for his deposit account. He knew he had wanted to check it but couldn't find it at home. As a last ditch before reporting it, he thought he had better have a look in his desk at work.

Entering his secretary's office for the first time that day he found, to his annoyance, two men waiting for him. One was tall and held a notepad, pen and Dictaphone. The other was very short and had a camera with an enormous lens, and a flash on top. Boyle's first thought was that they had come to interview him about the press release he had sent about some derogatory comments a London-based art critic had made about the North East and, more importantly, his college. He began limbering himself up to take a principled stand against cultural snobbery.

'I take it you're press?' he said, extending his right hand.

'Yes, Tony Mandrake, Witton-le-Cone Chronicle.' said the man with the Dictaphone, taking his hand and shaking it with a grip Boyle found almost painful.

'Laurence Boyle, Principal and Chief Executive of Titas College. Can I just say that I think you men of the press do great work helping to raise the profile of Witton? We need to stick together to counter the slurs given out by the likes of Eric Pilchard.'

'I appreciate it,' said Mandrake, 'but we were actually here to interview you about the hand dryer.' Mandrake's voice rose on the word "dryer" to make it sound like a question.

'WHAT?'

'You agreed to test it out if you remember,' said his secretary, Lisa Booth.

Marshalling all his faculties of self-control, Boyle turned to face her so to exclude the journalists from the exchange. He lowered his voice almost to a whisper, 'Lisa, love, you know I hate hand dryers. I thought you could at least have found a reason they couldn't put the damned thing in.'

'I know you did, Maestro, but how would it have made you look if I'd done that?' she whispered back.

His secretary was right. He had his image as the great supporter of local enterprise to consider. Boyle was the Hands-On Principal and the Great Champion of Witton-le-Cone. That was why he remained on site rather than conducting the college's affairs from his wife's chalet in the Austrian Alps. If it got out that he had refused to test a design home-grown in his own domain, he might as well have been eight hundred-odd miles away.

'Besides,' she added, 'it was designed to address what you hate so much about them.'

'What was that?'

'Stopping the tiny bits of poo from blowing back out.'

'That does not enamour it to me.' He seethed under his breath. Lisa smiled in the direction of the journalists.

Boyle forced a grimace and then turned suddenly to face the music. 'As it was a prototype, I really wanted to test the dryer by having it installed in the bathroom next to my office.' He lied.

'I see,' said Mandrake, 'Can you tell me why you wanted to test it yourself?'

Boyle knew how to improvise good answers. 'At Titas College we create an environment where staff and students on different courses work together on projects. I don't know if you've seen our new vision statement?

'I don't think so.'

'It is "SHINE". We won't be launching it formally till the New Year, but we're very excited about it.'

'Shine?'

'Indeed: Support, Humility, Inclusion, Nurture, Embolden. Projects like this one increase the "buy in" to the different missions moving forward at our college.' Grasping the left lapel of his jacket he continued, 'As a hands-on principal, I am greatly excited by the prospect of testing the dryer.'

'Excellent, Mr Boyle. Is it possible we could just have a picture of you next to it?'

'Of course, provided it's actually been put in. Lisa, love, could you go through and see if they've finished?' Boyle made a mental note: *Whoever is behind this calamity is going straight on my termination list!*

Lisa's returned. He whispered to her, 'Who's putting it in? Is it safe?'

'He is a qualified electrician and he has tested it, electronically at least.'

'I see.'

'But don't forget it is a prototype design, Maestro,' she added. 'They did warn that just because it's electrically safe it doesn't mean it'll work perfectly.'

Look at where being the Hands-On principal was getting him! Boyle was now feeling deep regret at having asset-stripped Titas of Harbour Hall, a small Georgian mansion two miles outside Witton-le-Cone, with a maze and walled garden. It had been part of the Durham College estate. Wouldn't it have been so much better for him if he could have had it fitted it up with a luxurious apartment of offices, well away from the sharp end at The Cathedral? Too late now - at least for the time being.

'Cheer up, Maestro! You won't actually have to use the dryer if you don't want to. Not very often, anyway,' Lisa added.

Boyle frowned and followed the journalists through into his office. The scene in the en -suite bathroom was not something he was prepared for. Some of the tiles had been taken from the walls and channels were cut into the plaster. He did his best to conceal the full extent of his annoyance, asking, 'How long are you going to be?'

'It'll be at least an hour: you see I've got to wire it in.'

Bloody great!

Boyle then noticed something that caused him to double-take. The dryer had the word "GARNIER" written on the front. He felt himself beginning to tremble. This word had connotations he could not allow anyone to find out, yet somebody probably did know. The fact it was probably Horace Villiers and that he was dead provided some alleviation, but could Villiers have told anyone before his demise?

There was no way Boyle could mention the matter now. He looked away from the press men, trying to hide his anger. 'You mean there's no wiring?' he snapped, quietly at the electrician.

'That's right. I've got to run a new circuit from the fuse box...' The electrician smiled conspiratorially. 'It'll be worth it for you, mind. THIS THING'LL WARM YOUR BALLS UP GOOD AND PROPER!'

'Really? And who's going to fix my tiles?'

'We'll have to get a tiler in. Don't know when it'll be, though.'

'I see.' Boyle sighed, relieved to catch a glimpse of the edge of what looked like his deposit account passbook in the "out" tray. Feeling more at ease now with regard to his personal finances, he turned to the press men with an open-armed gesture, 'As you can see, it isn't finished. I don't know if you'd like to come back, or...?'

'We were hoping to get it in this week's edition.' said Mandrake. 'And it would be good to meet the person who designed it as well as a student or two who have worked on the project.'

Such demands were not for Boyle to deal with. Someone else should have organised it all, just as someone else should *never* have arranged for its installation in his en-suite. Did he have any control at all of his own college?

For God's sake!

'I'll just go and have a quick word with my secretary. If you'd be good enough to wait here for a minute...' He went back through to Lisa's office, closing the door behind him.

'This has gone too far! The damned thing hasn't even been fitted yet. It's the middle of the fucking term and I need my office. Who sent that press release?'

'I'm not sure,' she answered.

'You're not sure!' he repeated, mockingly. 'And who asked if I would test it?'

'I was approached by a couple of students.'

'Some termite in engineering's been stitching me up! Find out who it is. And while you're about it you can phone engineering and tell them to expect these two hacks.' While he was sure Villiers had been behind it all, clearly someone else was carrying on the infelicity.

Boyle painted the winning smile back on his face. 'I'm going to send you through to engineering where they'll have some students and a lecturer to look after you.'

'Thank you, but we were hoping for a picture of you with the dryer.'

'Of course, I'd be delighted, but I don't see how that's possible when it hasn't been fitted.'

'We can hold it.' said the electrician in blunt, pitmatic tones. He had been talking to the men while Boyle had been through in Lisa's office.

'I suppose I can do that.' At this point it was taking all of Boyle's effort to prevent his smile from becoming a grimace.

The electrician picked the dryer up. It was surprisingly heavy. Boyle took hold of the other side.

'Say kimchi,' said the short photographer. Boyle grinned his head off. The electrician looked unsmilingly towards him.

Click!

Boyle let go of his side of the dryer immediately, letting the electrician take the strain. 'I really do apologise that you gentlemen were sent a press release before it's been installed.'

'Not to worry,' said Mandrake, 'I think we've got the bones of it. There was something else, though,' he added more quietly.

'What's that?'

'You know what happened with the engineering lecturer, Horace Villiers?'

Boyle's face fell. 'Yes.'

'I was just wondering if... I mean, I could give you the opportunity to say anything about it.'

Fucking journalists would have to bring that bastard up.

'Here at Titas College, we are devastated about Horace's death,' he adopted his most sincere expression. 'He and I always had a very warm working relationship. That's another reason I agreed to test the dryer.'

The fucking termite!

Boyle wanted to ask if either of the two knew the name of the person who had sent the press release, but to have done so would have been to admit to men of the press he was not in control. No, he thought. He would have his secretary find out. That's what she was for, after all.

'There was something unrelated I was just dying to ask you, though.' said Mandrake.

Boyle smiled accommodatingly, 'Oh yes, what's that?'

'You know some of the staff and union have thrown their dummies out of the pram over Titas College's new contracts?'

'Huh, are you asking me or telling me?'

'I was leading up to another question as I'm sure you know.' As Mandrake said this, the photographer stifled a guffaw, looking downwards towards his enormous camera.

'What was that, then?'

'How do you reconcile forcing Titas College's teaching staff into punitive contracts with your membership and enthusiastic espousal of the Labour Party?'

'No comment. We'll leave it there, shall we gentlemen?'

'Evidently so! Thank you Mr Boyle.'

Boyle fixed his grin until the men of the press had disappeared from view. This last question peeved him deeply. He could just imagine the headline "*Revealed: **Real** Reason why Titas Principal is Labour Member*".

Fifteen

Startled by the sound of footsteps, Grit tried to place herself out of sight, hiding the far end of the darkened area between a large rubber plant and stand of coats. As she froze, Grit became highly aware of all of her body. She didn't know if anything was behind her and wasn't going to move to find out. On the other hand, what if there was no way out of the far side? She really didn't know the layout at all well. Worse, perhaps there was an opening of some sort behind her. What if someone turned on a light and exposed her from abaft?

Although this had no justification these days, she was still mortified by the thought of someone coming up behind her, asking mockingly, 'And whose fat bottom is waving hello to me here?'

As she huddled in her hidden position, a female figure in a knee-length dress and high heels strutted between the cabinets. As Grit saw it walk under a light, showing the extra-bright peroxide blond of its shoulder-length hair, she realised it was none other than Alison Morrell. The figure went straight to the open drawer, tutted loudly, and placed the file it was carrying in it. Leaving the drawer open, Morrell walked towards Grit, stopping about two feet short of the rubber plant she was hiding behind. Grit opened her mouth slightly to try to silence her breathing, which was much quicker than usual. As the aroma of Morrell's *Black Opium* perfume became perceptible, she thought Morrell had spotted her and was about to confront her, but Morrell unlocked the cabinet marked "A-J" and took out a file which looked remarkably like hers – the one she had been looking at seconds before. Would Morrell notice that the file was unusually warm? Apparently not: she then walked off into a side-office some distance away, shutting the door behind her, leaving the strong aura of her perfume behind.

Whose file had Morrell just put in the cabinet? It might have been routine, but was it? When she was sure all was quiet again, Grit emerged from her place of hiding and looked in the open drawer, straight down to "V". Not many files were there and... Lo and behold a file marked "Villiers" had materialized. Morrell must have taken his file out and replaced it for some reason. What reason?

Grit took it out and went over to a desk with some light on it. This file also had, "DO NOT RE-EMPLOY" scrawled on the front. If she were caught now there really would be trouble.

What the hell!

Villiers's file made much more interesting reading than her own. Note was taken of so many projects he had initiated. It seemed that at Durham College he had been some sort of golden boy. At the bottom of one, however, was a note, apparently from a doctor acting for the college, which read,

'*Dr Villiers acknowledges his bi-polar disorder and takes steps to keep it well under control. However, it is recommended that the condition be reviewed regularly as part of his appraisals in future.*'

Grit looked for such an appraisal and found, '*Concerns have been expressed regarding Dr Villiers' erratic behaviour. It is recommended that he be placed on paid sick leave for a period of six weeks initially.'* This was dated Tuesday the first of September. Looking through further, Grit was dismayed to find no specific reports of Villiers behaving erratically.

At the back of the file was a badly photocopied letter, dated 3rd August 1985, titled "RE: WILFRED GARNIER. It listed a number of accounting discrepancies which, in the writer's opinion, should be brought to Garnier's attention. The letter was signed, 'H. Villiers, Head of Product Development.'

At this point, Grit was so absorbed with the contents of Villiers's file that she failed to realise a clanking sound, previously a safe distance away, had become louder. Neither had she noticed the short, wiry, male silhouette which had appeared and stood with the light behind it, looking as if it was holding a portable rack or some other piece of torture equipment.

'What are you doing here?' said the silhouette in what seemed a stern voice. It walked towards her, and she began to make out the man's square jaw and exceptionally handsome face, which were perhaps at odds with his slight build and bald pate. It was one of the caretakers carrying a ladder.

'Never seen you round here,' he said.

'No, probably not.'

'I've had a call to come and fix these lights. You are Grit, aren't you?'

'Yes.'

'You know me, Fred. I used to smoke. Gave it up though.'

Grit finally recognised Fred Thompson, who used to join her in the smokers' area at West Durham College. '*That's* where I know you from. I was wondering.' Quite relieved to see who it was, Grit was still careful not to let her guard down.

'It was a Tracy Millicent who reported it last week. We're so short-staffed it's taken till now for me to get around to it. You don't know where I can find her, do you?'

'No, er. Actually I'm not really supposed to be here.'

The door to the side office opened again, and Morrell's raised voice could be heard in the distance. Grit shot to the cabinet and had put Villiers's file in what she thought was the right place before Morrell appeared, followed by Tracey Millicent.

'But the drawer was left open when I went in. Really Miss Millicent, I've told you before, this sort of slack security is not acceptable. Keep up, please. The drawer was open. I left it as it was so you can see for yourself.'

Fred observed the scene with raised eyebrows as Morrell stopped and squinted towards the darkened area where he and Grit were standing near the open cabinet drawer.

'Will you come here please, Miss Bulmer?'

Grit walked towards Morrell and could see a file under her arm. She was now sure it was hers. Morrell appeared to be holding it carefully to cover the writing 'DO NOT RE-EMPLOY'.

'What are you doing in here?'

Grit was limbering up for a battle based on what she had found in her file, deciding to fight back. 'What's that you've got under your arm?'

'My paperwork is none of your business.'

Before Grit could bite back again, Thompson jumped in to the exchange. 'You are the young lady who reported the lighting problem, aren't you?'

'I think that was me, but it was ages ago.' said Tracy.

'Then it's my mistake,' said Fred. 'This young lady was in the waiting area. I thought she was the one who reported the light off, so I asked her to come through to show me where it was.' Then he turned to Grit. 'Off you go.'

Noting Morrell's frustrated expression, Grit left them to it. Then she realised. She hadn't photographed anything from Villiers's file. *Damn!*

Sixteen

Having dispatched the journalists satisfactorily, it occurred to Boyle that to call the hand dryer "Garnier" risked copyright infringement of a well-known manufacturer of cosmetics. Pleased to have found a legitimate reason to get rid of the name, he telephoned Engineering and made this clear.

Boyle's next task was to open his mail with the little poniard he relished using, but first he retrieved his deposit account passbook from his "out" tray. Examining it cursorily, everything seemed in order and he popped the document in one of his jacket pockets.

Several letters were about various business-related events, including one inviting him to speak at the Tyne and Wear Chamber of Commerce. Hitherto, Boyle had tended to shy from public engagements like this but, having discovered the esteem the position of Principal seemed to bestow on him from certain quarters, not to mention the chances to network they offered, he opted to answer in the affirmative. Taking out his trusty Faber-Castell ball-point, he wrote a reply on college watermarked paper to that effect. At this rate he would be President of the Worshipful Order of Brewers before long – perhaps even Sir Laurence. And quite right too!

A good job done, Boyle paper-clipped a note to the letter with the address and instructions to post it and placed it in his out-tray. Cap back on pen, he proceeded to the next letter. The edge was lost from his mood when he saw the letter heading "Federated Union of College Associates".

What the hell are those termites up to?

As he read down, his levels of annoyance increased inversely to his mood. Members were to have a ballot on whether to engage in a disruption and if this should be Stage One, Stage Two, or an all-out strike.

'BASTARDS!' he ejaculated, banging his fist on the desk.

He was particularly peeved that only about a quarter of staff were on the new contracts. Three quarters still had their hours stipulated. He had dearly hoped to have most, or all, on contracts with no working hours specified before the union managed to get around to making trouble.

The door to the en-suite was open and the electrician had been working away quietly. He looked up with a start. 'Is there a problem, Mr Boyle?' Boyle glared across. He had forgotten the man was there. Had he not, he would probably have curbed his outburst, but no matter. It was just an electrician. 'You could say that.'

'Sorry, what have I done wrong?' asked the electrician, looking a little hurt.

Pressing the intercom button, Boyle shook his head at the man. He should have known The Maestro's little conniption had not applied to him. 'Lisa, I need you to take down a letter for me, *immediately*.'

She came through, notebook and pen at the ready, to take shorthand. Agitated at what he had just read, Boyle had got up. He now sat on his desk, arms folded, his right leg swinging. 'Now I want this circulated to all FUCA members. No. Better make it to all members of teaching and lecturing staff.

'"Dear Parasite..." No! I want this addressed using each member of teaching staff's first name. Every last termite. Try to keep it informal. Heading, "Upcoming ballot for industrial action." "It has come to my attention that members of FUCA intend holding a ballot on the second of October." New paragraph, "Together, we have come a long way since the financial troubles suffered-"'

'-But doesn't that exclude staff who weren't at Durham College?'

Boyle glowered for a couple of seconds before this sank in, 'Oh fuck, yes it does. But you know what I'm trying to do, don't you?'

'I think so. Finding common ground with teaching staff.'

'Exactly. The problem is the termites that have joined College since then.'

'How about pointing out your achievement at saving Durham College - not wording it so nakedly of course - and asking staff to trust your judgement on the matter of the contracts?'

Boyle unfolded his arms to stop himself falling onto the desk and looked upwards, now supporting himself with them, 'Yes, something like that. "I hope that the example set by my rescue of Durham College will impress on you all the need to think very carefully about protesting against action necessary to ensure the secure future of our college."'

'You've got it, Maestro.'

'Yes, that's it, "Best wishes, etc."'

He stood for a moment. 'Let's hope that makes the termites think twice. Of course, I'll have any of them unwise enough to think they can do anything.'

Seventeen

In her disillusionment, Grit had applied for several jobs away from Titas College. Were she made an offer for any of them, it would be good riddance to Titas. That was the plan, anyway. The problem was that, as the staff governor, she felt tied to the place. As for other possible jobs, either they were many miles away or part-time and didn't bring enough to cover the mortgage. At this rate, to keep applying would mean going after any job, be it cleaning, care work or, God forbid, telesales.

Titas had a monopoly over adult education jobs between Tyneside and Teesside. Because of this, teachers and lecturers so employed found it problematic to go somewhere with better pay and conditions, either subjecting themselves to a long commute or by moving.

Grit had bought her house seven years before, when the housing market peaked before the Financial Crisis. She was therefore paying for a bigger mortgage than her house was now worth, and money was getting very tight. There was no point in asking Conor Gallagher, George's father, for money. Between his decreasingly regular voyages as a merchant seaman, what he had to spare was spent on drink. She worried about the prospect of a twenty percent pay cut. But that was if she got the job, which seemed extremely unlikely. The words, *DO NOT RE-EMPLOY* kept echoing in her head.

On top of this worry about her job, Grit still hadn't received copies of her employment records. She had seen them already, but that wasn't the point. Bumping into Smith at Smokers' Corner, he told Grit she should chase her request.

'I know, Bob, but it makes me so nervous. I never realised what it could do to you. Besides, what is the point when I've already seen most of them?'

'Seen *most* of them, what do you mean?'

Damn! She had not told anybody about her recent intrusions to HR, 'I just expect I have, that's all. You know, my Statement of Employment Particulars and stuff.'

Smith didn't look as if he bought this, but played along, 'Nonsense, there will be things on your record you won't have seen. The longer it takes for them to show you it, the less of it you'll see.'

DO NOT RE-EMPLOY, Grit thought. *They'll have to put it in another folder for a start!*

'Anyway, where are you off to now?'

'I'm due for another interview. It's in Gateshead.'

Smith wasn't familiar with the names of all the buildings associated with Titas and the Mill House premises accommodated several groups of offices, 'What interview – have you got another job?'

'I thought I'd try; it's for a playgroup manager.'

'I see. I'll miss you.'

Bob would miss me if I left, she thought, *Halleluiah!*

'I haven't got it. Besides, I've applied for my own job already. Doubt I'll keep it, though.'

Smith smacked his brow with the palm of his right hand, 'Oh God, you haven't, have you?'

'Well, yes. I thought about it and even if they're not playing fair I don't want to be dismissed and have to fight the case in court.'

'They're counting on that. You know you'd win.'

'No I don't. They've got all the big lawyers. I can't afford that.'

'You wouldn't need to. There is too much precedent. We know that there's a shortage of English teachers here and, under the Transfer of Undertakings, you are entitled to continue employment under your old terms. Just because everyone who worked at West Durham College was moved here it doesn't make any difference. What does in these cases is demand. And there is a bigger demand than ever for English teachers, especially with Boyle sucking up all the grants for SEN students.'

'I know you say that, but you don't have my worries.'

'Perhaps not. In the mean time, they will also be looking for you to flunk your interview.' Smith transferred his cigarette from his left hand to his right, 'Don't balls it up!'

'That's easier said than done. Christ, I feel like shit.'

Smith smiled, 'Try not to. If you don't feel so bad you'll be less likely to flunk it.'

'It's alright for you. They're not making your lot apply for your jobs for at least another term.'

'I'm on a new-type contract already. Remember, I only just started here.'

Then something struck Grit, 'Bob, when you were talking about looking forward to helping Horace, was it because he was going to take the college to court?'

'I said before I wasn't going to talk about that,' he looked around, furtively, 'but confidentially we did discuss it.'

'And what stopped him: too much stress? Maybe he couldn't afford to lose his job. A bit like me, eh?'

'Oh no, Horace could afford to give up his job. He had a big job in industry before. He'd have been earning all of half of what Boyle gets.'

'I heard about it at the funeral. But if he was earning that much, does that less likely it was suicide?'

Smith paused uncomfortably. '...Which brings us back to why you've gone and applied for your job.' He sighed, 'You really shouldn't have done. But remember this. '

'What?'

'They will be playing on your nerves getting the better of you. Don't let them and you're two thirds there.'

Eighteen

After a daily management meeting, Boyle, as he often did, took Morrell aside for a little chat. She confessed her concerns about what she thought Grit had seen. 'You know we want rid of the Bulmer girl?

Boyle gestured to Morrell that she was speaking too openly. As she moved into his confidence, he nodded.

'I'm afraid I might have a bit of bad news on that front.'

Boyle adopted his expressionless face. 'Go on,' he said slowly.

'Well, it's like this, Maestro, um...'

Boyle stood in stony silence. Having been brought to tears by his most recent outburst at her, Morrell was intimidated. 'You know you told me we needed to get rid of a certain member of staff?'

'I never *said* anything of the sort, Alison. Don't put words in my mouth.'

'Well then. Perhaps I should say we agreed it might be best if she wasn't here after the staff re-organisation.'

'You could put it that way. If you had to.'

'Thank you. Er... Margaret Bulmer has sent a letter of request for her staff records.'

'Well send her them.'

'The thing is, er, after we agreed the, you know.'

'Yes.'

'I wrote "Do not re-employ" on her file and collected a statement from Phyllis about her behaviour at that meeting. I made one myself too.'

Boyle exploded. 'AND YOU'RE ASKING ME WHAT TO DO ABOUT THAT?'

Morrell shuddered, 'More keeping you in the picture, Maestro. If she has managed to look at her file or to copy what's in it somehow, she could make out as if she was being constructively dismissed.'

'She'll see only what you want her to see.' He looked at her agitatedly. 'Christ, Alison, it should be bloody obvious!'

'That's not all, though.'

'Oh God. What now?'

'On Tuesday I went to check something in the staff records cabinets. She was standing right next to the one where her records are kept.'

'It was locked, I take it.'

Morrell felt so cornered at this point, she couldn't bring herself to tell Boyle the truth. 'Oh yes: I tried it after she'd gone. The question is, what was she doing there?'

'She shouldn't have been there. She had no authorisation. If it's ammunition you're after, she's given you all you need, woman. Remember, I don't take prisoners.'

'There's a problem. One of the caretakers was there to repair a broken light. He told us he had mistaken Bulmer as the person who reported it and invited her through from reception.'

'Well talk to Weightman. Get whoever it was to tell the truth.'

'There's only really one way to find out.'

'What's that?'

'The CCTV.'

'In that case, if Whiteley won't play ball, talk to the V-P Admin. Tell him it's on my authority and if he won't budge let me know and I'll give him a ring.'

'Okay, Maestro.'

'Christ, the things I have to think of.'

Boyle had been unable to remember the name of the head caretaker, Ron Waverley.

* * *

What Morrell had been unable to bring herself to tell him was that Bulmer had in fact been shortlisted for interview that afternoon. Given what Bulmer might now have found in her employment record, Morrell preferred to avoid a constructive dismissal case as this would undoubtedly end up as her headache.

Morrell now realised she needed to do all she could to counter Maestro's diminishing opinion of her. Now certain of what Grit had been up to, Morrell went straight from there to the office behind the main reception where cameras were monitored. She wanted the recordings from the cameras based in HR. After a couple of minutes, the security officer returned with a glum look on his face. 'This is most unfortunate, Miss Morrell. It seems the data for all our cameras has been accidentally wiped.'

'How come?'

'I've no idea. I've got a note here explaining what happened,'

'Have you any idea who wrote it?'

'It'll be one of the caretakers. I don't know which.'

Morrell pointed to the bottom of the letter, 'Isn't that a signature?'

'It does look as if it could be.'

'I need to take this and make a copy?'

'That's strictly against regulations. I can copy it for you here if you like.'

'That *would* be useful.'

The officer took the original and copied it. He then gave it to Morrell who asked, 'Can I see the original, please?' She then held the two next to each other and studied them closely for a good half a minute before handing the original back, 'Right, thank you.'

The officer looked baffled as she turned and left. Morrell then telephoned Ron Waverley to ask who was on duty when the CCTV outage was reported. Waverley told her that he had been aware of an accidental deletion of the files several days before, but not its instigator. This was not satisfactory. Morrell wanted to find out exactly who had deleted the files. Was Waverley playing ignorant?

Nineteen

Ever since she had read "DO NOT RE-EMPLOY" on her file, the words had echoed continually in Grit's head. She could see the words on the file when she closed her eyes. Even in her dreams they kept emerging. One dream involved a student handing her some coursework. It was in an exercise book like the ones when she was at school. All seemed fine until she went to mark it, finding those dreaded words written on the inside cover. In another dream, she had gone to the Hay-on-Wye book festival and met President Clinton. He signed a copy of his autobiography for her. She was delighted with this and couldn't wait to get home to read it. When finally she did so, she opened the book and read the inscription, "*DO NOT RE-EMPLOY*" apparently in the president's handwriting. There were so many other dreams like this and, on remembering the few she did, Grit found herself beginning to doubt her sanity.

She was afraid that the longer the college strung her along, the more hoops she would have to jump through before those fateful words became inevitable. When this point finally came, Grit would find herself too down-trodden to be capable of anything, either in the form of some sort of challenge to it or even doing a different job.

She really would have let down all those who needed her to stand up for them, whether they realised it or not; her colleagues, Mrs Villiers, Wesley Johnson and, more importantly, her son, George. They needed someone to do the right thing in their interests. She might drive herself to a point where she just couldn't be that person any more.

These worries carried on as she sat waiting for her interview in Mill House. One of many of Titas College's outposts, this soulless office block was just on the edge of the Kettle industrial estate, about a mile outside Witton.

A middle-aged woman Grit did not recognise emerged from a narrow corridor which opened into the area. She looked at her clipboard and called out, 'Margaret Bulmer.' Grit sighed, got up and did her best to smile at the woman.

Her heart was in her mouth. Who else would be on the panel?

'It's through here.' The woman opened a door at the end of the narrow corridor and gestured for her to go through it.

As she emerged from the corridor, the other members of the panel were revealed one by one. First she noticed her section manager, Maria Hetherington. Her presence was no surprise: they had always had a sound working relationship – or so Grit had thought. But as more of the room came into view, she saw, sitting next to her the bright reflection from the familiar bleach-blond hair. Grit's heart sank. Alison Morrell gestured towards the chair, her bracelets swinging below her wrist, as she pouted while licking the front of her top teeth. It was only as Grit moved to sit down that she noticed one of the files face down on the table in front of them. She could not be certain, but it looked very much like her file she had tracked down in HR. If it was, she had no chance.

'Please sit down, Margaret.'

She heard Smith's voice in her head.

Don't balls it up.

* * *

Looking back on the experience, Grit had to admit that the greater part of the interview seemed more like an interrogation. The woman who showed her in asked, 'How do you think you've done during this last year?' Grit's thoughts returned immediately to the elephant on the file.

'I think I've done very well,' she said.

'Why do you think so?'

'I've managed to meet all my targets. My students have made progress and, if you look at the inspection I had, it was rated as, "Outstanding" in all but one of the criteria.'

'Is that all you have to say?' asked Morrell, arms folded.

'Well there's all that, and of course all the extra work I've done serving as staff governor.'

The panel stirred uncomfortably as Morrell spoke, 'Yes, about that...'

Grit raised her eyebrows, waiting for a question. Morrell procrastinated.

What's the bitch playing at?

'I was at the meeting of the board where you made some wild suggestions about the death of Horace Villiers. It could have been an accident, you said, because Titas College is not a safe place. Another was that he could have killed himself because of his working conditions at Titas College. What was the other thing? ...Oh yes, you suggested the possibility he could have been murdered, but not by whom.'

'If it isn't known how Dr Villiers came to fall from the Tower, could *you* suggest another possibility as to how it happened?' Grit was not to be trifled with.

Morrell pulled her philtrum tight, as if she had swallowed a glassful of acid. 'Except for the murder scenario, perhaps, can you tell me what those you suggested have in common, Margaret, hm?

Grit let out a short laugh, 'You mean a negative portrayal of the college?'

'ABSOLUTELY!' Morrell began to raise her voice. 'And yet you were prepared to give voice to these wild scenarios at a board meeting.' She banged the table, causing her bracelets to jangle, repeating, 'A BOARD MEETING!'

Grit found herself shocked suddenly into a fantasy in which she grasping the file that was in front of her. Morrell's hands held onto it for dear life, but she finally twisted the thing, still held by Morrell, to show the writing she knew was on the other side. 'And what's this?' she asked.

The others present gasped as Morrell shouted, 'See! The Maestro and I were right all along. We can't possibly employ someone who behaves like that!'

Grit's reverie was kicked into touch by Morrell. 'Haven't you anything to say for yourself?'

This train of thought had, thankfully, spent some of Grit's anger. 'Yes. I am being interviewed for a job. A less good job than my current one, but decline seems the way of things in this place.'

'That's hardly fair, Margaret. It may have escaped you that under the terms of the new contract you would be under forbid you from making slurs or innuendos against the college. If you don't want to continue working at Titas College, then I don't see why-'

'-I do, but that isn't because it's a great place to work. It isn't. And I'll tell you what's not fair, interviewing someone for a job, and then making accusations toward her about an extra duty she does out of the goodness of her heart.'

Morrell licked her teeth again and, looking derisively at Grit, appeared to nudge Maria Hetherington under the table.

Certain she was going to lose her job, Grit felt a strong temptation to punch any member of the panel who said the wrong thing.

Mrs Hetherington sprang reluctantly into life, 'Alison tells me she found you in Human Resources.'

'That's right.'

'You do know that area is out of bounds to non-HR staff, don't you?'

'-Absolutely. Out of bounds. Yes.' Morrell cut in, licking her teeth again.

Grit had felt wrong-footed once. She was damned if it was going to happen a second time. *Stick to Fred's story. If it doesn't work, I'm a goner anyway.*

'I went there to hand in a request to see my file I had written. Do you have the request?'

'No.'

'Well you should.'

Morrell rummaged briefly in the file, 'Oh, yes. Yes apparently we do.'

'I'm glad to hear it.' Grit continued, 'I'd just handed it to one of your staff. She told me nobody was there, took it and left. Anyway, I was about to leave and along comes Fred Thompson with a ladder. "You wouldn't mind showing me where this light's out?" he asked, punching the combination into the door. Anyway, I could see part of the room was dark, so I said, "I'm not sure. Could it be over here?" I walked along to the darkened area and Fred followed me. It was then that Miss Morrell came along with another member of staff.'

A half-smile impressed itself on Morrell's face. 'That's a lie, Margaret, and you know it,' she crowed, triumphantly.

'I beg your pardon?'

'The last staff to attend the afternoon seminar left my department at two fifteen. That was an hour and fifteen minutes before I found one of the filing cabinets open and another five and a half minutes before I returned with Miss Millicent to find you and Thompson. So you couldn't possibly have handed your request to anyone other than me, or Miss Millicent, at quarter to four. And I checked with her. She said you did not hand it to her.'

Damn!

Grit hated lying, and Morrell of all people had to call her on it. She sat back and folded her arms. 'I've told you what happened. If it bothers you so much, then it's for you to prove otherwise, isn't it? Can we move on, please?

The room fell silent.

Twenty

Interviews for the English lecturers' posts concluded for the day, Morrell went back to her office and studied the handwriting on her photocopy of the note left when the files disappeared. She compared it with the signatures on all the Statements of Employment Particulars of all the caretaking and ancillary staff. She wasn't sure, but thought it matched Thompson's. Was there any point in getting back to Waverley over this, or would he just stall her? During the interview, Bulmer referred to the caretaker as Fred, didn't she? How very cosy! With this in mind, she found herself clacking assertively down to Ron Waverley's office, knocking twice.

'Ello?' came the answer eventually.

Morrell found Waverley sitting with a telephone receiver wedged to his ear by his right shoulder, pencil and note-pad in hand. He gestured her to an old kitchen chair near the door. 'Just a minute.'

Morrell did as she was told, albeit with steam coming out of her nostrils, while Waverley scribbled on his notepad, saying "Yes" and "No" at frequent intervals. Eventually he hung up, 'Sorry about that; someone's just done graffiti all over the men's toilets on the main concourse.'

Suffering the indignity of being put on hold while the head caretaker dealt with graffiti of all things, her stare hardened. 'Is that all?'

'No. Apparently this graffiti accused the college's distinguished principal of murder, so we've closed the toilets and we're getting it cleaned up. I called the police, and all they'd do was come and photograph it. If they classed it as a hate crime they might take it more seriously.' Waverley chortled quietly. 'Anyway, how can I help you, Mrs ...Morrell, is it?'

'Miss Morrell, actually.' She showed Waverley her photocopy of the note. 'I was wondering whether you could tell me if you recognise the signature on here.'

He glanced at it briefly. 'I can't say I do. Sorry.'

'That's unfortunate, because whoever left the note managed to dump much needed CCTV footage.'

'Much needed; why, exactly?'

'I found one of your caretakers next to the staff files in Human Resources with a member of teaching staff, Margaret Bulmer.'

'Oh dear, what were they doing?'

'Just standing, talking. He had come to fix the lights.'

'You mean they weren't...?'

'Oh no, not at all. It's just that I've been concerned about a breach of confidential files in my department and wanted to see the footage. Then I found out from the security office that the files have been deleted. I know all files are over-written after five days anyway, but...'

'I see, so you want to find out who deleted the files because they might have wiped something important?'

'Exactly.'

'Do you know if anything has been taken?'

Morrell stalled for a moment: the question arose as to why she should be so concerned to see the footage if nothing had been stolen.

'I'm not aware of that, no, but we have so many files there, it would take several weeks at least to check everything.' She thought she should drive her point home, 'And Miss Bulmer was not authorised to be there.'

As he sat facing her, Waverley leant sideways on his desk, 'How about you leave it with me, and I'll ask around?'

Morrell wasn't happy, but what else could she do?

'Very well, if you'll let me know what you're going to do about it when you've spoken to him.'

Morrell so wanted to make Maestro happy by getting rid of Margaret Bulmer. But if Bulmer had somehow managed to copy the entire contents of her file, she could well bring a case of constructive dismissal against the college when she left.

Twenty One

It was Saturday. Grit found two letters on her doormat. One was from Oak Tree Playgroups Ltd. She opened it and looked, reading silently to herself, 'Dear Miss Bulmer, thank you for the application for the above position. I regret...' *Oh well, it was worth a punt. Besides, I doubt I was cut out for managing small children full-time, let alone the other employees there.*

The other was from Titas College. *They didn't hang about getting rid of me!*

She didn't want to open it, but braced herself, ripping open the envelope.

'What are you doing?' asked George as he reached the bottom of the stairs.

'Reading the post.'

'Why are you looking at the ceiling, then?'

'I thought I noticed a crack there,' she said, pretending that she had a reason for looking away from the letter. What would George have thought of her if he had realised the real reason?

He looked over her forearm at the letter. 'Dear Miss Bulmer,' George started reading. Before she could tell him it was her post and he shouldn't be looking at it, he had managed to glean, disjointedly, 'We are delig. tud to conf. to confim'.

That was unexpected!

Grit forced herself to look at the letter. In disbelief, she turned it over to see if there was anything missing, some hidden message or a funny date, but no.

'Oh, well that is a relief!' she said, breathing slightly heavily.

'Have you got yourself a new job?' George asked.

'No. It means I haven't lost my old one. That's all.' It was odd to be relieved to be stuck at Titas, but Grit was. At least she could just about continue the struggle to pay her mortgage: better than ending up homeless or in some privately rented hovel on the local housing association's interminable waiting list.

'Mam?'

'Yes, pet?'

'How come your surname's Bulmer when mine's Gallagher?'

'Because your dad's surname is Gallagher.'

'But that doesn't make sense.'

'It's usual. Conor and I weren't married, so I didn't take his name. But the child normally takes the father's name.'

'No, what I mean is, I should take your name, 'cos I live with you, not him.'

'That's very well argued, darling. Can we talk about it another time?'

'Alright.'

Twenty Two

First thing on Monday morning, Boyle concluded a meeting with Seiji Azuma (V-P, PR), Tom Scruton (V-P Finance) and Myrtle Howard. They had been discussing Titas College's bid to expand its incursion into prison education. They were also shifting management of the finances and administration to a company, *Novum*, set up by the college for this specific purpose.

'I'll leave the matter in Myrtle's capable hands,' said Boyle. 'After all, she's done a magnificent job of putting together low cost bids to Prolapse, the Prison Objectives Learning and Practice Service, to take over offender learning.'

Suddenly, Alison Morrell burst in with her engine running.

'GET OUT!' he shouted. 'If you want to see me, talk to my secretary.'

'But Maestro, I thought you'd want to see this straight away.' She was brandishing a newspaper.

Appreciating that Morrell could have good reason for intruding on his private meeting, Boyle moderated his tone. 'I'm in a conference here.'

'I think that's everything for now isn't it, Maestro?' Howard interjected, helpfully.

'Yes. Very good work, Myrtle, thank you.'

'Oh, thank *you*, Maestro,' said Howard in her silken drawl, and left quietly.

'Right, you stay there. Don't move an inch.' Boyle said.

Morrell froze.

'No not you, you!' he spluttered, pointing to Azuma. 'I want a word with you.'

Azuma bowed.

'Now, Alison, just what is it that can't wait?'

Morrell placed a copy of that morning's *Draguian* in front of him. The headline said it all. "HAND-DRYER CONNECTION IN MYSTERY COLLEGE DEATH".

Already seething at this, Boyle noticed the picture was the one of him holding the hand dryer. Now apoplectic at having been misled, he read on, *'The inquest into the death of HORACE VILLIERS, former lecturer at TITAS COLLEGE, has recorded an open verdict. Villiers fell to his death in unknown circumstances on 9th September. His wife, Marion Villiers, told our reporters, 'Horace has been under stress for some time. My heart attack certainly upset him, but he had been unhappy at work. I think he was being bullied.'*

'Titas College's principal, LAURENCE BOYLE, told reporters that he had always had an extremely positive relationship with Villiers, to the extent that he had agreed to test a HAND DRYER, designed and built by Villiers's students in his suite at the college.'

'Christ, even the bastard's wife is a mealy-mouthed gorgon... Which is why I wanted a word with you, Azuma.'

'Very good, Maestro?'

'You weren't aware of a press release sent to the Chronicle by our engineering department, were you?'

'No, Maestro. And as far as this article is concerned, I had no idea.'

Boyle peered at Azuma, pasty-faced. 'Are you sure?'

'Oh yes.'

For fuck's sake!

'Just as I thought. It needs to be made clear that all communications about College activities should go through you – or me, of course.'

'Indeed, Maestro. I agree entirely. Would you like me to send out a memo?'

'Yes, do that. And if you find anybody – and I mean ANYBODY – flouting your instructions, report them directly to me, is that clear?'

'Crystal clear, Maestro.' Azuma bowed again and left.

Boyle now turned to Morrell, who had been standing anxiously throughout the exchange. 'Let's also get *this* crystal clear, Alison. I will not tolerate people bursting into my private meetings. Even insiders.'

'I'm really sorry, Maestro, but I thought-'

'Yes, I know. I'll let you off this time.'

'Oh, *thank you*, Maestro.'

Waving Morrell away, he pressed the button on the intercom. 'Lisa, Love. I've got an errand for you. I need you to look up the report of the inquest into Villiers's death and see if you can find anything – and I mean, *anything* - negative about this college. Do you think you can do that for me?'

'Yes, Maestro.'

Having switched off the intercom, Boyle sat alone in his office for a few moments.

Fucking journalists!

Twenty Three

The next morning, having dropped George off at his school breakfast club, Grit had got to her "workstation" by ten past eight. Behind with her lesson planning, she was pleased to have got into work early. She had been there about fifteen minutes before hearing a voice behind her.

'Can I talk to you, Miss Bulmer?' Grit recognised the voice, but didn't expect to hear it then. She swivelled round.

'Yes, of course. But how did you get in here; this is a restricted area?'

'Dunno. I just came in. Dude over there handed me the door as he went through.' Wesley pointed towards Smith, who had just arrived at his own workstation, plonking his briefcase on the desk. Grit hid that this made her heart leap.

'Okay, okay. But we'll have to go somewhere else. If we stay here, questions are bound to be asked.' Grit had expected her re-appointment to ease all anxiety she had about her excursion into HR, but it hadn't. It had begun to seem, with each day that passed, as though she was becoming more and more afraid to be seen putting a foot wrong.

'Right, typical that is, Miss!' said Wesley, true to character.

Grit took him to the room where she was to hold her first class of the day. She moved one of the chairs round so they sat opposite each other in the corner.

'Fire away, then.'

'It's about that dude who jumped off the roof.'

It struck Grit that she hadn't thought about how to answer questions like this. On one hand, the little matter of whether Villiers had lost his job at the college did not put the establishment in a good light, particularly if he *had* killed himself. On the other, even a cursory glance at her new contract divulged the dire consequences of even whispering anything to suggest that Titas was anything less than educational utopia.

This niggled her; had Villiers's employment been terminated, or might he have been re-employed like she was? After all, "DO NOT RE-EMPLOY" had not come to pass in her case. On the other hand, was Morrell's suspicion of what Grit might have found out in HR the reason she had kept her job?

But then again, it wasn't surprising if rumours about Villiers had spread like wild fire. Speaking of rumours, she didn't *know* anything apart from the fact that Villiers had died as a result of a rapid descent from the tower. At this point Grit considered her best strategy was to play dumb.

'Man jumping off the roof? I don't know about that!'

'Seriously, Miss? It was all round the college.'

'Is it? When did it happen?'

Wesley leant back in his chair, left arm draped over the back. 'You're joking, aren't you, Miss?'

'Of course not.'

He leant forward to drive his point home, 'You know when most of us left your class early? That's 'cos some had got texted to go and see what was going on. I didn't know till the next day when Tez told me.'

'I had heard a rumour, but I prefer not to act on rumours.'

Wesley shook his head, 'You're unbelievable, Miss. You know, I thought you were cool.'

Grit stood her ground, 'I'm not prepared to admit or support anything I have only heard on the grape vine. It is clearly a very delicate matter and there's no way I'll give credence to other people's fishing expeditions when I honestly don't know very much myself.'

'But when something like that happens, don't you think everyone should know about it, like, to stop all the rumours going around?'

'That's a good question, Wesley, and I'd give you a very good mark if it was in an essay you'd written.'

'Can't you do that anyway, Miss?' Wesley grinned.

"I'm afraid not. I will ask around to see if there's anything authoritative I can tell you, but this should be released officially in time.'

'You mean when all of them upstairs have got their story straight, don't you?'

'Only if I'm sure it's true. I mean when.'

'What if you're never sure? I mean, it can't look good when a sacked member of staff falls off the tower.'

'Even if he was sacked, it doesn't mean-' *Shit!*

'-Aha, so he was sacked, then!'

'I didn't say that.'

'Yes you did.'

'I was talking hypothetically, based on what you said. I don't know that, either.'

'I didn't know he was sacked.'

'Why did you say it then?'

'Flying a kite. I'd heard a rumour.' Wesley looked really smug for scoring his point. Grit could have punched him.

'Could it be that your rumour might have come from the same place as mine?' She impressed herself at the save.

'You've got me there, miss.'

'Well then?'

'But I'll get to the bottom of it. You know I went to some of that dude's classes. He was okay. I'd just turn up and he'd include me, whatever they were doing.'

'Oh Wesley. You are a difficult student...' A one-sided smile spread across his face as Grit continued, '... But I admire your sort of curiosity. I wish I had it.' Grit knew fine well that, amongst many, many other things, her sojourn to HR. indicated she had *that sort of* curiosity in spades.

'Do you mean the curiosity what comes when you've got a chip on your shoulder?'

'Am I wrong?'

'Yeah. Well, maybes.' Wesley winked.

She knew him alright, but then he tilted his head to the side some of his dreadlocks fell away, 'There wasn't anything else, was there?'

'You've forgotten, I s'pose.'

Then it struck her suddenly: 'Your grant. Don't tell me you still haven't been paid.'

'Nope.'

'Right, well come with me now. We'll go to Student Services while I've got a few minutes.'

* * *

Grit walked with Wesley across the quadrangle from the college's main building, past the various fountains, none of which were running, and green areas, to the impractically small office.

'I've never been to Student Services yet; not in this new building, anyway.'

'Are you impressed, Miss?'

Grit pursed her lips as she looked up at the giant poster on the wall, proclaiming, "SHINE at Titas"- the first she had seen. She was not.

The young lady at the desk smiled pleasantly at them and Grit said why they were there.

'I'll just see if Andrew can speak to you,' she said, and went out of the door behind the desk.

The tall, mousey-haired, middle-aged man who, according to his name badge, was Andrew Wright-Muff, came out wearily and looked towards Wesley.

'You again!'

'I'm Margaret Bulmer, Wesley's tutor,' said Grit, authoritatively. 'Apparently a grant awarded to him hasn't shown up in his account.'

'I know; he came to see me yesterday, twice last week and, I think, once the week before, and twice on the first week of term. All I know is that the money has been paid in. If there's a problem, I suggest he needs to go and talk to his bank.' He turned to face Wesley, 'Which is what I told you to do earlier.' He turned back to Grit. 'Do you know he actually blamed me because he said he'd missed football practice?'

'I've been to my branch. They say the money isn't there. And I didn't miss practice. I was late, though.'

'That is strange.' While Wright-Muff was irritated, he also seemed deflated – as if something was on his mind he could do nothing about. Grit looked straight at him, 'Has this happened with any other grants you've awarded?'

Wright-Muff sank down on a stool behind the counter as if he were a beach ball whose air was gradually being let out of it. He sighed deeply. 'It's confidential, but yes, it has. All I know is the money has been paid. We are investigating it and if the error is on the part of the college, of course you should be reimbursed.'

'But what about the fine my bank has charged me for being over-drawn?'

'I'm sorry but there's nothing I can do about that. Not yet, at least.'

Grit thought she would make a constructive suggestion, 'Would it be possible to cancel the payment into Wesley's account and give him cash or a cheque?'

'There is no mechanism to do that.'

Margaret could see Wesley's ire rising. She was grateful, then, that he was resigned to the immediate situation.

'Come on Miss; I can see they won't do anything.'

'I really am sorry,' said Wright-Muff, as he turned and went back through the door behind the desk.

Then Grit had a brainwave. 'Just a minute!' she called after him, 'Can you take us through what you actually do to pay out grant awards?'

Wright-Muff spun round. 'It's straightforward Internet banking.'

'I'm sure, but please, show us.'

'I'm probably not allowed to.'

'What do you expect us to do instead, go to the auditors... or the police?'

Wesley smiled, 'Nice one, Miss!'

Wright-Muff sighed again, 'If I show you, will you leave me in peace?'

'Don't you want to get to the bottom of what's been happening as well?'

'I suppose so. Come through.'

They made their way behind the counter and crammed into Wright-Muff's tiny office. 'As I said, it's straightforward, you just log into the bank. As you can see, we're with Philanthropists' Provident, go to Charities' Current Accounts. You'll have to look away because the password is confidential.' He typed on the keyboard, 'Okay, we're in. Go to balance. The payment was made on the twelfth of September'

Oblivious to what Wright-Muff was talking about, Wesley focused on the address bar and noticed something straight away, 'Are you with Philanthropists' Provident or Philanthropists' Prudential?'

Wright-Muff pointed to the logo on the top of the screen, 'I thought it was Provident, but it's Prudential,' he said.

'Just like in the address bar.'

'That's right.'

'Exactly!' said Wesley, snapping his fingers.

'What's your point?'

'I'm sure it's Provident,' said Wesley, 'but it says 'Prudential' in the address bar. And I'll bet on my mother's life there is no such bank as Philanthropists' Prudential.'

This time it was Grit who was impressed. 'Are you suggesting there is something "fishy" –with a "ph" - about this website?'

'But this is the one we've always used.' Wright-Muff protested.

Twenty Four

At lunch time, Grit was in smokers' corner mulling over what to do about Wesley. This just led to her feeling like she did at governors' meetings: in over her head. In fact this damned college had driven her to distraction. She stood calculating in her mind just how she would afford her mortgage when the new contract came into effect.

Smith appeared unexpectedly, causing Grit a burst of excitement.

No, play it down!

It's not fair, Bob,' she complained to him angrily.

'Not fair?'

'The new contract; I'm really going to struggle on what it pays. You know those of us on it get about twenty percent less than we did before.'

'Well, these are hard times. We'll all have to tighten our belts. Of course, when some of us are so chicken they go applying for their own jobs...'

He was winding Grit up, but she wasn't falling for it. 'What is the point in having you here if you aren't going to do anything?'

Smith smiled at Grit. 'Do you know the results of last week's ballot?'

'I haven't checked my emails all weekend. Why?'

'Ninety two percent turnout and of them eighty five percent of that were in favour of rolling strikes. All those who voted wanted low level action.'

'What does that mean exactly?'

'It means the union will be scheduling some strikes. The rest of the time we work to contract, what used to be called a "work to rule". That way we make it more difficult for them by not supplying any grounds for unfair dismissal.'

'Don't you think it needs more than that?'

'Sympathy of our comrades in other unions can be useful as well. Soon we'll have them wriggling like mad. Just you watch.'

'By wriggling, you mean what?'

'Brother Boyle and Comrade Morrell will start by threatening us with dismissal for striking. Then they will tell us that a work to contract is a breach of contract.

'So they can take disciplinary action against us just for working to contract? That's so wrong.'

'No they can't, but questions will arise around exactly what our contracts involve and what they don't. Believe me, there's plenty we can do already that can give them a hard time before we get onto dodgier ground.'

'Will we have to go onto dodgier ground?'

'From what I know about Brother Boyle, yes,' Smith sighed with a certain satisfaction, 'Couldn't you just smell the desperation in that letter he sent to everyone? "My rescue of Durham College" –As if we're supposed to credit him with that.

'But there's more we can do before it gets to that stage.' Smith said with what Grit took to be a hint of glee. He continued, 'I think I'll have a chat with my friends about Health and Safety.'

'Health and Safety?'

'Absolutely! It's a minefield, Health and Safety. There are so many things that need attending to. I mean I know the college is only a few years old, but have you any idea how much pen-pushing is needed to get all this compliance stuff up to date?'

'No, er. Quite a bit, probably. I remember there was some of that at the nursery, but someone else dealt with it.'

'And do you think they'll be on top of it a hundred percent?'

'How would I know?'

'I'm sure we can find plenty wrong. Boyle might be furious about strike action over the new contracts, but I think you'll find that in reality this wonderful new building is actually a proper death trap. So bad, in fact, that we'd be entirely justified in refusing to work at all. How, for example, did Horace fall from the tower to his own death and potentially endanger the lives of others?'

Then the penny dropped, 'Don't tell me that was what you were talking to his wife about at the funeral!'

'Amongst other things.'

'That's distasteful Bob; the man was barely even cold.'

'I'm sorry you think that. But can you think of anything more emotive than someone being driven to his death by an institution whose health and safety was inadequate to prevent him?'

Grit sighed, 'Do you want to meet later to talk about what to do?'

'Oooh, dodgy! Just think if we're seen.'

'Yeah, yeah. How about Jan's café along at the *Shops a Go-Go* after work?'

'Okay, what time?'

'I finish at two, so call it two-thirty.'

'It's a date.'

Grit paused, musing over Smith's latest utterance. Although her ache had been replaced by butterflies, this was no time to go soft on the man, 'You're really enjoying this, aren't you Bob?'

Smith said nothing. He held his cigarette between his index finger and thumb, taking a sharp draw on it before blowing out a long line of smoke rings. Oh yes, he was enjoying it, alright.

* * *

As Grit left college that afternoon for her meeting with Smith, she noticed a couple of tents were set up on the green at the side of the college wondering why they were there, but put those thoughts to the back of her mind as she headed up the street to Jan's Café. This establishment was really a small greasy spoon, but for some reason served better coffee than any of the big chains, and much cheaper.

As she arrived, Smith was already seated by the window with a coffee and a banoffee pie.

'I'll eat it if you don't want it,' he said.

Her heart melted, 'No, I love banoffee pie. How did you know?'

'A lucky guess, maybe.'

Grit devoured most of the pie and stared across the small, open complex where the cafe was. 'This morning I took one of my students to Student Services. I don't know if you remember him. He was the one who had joined me when you and Bill were late for lunch in the canteen. Money from the benevolent fund was supposed to have been paid into his account.'

'And hasn't it been?'

'Their records said it had, but his said it hadn't. The man in there looked so pissed off with himself he couldn't work out what had gone on.

'The poor chap,' said Smith, 'I don't think any of my students have had recourse to use the fund, but Bill mentioned something similar that happened to two of his students just last week.'

'I think the student I took along is in one of Bill's classes, but if there are two...'

'...There could easily be a computer problem. I'm only glad I can't do online banking because that, I understand, is about as secure as a northern rock.'

'Quite.' Grit agreed. 'It looks like the college – or Wright-Muff at least - has been inadvertently using a fake website for the benevolent fund account. Wesley spotted it. Very sharp of him, actually. Anyway, I'm going to have to report it to the auditors.'

Smith agreed, but had to drive his Luddite rhetoric home. 'You see, a fake website for online banking, more chances for innocent, well-meaning people to get ripped off. And you wonder why I hate computers! Anyway, the external auditors have resigned. How will you go about reporting it, if you don't mind my asking?'

'I'll start with the Internal Auditor and then go to the police or Consolidated Charities if he doesn't do anything. Do you know who he is, by the way?

'Someone called Stuart Singleton. I wouldn't get my hopes up about him doing much, but it's worth a try, I suppose you could go to the audit committee as well. You aren't on it, are you?'

'Can you honestly see the board appointing me to the audit committee?'

'Fair point.'

'Do you know how to get in contact with Singleton?'

'He's in the Orange Pages, I believe, under accountants. What about the chairman of the audit committee?'

'Martyn Donoghue, Boyle lapdog? Yeah, I'll copy him into whatever I report to Singleton, so when they get nowhere at least they'll have each other to blame.'

'Just make sure you have covered yourself. Whatever they do, you will be acting correctly if you send to Singleton and copy Donoghue. Anyway, some of us who aren't teaching tomorrow are organising a picketing rota. Is there any time you're free?

'Only the first session.'

'I'll ask Bill if there's room then, shall I?'

Thrilled that Smith was now treating her as a confidante, Grit sat engrossed in everything he had to say. But was she letting his plans of insurrection take priority over what she had already decided were the important things: finding out the truth about Villiers and non-payments by the Students' Benevolent Fund?

Twenty Five

Thursday, 7th October: *The Deum Horriblis*

After an even heartier breakfast than usual, Boyle bade his wife, Violet, goodbye and set off for work in his brand new Jeep Grand Cherokee.

On the surface, the Boyles led a congenial existence. Their only daughter, Lucille, had left home to do missionary work in Botswana some eight years before. Their home was at High Admiral's Wood, generally thought of as a "posh" suburb of neighbouring Washington, less than two miles from Witton. This was the sort of estate one could easily imagine being gated, safely away from the hoi-polloi, but also from convenient pubs, bus routes or public open spaces. It was just the sort of place nobody in mainstream society ever ventured to, except perhaps to deliver post or clean the drains.

Boyle did not drive directly to work, however. He had a busy day ahead of him and arranged to talk to Alison Morrell about certain members of staff, but also to discuss the emergency management meeting on dealing with the strike. Showing off his new car had nothing to do with it whatsoever.

He pulled in outside Morrell's house, which was just the other side of the road connecting High Admiral's Wood with the outside world, Bonemeal Lane. Morrell herself was standing outside waiting for him, surrounded by masses of colourful leaves falling from the trees around.

After pulling up, he leant over and opened the passenger door with a struggle. Morrell opened the door wider, beyond his reach, and got in as he shuffled back to the driver's side, now feeling bilious from his exertions.

He covered his mouth to stifle a burp. 'She's a beauty, isn't she?'

'Who?'

Morrell's apparent ignorance irritated him. 'My new car, whaddya think?'

'Oh yes, very nice. Smells nice too. All this leather...'

'Smells nice, indeed! It's a mega powerhouse, this. The SRT-8 model. Guess how quickly she can get to sixty?'

Morrell wanted to stay in Boyle's good books, but she knew very little about cars, 'I guess it's really fast, so I'd say about half a second.'

This deflated Boyle, somewhat, 'Let's just say there's hardly anything she can't blow away. I've got you here so I can pick your brains, as you know.'

Driving to College, Boyle's mood had remained buoyant until he and Morrell saw a group of pickets gathered outside the main gate, including Bob Smith. 'There he is; treacherous bastard!' Boyle snarled.

Morrell got her phone out and filmed the gathering. Approaching the college, they noticed Margaret Bulmer and Bill Ogle at the roadside, 'Just what we need: a demonstration by the Campaign for Nuclear Depressives. Look at that arsehole! If he had glasses any thicker than that, he'd be using them to stop jars! And that bloody girl wouldn't be there if you had seen to things properly.'

Morrell took this last remark on the chin. 'It's no surprise really. They are scheduled to strike today.'

Boyle drove straight past and headed for another turning further along. 'How many are there?' he asked.

'I counted fifteen altogether.'

'Fifteen pickets. They can't do that – You've got that on your phone, have you?'

'I have.'

'Good girl. It's a proper bloody state of affairs when a principal is prevented from going into his own college.'

'They haven't actually stopped us, Maestro.'

'If that's the case, why am I driving to a back entrance where I can skulk in without being threatened?' Boyle steered his new Grand Cherokee up the kerb, around a barrier. On reaching the rear gate, he then leant on the horn until a passing caretaker noticed.

'The road's supposed to be blocked off,' the man said, annoyedly, 'How did you get here?'

'Do you know who I am?' barked Boyle.

'All I know is my instructions are that this gate stays shut.'

'Fucking jobsworth,' muttered Boyle under his breath.

Morrell was about to explain the situation to the man when a couple of teenage students who lived locally passed by, giggling, 'Why won't they let you into your college, Mr Boyle? Have you got the sack?'

This made him even more furious, but one thing Boyle always avoided was confronting students, so shouted, 'There now, you heard what they called me!'

The caretaker rushed to attention, 'I'm very sorry about that Mr Boyle. I didn't know what you looked like.'

'Have you not seen the pictures at reception? Perhaps now you might be kind enough to open this pillocking gate!'

'Certainly, Mr Boyle, b-'

'-Come on, man; we haven't got all day.' Boyle's head now looked as if it might explode as moisture practically poured onto his collar. Pale with rage, his red-hot face had reached an almost unrecognisable state as though it might presage spontaneous combustion. He belched loudly.

'But I'll need to get the key, sir.'

At this, Boyle snapped, sounding the horn in time with each of the syllables, 'YOU ADDRESS ME AS MAESTRO. I AM THE MAESTRO!' Reversing away furiously, his new car mounted the kerb opposite the entrance and bumped into a commercial waste container, knocking it a couple of feet from its designated spot.

Morrell grasped the handle on the inside of the door, and dug the backs of her stiletto heels deep into the carpet. 'I really think you need to calm down, Maestro.'

'Eh?'

'There's no point in getting aeriated.'

'You what?' Boyle put the car in drive and pressed the accelerator. It screeched forward.

'Umm. Don't you think this is how that crowd of trouble makers at the front would want you to react? If you let them see how angry you are, it might not do any good.'

The car was now driving back along the small service road with the speedometer indicating 65mph.

'And you can either slow down or let me out. Do you really want to damage your lovely new car?'

These last utterances were lost on Boyle, who was too busy ruminating on the situation. 'You think I care what those locusts think of me (burp)?'

Having forgotten about the barrier, Boyle hammered on the brakes and crashed over the kerb to avoid it. The car then reached a junction with the major road at the front of the campus.

'Is this car run in yet?' asked Morrell as Boyle pulled out in front of a van which sounded its horn at length, the noise receding quickly into the distance as he floored the accelerator, causing the Grand Cherokee to surge forward at a pace unmatched by lesser vehicles.

'See that! We've just blown White Van Man there away. Won't be seeing him again!'

As the car approached the main entrance for the second time that day, the crowd of demonstrators had grown. Boyle braked heavily and, as soon as he had turned the corner, accelerated towards the crowd. Some of the students from the vigil were blocking the road as well and, when they saw Boyle, began shouting "Murderer!" The crowd scattered, but not quite quickly enough. A clunk sound was followed by a small commotion. Boyle heard the clunk, but was too intent on getting away from this shower.

'Did those morons just shout, "murderer"?' he chuckled.

'Yes.'

'I didn't get where I am today by caring what others think of me.' Being called a murderer was oddly soothing. Morrell sighed. She hadn't looked back, either.

'And I'll have them for demonstrating inside the picket line,' he added, 'For crying out loud: would you look at that?'

Morrell wasn't sure what Boyle was referring to, 'Do you mean the name-?' Before she'd finished her question, Boyle answered it himself.

'-Some bastard's taken my sign again!'

'You mean your name on the parking space? Does that need worrying about now, really?'

'It wouldn't normally, Boyle growled, 'but it's the second time this term and, what with all that demonstrating, it's bound to be deliberate. I'll have the termite that's done it, though, just you see.'

Twenty Six

'He's made off with me sign,' complained one of the student protesters to Grit.

'Who has? Do you mean the car that just went past?'

'Yeah, it was the principal,'

Another student shouted, 'That was him: the murderer principal.'

'How could that of happened?' queried Grit, 'He didn't stop, so how has he tak-'

'-It's caught on the back of his car, didn't you notice?' Another protester whined, 'Couldn't you hear?'

'I heard a click sound and then some shouting.'

'He's a murderer,' the second student repeated.

'Look, will you pipe down, please.' said Grit, 'This is an official picket, and you are not helping.'

'But what's more important, your pay or your workmates' lives?'

'We can debate that some other time, but you need to leave this picket line right now.'

The white Transit whose horn had sounded when Boyle cut in front of it pulled up at the picket line. The driver, a burly man, was someone those with a self-destructive urge might pick a fight with, wound the window down.

'Who was that clown that just drove in?'

'Just now?' Grit asked.

'Aye.'

'In the jeep thing?'

'Aye.'

Ogle waded into the discussion. 'I heard your horn. Thank you for showing your support!'

'Eh! What are you, another clown?' said the man. Still incensed at being cut up, he hadn't even noticed it was a gathering, let alone considered what its purpose could have been.

'No, we're on strike.'

'Some of us don't have that luxury. Only last month, I was called in at thirteen hours' notice to replace the handrail at the top of that tower. Now I've been brought in to fix that leaking glass roof over the students' entrance. Look, that driver was really dangerous. Where could I find him?'

'A hundred yards on the left, there's a barrier. You can't go in there, but that's where he'll be parked. If you go straight ahead into the main doors, there's a map. Just look for the principal's suite,' answered Grit.

'Right, I'll soon sort that twerp out,' said the man, putting the van in gear and driving on.

'Do you mind, Grit?' Ogle retorted, 'We're supposed to be demonstrating about our lousy pay and conditions, not telling people how to find the principal.'

Grit blew a raspberry.

* * *

Reaching the Executive car park, the man couldn't be sure to recognise Boyle's car because of the large placard wedged below the back window, proclaiming "I don't cross picket lines." The man might have been a hothead, but he wasn't going to risk launching into reprisals against the wrong party and there was nobody to be seen.

Besides, he thought he should be getting on with his work, so left the scene – for the time being.

* * *

As he puffed into the executive car park, Boyle was on his mobile to the police.

'We've got an incident at College (burp).'

'What college was that, Sir?'

'What college? Titas College! This is the Principal speaking. We need police assistance – immediately.' Struck by a slight tightness in his chest, Boyle wheezed this last line as though he was about to expire.

'Do you need an ambulance, sir?'

'No. Why are you asking me that when you didn't even know which college?'

'Sorry sir, it's just that from how you sounded-'

'-How I sounded? I'm perfectly alright!' Boyle stopped just short of the door from the corridor to his secretary's office, and leant his back against the wall to catch his breath.

'Can you tell us what's happened?'

'It's the. It's the,' He gasped for air, 'It's the bloody union. A riotous assembly, illegally at the gate.'

'How many would you say there were?'

'A – About thirty.'

'Is this a picket line?' the woman checked.

'Of course it's a picket line. You didn't think I'd call the police for a vicarage tea party did you?'

'Has there been any violence?'

'My brand new car was attacked. I also heard a van behind honking when they blocked his way in.' A bit of creative imagination would always help the cause, he thought.

'I see, sir. We'll send an area patrol car straight away.'

'Good. The sooner the better, and there'll need to be more than one, I'm sure.'

'The unit will assess the situation on arrival.'

Boyle hung up. *Now,* he thought, *what can we do to make things difficult for the termites?* He headed for his office.

'Here's your coffee, Maestro. You look as if you need it.'

'I do that.' He took a glug of his mocha, 'Lisa, love.'

'Yes, Maestro?'

Boyle really loved Lisa's pout. She reminded him of a young Eleanor Bron. 'Why the hell didn't you call the police?'

'It all seemed peaceful enough to me.'

'Well it wasn't when I came in (burp). What can you tell me about it?'

'I know there are two demonstrations.'

'Really, how?'

'I keep my ear to the ground. It is my job to know these things, Maestro. One is the official picket by FUCA which we know about.'

'Yes, yes, and that's it, isn't it?'

'Well, no. The other is a group of about fifty students who camped out overnight in protest about the way Horace Villiers was treated by the college.'

Boyle spilt the coffee he was drinking over his desk. The mere mention of that name was enough to re-ignite his animus, 'Oh God, not him again!'

'I'm afraid so,' Lisa said as she left the room to get blue roll.

On her return, he realised that there was something else he needed to ask her. 'Did you read the report into Villiers's inquest?'

'I did, Maestro.'

'Did it say anything bad about the college?'

'Nothing, Maestro.' Lisa put one piece of blue roll in the bin and tore some more off.

'Nothing about the handrail?'

'Yes, it said how it was fully compliant.'

'What was the verdict?'

'Open, Maestro.'

At least I've managed to avoid one shit storm.

Twenty Seven

Brooding on the general situation, Boyle heard a gentle knock at the door.

'Yes,' he replied as Lisa wiped a dampened wad of roll over his desk.

'Hello, sir. Umm I'm Sergeant Board.' The tall, slightly stooping figure in uniform had thick black hair, a rugged face with a hawk-like nose and a small moustache, a combination emphasising his lugubrious manner.

As the sergeant's arrival had been very prompt, Boyle had been robbed of the chance to chide him for his tardiness. 'Have you dispersed them, yet?'

'Regrettably not, sir. The students have now assembled outside the entrance to the main building. There are currently about two hundred of them.'

'Oh God. What about the staff picket?'

'That is outside the premises, sir. I don't think it need concern us.'

'Well I do. There's a bunch of picketing termites out there and they'll be behind it all. You mark my words.' Boyle would much rather blame those rotten, disloyal outsiders for any disruption than the students or, as he preferred to think of them, his customers.

'They were calling for you to put in an appearance, sir. But I wouldn't recommend obliging at this stage.'

'Shall I come back later, Maestro?' asked Lisa.

'No, I've nothing to hide from my secretary! Just bring me a fresh coffee. Of course I agree with you, Sergeant. I've more important things to be doing than running round after a bunch of protesters. When are you going to disperse them (burp)?'

'That's the thing, sir. They are demonstrating on private land. Unless someone is assaulted or damage is caused, we have to proceed with caution.' Proceeding with caution was Board's default *modus operandi,* an approach which had served him well throughout his career, he thought.

The phone on Boyle's desk rang. Anxious about the situation, he had to force himself to wait the obligatory six rings. 'YES'.

'What's going on, Maestro?'

'Going on, Phyllis?' trying to play the situation down, he let out a particularly loud belch.

'I've just parked outside the main building and there seems to be some sort of demonication going on.'

The Chairman of the governors wading in; this Boyle did not want.'

'Nothing very much, Phyllis. It's the staff picket. They've broken the law, but don't worry. The police are dealing with it.'

'I think the students are cocaphonizing.'

'It's all under control, Phyllis, I do assure you,'

'You say the police are here.'

'Yes they are. Just a precaution, you know.'

'I think we'd better have a meeting, if you don't mind.'

'I am very busy at the moment.'

'Of course, Maestro, I do understate.'

In the mistaken belief he had dealt with Roberts, Boyle hung up and turned to the sergeant, 'Now where were we? Oh yes, you were telling me how you were going to deal with these illegal pickets.'

'I'm sorry sir; there really isn't much we can do at the moment except ask them to leave.'

'Fan-bloody-tastic! Well if that's all you can offer, then I'd be obliged if you and your fellow officers got on with it.'

The sergeant left, holding his hat in his hand, and Boyle sat quietly for a couple of minutes. Why did an unbalanced ex-member of staff have to go and die that way? It was unfortunate, but he couldn't have re-employed him, could he? Anyone showing insubordinate leanings had to go. This was how he any decisive manager had to work. He touched on the idea of expressing regret to the protesters, but the anger he was completely justified in feeling towards Villiers for wrecking his car and all those ganging up with him over the affair would render any such regret disingenuous.

So what?

Why did they pick on him? He would never have admitted the situation was his fault or that he had determined to make life as unpleasant as possible for Horace Villiers. Besides, nobody needed to know about that, did they? And, as far as Boyle knew, they didn't.

Now drinking his fourth massive mocha of the day, Boyle wandered to regret at the asset-stripping of Harbour Hall from Titas College and the possibility of acquiring some other grand residence in the country from which to conduct matters. After all, being a "hands-on" principal had become such an ordeal, perhaps things would run better from a distance anyway. Maybe he and Violet would be happier moving to Austria permanently.

He had heard of the principal of a college in Leeds conducting its affairs from Krakow in Poland on a permanent basis. It was wonderful to think what could be done using technology.

There was a knock on the door and the sergeant re-appeared together with Phyllis Roberts.

'They are refusing to leave unless you talk to them, sir. Again I would recommend caution,' said the sergeant.

'Yes, caution,' said Boyle, annoyed that Roberts had failed to remove herself from the situation, 'I'm not addressing a hostile crowd.'

Roberts joined in, 'Of course I would concord with you nasally,' she said, the hem of her skirt brushing gently against the floor, 'but local news have got the cameras here.'

'By the way, sir,' added the sergeant, 'We are concerned to speak to the driver of a red Jeep Grand Cherokee, registration, LW60YLE. It was traced back to a Laurence Boyle, I believe.'

'Laurence Boyle, that's me.'

'Oh, well in that case it has just been reported to us that the driver of the vehicle drove at a group of students, causing them to scatter. It is alleged also that a sign belonging to one of the picketing members of staff became wedged behind the vehicle.'

'Absolute rubbish. I know nothing about that.'

Sergeant Board went into Lisa's office and retrieved the sign, 'I did find this wedged there, sir. I'll have to put it in my report.'

'For God's sake, I have called you here to help deal with a major incident. A MAJOR INCIDENT, and you are more concerned about a pillocking sign.'

'Nevertheless, sir, this has been brought to our attention and I shall have to report it.'

'Fine, do what you want. Just let me get on with my job.'

Lisa appeared in the doorway, 'ITN are on the phone'. she said urgently. 'They want to speak to you.'

As the sweat marks grew around his shirt, Boyle pointed the flat of his hand towards her, 'Not at the moment. Tell them I'll release a statement later.'

'Very good, Maestro.'

With the TV cameras there, Boyle knew he had a mission to complete. Opening the bottom drawer of his desk, he rummaged around to find the hands-free microphone headset which connected to the college's PA system. He turned it on, 'Testing, testing, one two three. This is The Maestro speaking.'

'Exactly where is this supposed to be heard, sir?' asked the sergeant gloomily.

'Everywhere in College,'

'If you say so, sir, but I don't think it's working.'

A couple of further attempts showed this to be the case.

Boyle growled and then sat quietly for a moment, 'Sergeant, do you have a megaphone in your car, by any chance?'

'I daresay we can find one, sir, but I'm not sure I'd recommend...'

'-Please locate it for me?' Standing up quickly for him, Boyle felt his insides swash, 'Now let's see if we can snatch some semblance of victory from the jaws of disaster?' he said, putting on his jacket to cover his wet shirt.

Walking along the various corridors leading to the main foyer and the busts of William Armstrong, Joseph Swan and Earl Grey, Boyle couldn't help humming the song "Gold" by Spandau Ballet, to himself, while imagining the lyrics in the first person:

I am Gold ('gold)
Da de de da dum dum dum
De de da dum dum de dum
Da da da dum-ba-du-um...

Arriving at the main entrance, he was slightly dismayed to see some of his loyal vice-principals there, including Alison Morrell and Myrtle Howard, along with Sergeant Board, a couple of other members of Her Majesty's Constabulary and some of the ancillary staff who were hanging around looking distressed.

Which of you bastards reported my car to the police?

The top of the steps to the entrance formed a platform and from this Howard was delivering something akin to an introduction given in nineteen eighty two, regarding the Falklands Conflict by a certain prime minister, to students. The sergeant handed him a megaphone and the noise from the crowd lessened.

'Is it on?' Boyle asked the sergeant. The megaphone emitted a screech drowning out the sergeant's reply. Boyle looked around himself. Howard looked towards him as if in awe, Morrell smiled in expectation, and he heard Roberts who, having followed him all the way from his office was behind him wishing him good luck.

The TV cameras were there at the back of the crowd, and he was also fairly sure he saw Lisa out of the corner of his eye blowing him a kiss. Boyle may have hated addressing large gatherings, dissenters, outsiders, locusts, and all the other varieties of termite, but it was necessary to rescue the moment for Titas College, for Witton-le-Cone, and for himself. After all, students were customers, and the customer is always right. Now was his moment to shine.

A queasy sort of hero, he raised the megaphone to his mouth, belching again, this time quietly, but the slight transfer of weight caused him to stumble and trip on the steps. One of his brogues came off. Trying to slip his foot back into it, he somehow caused it to spin up in the air, landing a short distance away. One of the constables picked the shoe up and handed it back to him. Boyle then held it up triumphantly with one hand, and spoke into the megaphone, held by the other.

'We seem to have got off on the wrong foot!'

Enthusiastic laughter from his cohorts spread partially to some of the protesters.

That went down well. I am a genius!

'Dudes and dudettes,' he began into the megaphone. 'I realise you're not happy, so I've come out here to touch base with you.'

Someone in the crowd shouted, 'Dead right. We're not happy.'

Boyle continued, 'It is true that, sadly, on the ninth of September, a valued member of staff, Horace Villiers, tragically died on our campus.'

'And how did that happen, then?' someone shouted.

'As is now, I think, widely known, he fell from the tower. My understanding is he had quite a few issues.' He stifled another burp.

'You sacked him, didn't you?' shouted the second voice again.

'I am unable to discuss Horace Villiers's status with the college.'

The noise levels heightened. Trying to mask his irritation, Boyle continued, 'At Titas College we have high standards. That is to make sure you are all getting the best possible education here.'

'Bollocks!'

'Sadly, if a member of staff is unable to meet our high standards, it is in your interests that corrective action must be taken.'

This was interrupted by the first voice, 'That's slanderous crap.'

With a worried look on his face, Sergeant Board began talking into his police radio as a brief flash of dark anger bolted across Boyle's face. His inclination was to tell the owner of the voice to leave his campus and settle the matter in court, but with a herculean effort, he pursued his calumny while pretending innocence.

'I am genuinely sorry you feel that.' He shook his head, wobbling his jowls from side to side. 'Absolutely, I do, but it has always been a matter of maintaining standards. If I have made a mistake about that, then please, show me how it is wrong and I will do my very best to correct it.' While saying this, Boyle had managed to suppress entirely the tip of the sarcasm iceberg he could feel pushing up quite hard against the surface. The crowd went quiet. He began to feel he might just pull off a victory, as the reporter from local television, who had made his way forward in the crowd, raised his hand to ask a question. He nodded cautiously towards him.

'David Mercury, ITN. Mr Boyle, do you think Titas College's stance on new contracts for staff could have led to events here today?

'They may be connected, but what everyone needs to appreciate is the tough financial environment we are operating in. Sadly, over-generous contracts like those previously given to staff mean Titas College would have gone bankrupt if they were kept in place. And I've been there before, believe me.'

'Have any members of the local Labour party, of which you are one, expressed any concerns about the new pay and conditions for staff?'

Oh Christ! Not that again... 'Can I suggest you make your way to the front gates, where you will find an illegal number of pickets? That's all, thank you.'

This exchange had rather taken the shine of his address to the protesting students, but Boyle thought it best to quit while he was ahead. As he turned to leave, a soft object hit him in the face with some force, but that wasn't all. A smell emanating from the projectile struck him. It was so foul he felt his stomach lurch. Too suddenly to cover it up, what he hoped was another gaseous eructation proved a little more than that. It trickled to his top chin, taking two subsequent paths. The first ran down his other chins and into the front of his collar behind his tie. The second dripped from his first chin onto where the tie was directly below it a little way down. It was only when he tried to wipe his face with his handkerchief that he realised he was still wearing the hands-free microphone that hadn't worked. It seemed that a certain amount of regurgitated coffee had made its way onto this as well. It was all too much. He didn't have to put up with this and now he wasn't going to. Boyle thrust the megaphone into Roberts's arms and tore off the headset, throwing it to the ground.

The projectile, followed by the arrest of its apparent projector, brought to a head the tensions which had been fermenting for some time, leading to a number of the crowd to start shouting 'Boyle Boyle Boyle, Out, Out, Out!' followed by other cries similar in sentiment. A few objects, eggs mostly, were thrown as the reinforcements Sergeant Board had called for arrived in full riot gear – something which proved enough to turn the tide against what looked as though it could turn into a stampeding of the main building.

Boyle, however, was oblivious to these latest developments. Knowing his fury had got the better of him, he had already taken flight from the scene, shoe in one hand, vomit-soiled handkerchief in the other, ignominiously back to his office before sending Roberts the following text:

'Hi Phyllis,

Thank you for your input today. The only practical solution at this point is, in my view, not to recognise the union in any upcoming negotiations. I would be grateful if I could proceed on this course without interference.

Cheers,

Maestro'

As he recalled, the only reason he had gone to address a hostile crowd was because she had urged him to. The glamour of the TV cameras had no influence on his decision whatsoever. His ballooning ire was to be directed squarely at the striking staff in spite of what some of his customers clearly thought of him.

Boyle's latest challenge was to make it seem as if it was an aberrant union behind everything that had happened that morning. Remembering the TV cameras, he promptly got on the phone to North Eastern Television Holdings, hoping with some desperation his contact there could help to play down the matter.

Twenty Eight

Phone call completed, Boyle realised the smell of vomit and sweat about his person. He hadn't enough time to go home and change in time for his address to the local chamber of commerce that evening. At least *that* was an audience who would appreciate what he had to say.

He had already chewed up several Clorets, which should have cleared any aftermath of the mini-puke from his breath, but he still needed to get clean. As a rule, Boyle kept a spare shirt and tie in a small wardrobe provided in his office, so that was taken care of. After the stressful morning, he would have liked a bath, but decided the time constraint meant a shower must suffice.

Boyle had never bathed or showered in college, and his Boss shower gel was not on hand, so he had to make do with the standard issue soap. It was refreshing nonetheless to wash away his cares.

Stepping out of the shower, he realised that there was only a single small hand towel available for use. Boyle had not noticed the assumption had been made somewhere that with the high-tech hand dryer at his disposal Maestro would not require towels. A man whose body had as many deep creases and indentations as his would require a far greater drying capacity than such a diminutive item could offer.

Then he remembered what the electrician who installed the hand dryer had said.

That thing'll warm your balls up good and proper!

Morrell was in Lisa's office waiting to see Boyle about the new contracts. A distant rendition of a Kylie Minogue hit could be heard over a whistling sound.

I should be so lucky-

lucky, lucky, lu-

'What on earth is that?' asked Morrell..

'Just singing, he does sometimes.' Lisa replied with a slight smirk.

Suddenly, the singing began to sound more like howling.

'Is that Deep Purple?' asked Morrell.

'I've never heard him sing like that before. He's strictly eighties.'

They looked at each other and rushed into his office. Ever resourceful, Lisa produced a coin from her purse and reversed the latch from outside. The door opened, and the sounds of the drier's motor at full suck together with Boyle's howls and to the sight of his substantial body was something to behold, naked except for the brogues and socks with garters.

'Turn this thing off at the wall switch, I can't reach it,' he called on becoming aware of their presence.

Morrell turned the switch off, but the machine kept going, 'What are you playing at? Just bloody turn it off woman!'

Lisa rushed off and barely a minute later returned with Fred Thompson, who found Morrell with her head hidden the other side of Boyle and her left arm jiggling quickly up and down. He found the fuse box and switched off the circuit concerned, silencing the machine, to uncover a regular jerking sound caused by Morrell's continued attempts to free Boyle.

'It's no good Maestro; it's stuck inside. The grid's come off and you're lodged further up.' Trying to move out from under the dryer, Morrell found she too was stuck. Some of her hair had become trapped in the other intake, forcing her into a position looking directly into Boyle's groin. Lisa was telephoning for an ambulance.

Thompson stood with his tool box, thinking. 'Best thing we can do is get you down off that chair,' he said.

'But what about my hair?' plead Morrell.

'We could cut it off, or I could see what we can pull out, maybe.'

'That would be preferable. I've only had it done yesterday.'

Nobody noticed that Boyle, who had been relatively quiet since the drier ceased operating, was simmering towards a rage. 'I'm standing in agony here and nobody seems to have noticed,' he bellowed eventually.

'It's alright, Maestro. We're just having a bit of an idea shower about what's best to do going forward,' answered Morrell as the smell of burnt hair and singed flesh began competing with her perfume.

However well intentioned, this seemed like provocation. 'No it is NOT alright. This, THING, needs to come off the wall.'

'Is that alright with you, Miss Morrell?' Thompson queried.

'Of course it is,' shouted Boyle, 'Now get on with it, man.'

Thompson could see that, from her position, Morrell was unable to see what he was doing, so to avoid alarming her unnecessarily, he announced what he would do first.

'Right, I'm looking for the attaching screws. Going to case for medium Phillips, removing bottom right-hand side-'

'Just because we are at your pity, it doesn't mean I've forgotten!' snapped Morrell.

'Forgotten what?' asked Thompson, 'Removing bottom left-'

'-You wiped the CCTV, didn't you?'

'Why don't you shut the fuck up, Alison?' said Boyle.

'*He* knows what I'm talking about, Maestro.'

'For God's sake, woman. I'm relying on this man to free my jumbo from this... this... CATASTROPHE!'

Having removed all the visible attachments to the dryer, Thompson began to detach it from the wall.

'GYAAARH' yelled Boyle

'OWWW' cried Morrell

'I'm sorry, but I've got to move it to take the cable off. Would you mind holding the dryer, Mr Boyle, while I get my wire cutters?'

'Anything to oblige, Fred, is it?'

'Yes, sir.'

'It's Maestro, by the way. I am addressed as Maestro.'

Fred returned and cut the cable, 'Okay... Maestro. What do we do next?'

'We need to set Alison free, so I can get down from the chair.' said Boyle.

'Nobody's cutting my hair,' said Morrell, resolutely.

'Shut up woman, this is an emergency. At least you haven't got private parts stuck in this craptraption.'

'All I can suggest then is for me to get my hand in and pull Miss Morrell's hair out. You'll need to keep tight hold of the dryer, though.'

'Just great,' said Boyle, 'Do that now, instead of when it was stuck to the wall. Why am I surrounded by incompetence?' A tear ran down his cheek.

Thompson reached into the pocket of space already containing Morrell's head and Boyle's balls and began to tease Morrell's hair out.

'Get on with it!' called Boyle. 'I can't hold it much longer.'

Thompson freed some of Morrell's hair with a jolt, stumbling onto the clothes Boyle had cleared from the chair, which caused him to trip. As he tripped, Thompson caught the chair, toppling Boyle onto him, which in turn knocked him to the floor, pulling Morrell down as well. She screamed.

For a good few seconds all that could be heard were the various parties breathing heavily.

'Is... Is it still attached?' Morrell asked, breaking the distraught quiet.

'Your hair or my jumbo?'

'Either.'

Thompson wriggled free and took stock of the agglomeration, 'They're both still attached,' he sighed. He was in fact getting really annoyed with Boyle, Morrell and the situation in general but, as a mere minion, knew not to let it show.

At this point the paramedics arrived.

'It's a bit of a difficult situation,' Lisa explained to the first paramedic, 'I wondered if we'd have been better calling the fire brigade.'

'Let's have a look.'

'You don't need me for anything more, do you?' Thompson asked Lisa, carrying his toolbox and leaving the scene before she had time to answer.

'Now, what do we have here?' the first paramedic said inquisitively as she stared into the office. Now on their feet, Morrell and Boyle were standing bent in differing positions against the dryer as if modelling for conceptual art.

'Yes, I see, hmmm. You're only attached by your hair, is that right?'

'That's right, but I don't want it cut off: I've just had it done.'

Boyle rolled his eyes.

'But your attachment is rather more... fundamental?'

Boyle glanced sideways. 'It should be flaming obvious.'

'It would be simpler if we could just cut your hair off here.'

'NO!' Morrell was insistent.

'Then there's only one thing for it. We'll have to take you both with us.'

'Hang on a minute,' said Boyle. 'I need something to cover myself with.'

'Can you get some blankets, please Nate,' she said to the other paramedic, who disappeared.

The following minute and a half's silence seemed like an hour.

Once the second paramedic had returned with the blankets and they were draped over his body.

'I need something to cover my head, and I'd advise Alison to do the same,' said Boyle.

Morrell was able to hide her head in one of the blankets already draped over Boyle, but no matter how many further blankets they added, his shiny pate kept prodding its way through.

'Where are you parked?' he asked.

'Outside the front entrance.'

'Oh God, look, is there any chance you could come around the side?'

'We're not allowed to waste time.'

'I agree,' said Boyle, 'The faster the better. You realise I'm addressing the Tyne and Wear Chamber of Commerce at six?'

Lisa gave directions and they drove a few yards around to a fire exit across the corridor from Boyle's office. Opening the fire door triggered an alarm and Thompson was summoned to return and disable it, which he did reluctantly.

While he was turning the noise off, Lisa noticed a large paper bag next to her desk, containing a file marked "Philanthropists' Prudential / RFZ". She removed the file furtively, placing it under her desk. 'Try this for size, Maestro.'

Boyle turned himself and the hand dryer around slowly to see what Lisa was holding. Dragged around as well, Morrell winced.

'Worth a try, I suppose,' he said. Lisa manoeuvred the bag onto his head as the noise stopped.

At this point, the pair could have been large children pretending to be ghosts. If someone had replaced the paper bag on Boyle's head with that of a pantomime horse's facing backwards, they could have played a part in *George and the Dragon.* The only signs that this pantomime was no pantomime were the occasional flashing of stiletto heels with bows at the back, as well as socks with garters and black leather shoes from just above ground level, together with the strong scent of *Black Opium*. A well-versed observer would have been able to guess exactly who was hidden underneath the blankets and paper bag as the shrouded ensemble of Morrell, the hand dryer and Boyle was led carefully out through Lisa's office, across the corridor, through the fire exit, outside and into the ambulance.

But had they been noticed?

Twenty Nine

'Shit!' exclaimed Boyle once the ambulance was under way.

'What?' asked Morrell.

'They haven't brought my clothes, have they?' He waved at the second paramedic, who leant across, attentively. 'I'm afraid not, sir. There was such a commotion getting you and your colleague into here, nobody thought to bring them.'

'That's disgraceful!' Boyle shouted, 'If my current predicament weren't so compromised, I'd be making an official complaint, which I may do anyway in due course. I hope you're aware of that.'

'We'll do our best to get you both safely to A&E. But I can give you a complaint form now if you like.'

Becoming resigned to the situation, Boyle went from choleric to woeful, 'This is going to be a proper debacle if it gets out.'

'I agree with that. But just be glad of one thing,' said Morrell

'What?'

'That your office is on the ground floor.'

Boyle grimaced: the optimism implicit in the suggestion of an even worse scenario was yet another cause of annoyance, 'It's your fault of course. Why couldn't you have just let them cut your hair?'

'I was trying to help, and I only had-'

'-Had it done yesterday. Sound like a bloody stuck record, you do.'

The discomfort Morrell now found herself in was becoming too much to bear without her releasing a dose of honesty, 'I don't want to say any more on this, Maestro,' she said, 'because there is the question of how you got into the situation your secretary and I found you in. What in heaven's name were you doing standing there stark naked on a chair? And what was with the shoes, socks and those strap things old men wear?

'That's enough,' bawled Boyle. 'You're already in my bad books about Comrade Termiteski and the Bulmer girl. If you'd circled your wagons, my college wouldn't now be burdened with their uncongenial presence. And then there's your failure to get the new contracts in place. When I say I want *pronto,* I don't want any pissing about. Have you got that?'

'To be fair, Maestro, it wasn't that straightforward. And the union has been especially difficult.'

'I expected that. The problem is you are weak. In fact, you need to watch your step, Alison, unless you want to find yourself *an outsider*.'

Morrell gulped.

'Where are we going to when we arrive at Casualty?' Boyle asked the second paramedic as the ambulance approached the hospital.

'We'll see if there's a separate room available. The nurse can triage you there.'

'Glad to hear it, considering I've been picked up naked and no bugger thought to bring any clothes.'

'Isn't there anyone you could call?'

'I'll call the wife. Once Alison's been let out, that is.'

Morrell wrinkled her mouth. It was bad enough being stuck in a position where she had been mauled around with her face in Boyle's uncovered posterior for the best part of an hour without being referred to as though she were a domestic cat.

'... But I don't have my phone on me, obviously,' Boyle continued, 'And I hope all this won't take long. I'm due to address the Chamber of Commerce at six.'

'I'm afraid we can't make any promises on that front. There's a two hour waiting time and it's gone half-past-three now.'

'Terrific!' griped Boyle. Realising she might be able to help him, he changed his tone towards Morrell, 'Alison, love, you haven't got one of those phones that'll look stuff up, have you?'

'You mean a Smartphone?'

'Whatever they're called.'

Morrell didn't answer. She'd already wedged hers against Boyle's left thigh and was looking up the number for the Tyne and Wear Chamber of Commerce. This might be a chance to get back into Maestro's good books.

Thirty

Grit had been walking on air all afternoon. She had gone to meet Smith at Jan's Café and found him sitting nursing a cup of tea. Plonking herself down opposite with her double espresso, Grit felt as if she might not be able to contain her feelings for him much longer, not that she cared.

'Are you sure all that caffeine is doing you any good?' asked Smith.

'I need it to keep me going. How do you think it went this morning?'

'Okay, I suppose.'

'Why suppose?'

'Too many unknowns. There was that student protest. Someone should have known it was brewing. Just shows it doesn't matter how well connected you think you are... What I mean is, had I been here longer, someone would have told me about it.'

'Do you think we'll suffer because of the protest?'

'Thanks to those students, we appeared to have more than the regulation number of pickets inside the line.

'We shouldn't have much difficulty proving we didn't, should we?'

'No, but it's a question of perception, not just official judgments. With enough media sympathy, Boyle could make it look like an illegal staff picket.'

Grit got her tablet out of her handbag and passed it to him, 'I wouldn't be so sure. Have a look at this.'

'What's this device?' asked Smith. 'It looks like an Etch-a-Sketch.'

'Never mind that. Just look at it.'

'It's a bit of a blur. Is that someone we both know in the background?'

'You need to press Play.'

'I can't see a play button.'

'It's on the screen. It's a touch screen.'

'Is it, indeed?' Smith tried pressing the Play icon on the screen, but nothing happened. He looked at Grit helplessly, but then the video started, apparently on its own.

'We seem to have got off on the wrong foot,' said screen-Boyle.

When the clip finished, Smith asked, 'Where did you get this?'

'It's on *Candid*.'

'Does that mean anyone can look at it?'

'Yup.'

'When was it filmed?'

'Early this afternoon.'

'Can you play it again?'

Grit pressed the screen and they watched again.

'Did he say what I think he said?' asked Smith.

'He only implied he sacked Villiers. I doubt he'd ever admit it if he actually had.'

'It would explain a lot, don't you think?' said Grit as her thoughts turned to the fateful words scrawled on Villiers's file: *DO NOT RE-EMPLOY*. She could not mention this, even to Smith.

'Quite possibly,' he agreed. 'Besides, it shows that something apart from staff picketing was going on. Indeed, a protest by students about the death of a lecturer would make a far better new story.'

'Should we point that out to the local news?'

'We could phone the news desk and check. Can I use your phone?'

'Of course...'

After a few minutes of Smith fiddling in futility, Grit finally enabled her phone to work for him, 'You really are hopeless, aren't you?'

'Absolutely.'

'I thought you just said you were 'cos you're a luddite.'

'That may be true, but I am hopeless as well.'

'Right, having dialled the number you press this...'

'But it's on the screen!'

'That's right.'

Once he had got through and was talking to ITN, Grit remembered, 'Oh shit, I should've picked George up from his friend's mum's half an hour ago.'

Smith raised his left hand, before covering the microphone end of the phone. 'That means I'd have to write it out first! And we still need to discuss our strategy. I'll only be another minute.'

'Look why don't you come with me? Have you got your car?'

'No, Helen has it today.'

'We'll take mine then.'

As they made their way to Grit's rusty Suzuki Baleno, Smith completed the call, holding the phone uncomfortably.

'You haven't met my son, George, have you?' asked Grit as Smith handed the phone back without ending the call.

As she did, Smith fiddled with the door. 'There's a knack to it.' she said, pushing the door in and releasing the latch. *Why didn't I think of this sooner for the filing cabinet in?*

Once in the car, Smith replied glibly, 'No I haven't met your son, George, is it? I don't suppose I've much choice as things stand.'

Grit looked at him for a moment, 'Trust you not to like kids.'

She started the car wiggling the gearstick, causing a scraping sound to emanate from beneath. Revving the engine hard, she started to pump the clutch and the car crawled backwards. There were more noises as she selected first gear and once these had subsided and the car lurched forward, Smith thought it time at last to continue the conversation, 'I don't dislike children, exactly. It's just they get in the way a lot.'

'I was surprised yours weren't all grown up.'

'Do I look that old?'

'How old are you, actually?'

'Fifty five.'

'There you are, then. And you certainly don't look old for fifty five. Or you wouldn't, at least, if you didn't dress like it was nineteen seventy six.'

'I shall ignore your chiding my sartorial preferences, particularly as I'm probably old enough to be your father.'

This remark struck Grit. Her father was thirty five when he had died – only a year older than she was now.

'How old is George?' he asked.

'Just turned nine.'

'Oh, Toby, my youngest, is nine next week.'

'I remember now. He called you a pajero.' Thinking back to the other week when she and Ogle were in Smith's kitchen, Grit couldn't help but giggle.

'Is something funny?' Smith said, dead pan.

'*Toby!* Why did you have to call him that?'

'What's wrong with Toby?'

Bursting into hysterics, Grit swerved the car, narrowly missing a cyclist on the other side of the road.'

'I think you'd better pull in,' said Smith, grabbing the steering wheel, 'What's wrong with you?'

'All right, all right, I'll stop a minute.' Grit gasped, 'House on Durham Road, children Emily and To. ...To. ...' Grit was overcome by another wave of laughter.

'I didn't choose Toby's name, my wife did, and Durham Road is *not* expensive. Well... not very.'

Shrieking with further laughter, Grit struggled to form the words, 'Not... ha... Not wh.(splutter). Not wh-when you've moved up from London. Not when it's worth more than your mortgage, unlike mine!' She reached into her coat pocket for a tissue as her eyes and nose had begun to stream.

'No, well, Helen and I are fortunate in that we were able to pay our mortgage off when we moved up.'

'You know what you are, Bob?'

'What?'

'A champagne socialist.'

'Do you think you'll ever be fit to drive again, Margaret?'

'You know what you can do if you don't think so.' She dabbed her face with the tissue.

As they got to George's friend's house, Grit stopped the car, looked at Smith and giggled.

'I'll stay here,' he said.

Grit took a couple of deep breaths before jumping suddenly from the car and running to the front door. 'I'm so sorry, Rita. I forgot all about him!'

'Don't worry. George and Brandon have been playing that zombie game.'

A few seconds later, George ran out of the house to the car with the hood of his coat on his head, the rest of it flailing behind. He reached the car clearly expecting to get into the front passenger seat. Stopping suddenly, he frowned.

'Mam, there's a man in my seat.'

'I know love. You have to sit in the back.'

About to protest at this, George noticed his mother's face. 'Have you been crying?' he asked as he got in behind Smith.

As Grit went around to the driver's side, she noticed George punch the back of Smith's seat. 'What the hell do you think you're doing?' she said on opening the driver's door.

'I'm warning him.'

'He thinks I've been making you cry.' Smith explained.

'You'd better not have been.' growled George. 'I've seen my mam's face.'

'No love, I've been laughing.'

'Yes, laughing until you cry,' Smith added.

'I don't understand, Mam,' said George, 'have you been laughing or crying?'

'Stop worrying about your Mam,' said Grit, 'And DON'T threaten Mr Smith. He's a good friend of mine.'

'He's in my seat.'

'Would it be better if I went in the back?' asked Smith.

'No! He needs to learn it's not his seat. Grown-ups go in front.'

'Alright, I'll let him stay in the front, but it *is* my seat.'

Grit's old Suzuki pulled up in front of her home, a back street terraced up on a hill near the railway, and backing onto Richards's brewery.

'So this is it?' asked Smith.

'Oh, I know it ain't much, compared to Durham R-'

'-Nothing was further from my mind!' Smith was indignant.

'Go on Mam, whack 'im one for being cheeky about our house,'

For the first time, Smith bit back, 'Tell me, George, exactly what have I said that's cheeky about your house?'

'I dunno, but Mam was saying.'

'Your mum was joking about my house.'

'Aye, being big and that.'

'Well, yes, but it isn't really.'

'Honestly, Bob, I wouldn't try to argue with him.'

George had got out of the car and was standing, pet lipped, his coat hanging down from his head by its hood, 'When are you getting me my Zombie Expunger Two?'

Smith's face lit up. 'I've got one of those.'

'From what I've seen this afternoon I'm surprised you're capable of playing video games!'

'Is that what Zombie Expicator is? I meant my youngest offspring also lives on video games.'

'Who plays Zombie Expicator?' George interrupted, scowling.

'Toby does.'

'*Toby does,*' George repeated in a poor imitation of a "posh" accent, 'You can tell *Toby* from me Zombie Expunger is better.'

'Thank you; I'll bear that in mind.'

'I'm sorry he's like this,' Grit said, emphatically, as she led the way into the house, adding, 'What's a pajero?'

'Why?'

'Because yours called you that when I was in your house, remember?'

'Yes, he did, didn't he?'

'So what is one?'

'You don't want to know.'

They went through to the kitchen, which directly overlooked the back wing of the brewery. If anything, the malty smell was stronger inside than out.

Smith blushed as George ran upstairs.

Throughout the following half an hour he could be heard occasionally shouting at his computer game.

'We're just having Fray Bentos and peas. Is that okay?'

'That suits me fine,' he said cheerily, 'I'd love something a bit rough and ready.'

'Is my food not posh enough for you, then?'

'I can't deny it.'

'You cheeky sod!'

'Don't tell my wife, but the diet at home tends to comprise beans, pulses, rice, lentils, and a wide variety of vegetables, the origin of which I am typically unaware until they are sprung on me. It's all very healthy - and wonderful for Helen, who usually makes up for it by gorging on cream cakes.'

'What are you trying to say?'

'It's wonderful to have a change from the macrobiotic régime.'

'I won't tell if you won't.'

'You haven't any beer, have you?'

'I might have some lager,' Grit opened the fridge, 'There's some Fosters and a six-pack of TNT Pils, but I was going to open a bottle of wine.'

Looking nonplussed for a moment, Smith appeared struck by a sudden burst of enthusiasm. 'Can I go out for a minute? I'll be right back.'

'Sure.'

He rushed out of the door and re-appeared five minutes later with three bottles of Richards Ruby Red.

'That was quick. How did you get to the corner shop so fast?'

'I didn't. I nipped through to the brewery. Nearly got run over by a truck, but they've got a counter where you can buy it.'

'You know that never occurred to me.'

'It's just the smell.'

'Maybe George was right, you rude bugger.'

'No, I mean the smell from the brewery.'

'That? Oh, you get used to it.'

'It made me thirsty for beer... Would you mind if I rang Helen? We normally get our own dinners on Thursday, because we never know when we'll be in, but it would be courteous.'

'Okay.'

'Thanks. Where is it?'

'Where's what?'

'Your phone.'

'Can't you use yours?'

Smith gasped, 'Oh yes, I forgot I'd got that one. I was expecting to use your telephone. Sorry.'

After Smith had called Helen, they sat down to dinner, He felt more relaxed than he had in a long time, in spite of George pulling the odd face at him, and getting told off for it by Grit.

'What was it we were meant to be talking about, by the way?' he asked.

'I'm not sure. Did you manage to get through to ITN and the Chronicle?'

'Yes. The line were taking was that the student protest about Horace is far more newsworthy. The trouble is someone high up has pulled the plug on it all. Anyway, that perhaps lets us off the hook with our picket line.'

'Why have they done that, do you think?'

'Boyle will have his contacts and wouldn't be above using blackmail,'

'That doesn't surprise me. You know, I always thought I understood the world, but even though I never liked Boyle, it never occurred to me he would do something like that till you pointed it out.'

'It takes a certain mindset.'

'Do people with insight into motivation and behaviour tend to struggle more with tech...?'

'I have no idea.'

Thinking of insight, Grit had only just realised she had Smith eating out of her hand. This left her with a tingle of excitement. 'Something else I should tell you is that Bill told me about four more students this afternoon, who haven't been paid their grants.'

'Did he tell you whether anything further was being done about it?'

'I think Wesley got a cheque. Don't know if it's cleared though.'

'One of us should report it to the Internal Auditor, but I might call in on Wright-Muff on Monday to let him know what we're doing If he really is in the dark about it, he might have reported it himself. Doubt he'd have the initiative, though.'

With the sense he had opened up to her, Grit felt that now was the time to get to know Smith more intimately. 'It sounds like you know what you're doing. Actually, Bob, do you think we could talk about something else for a change?'

'Sorry, this sort of thing is just meat and drink to me.'

'Yeah, you can tell.'

At eight o' clock, Grit shooed George off to bed. Before leaving the room, he pointed at his own eyes and then towards Smith...

The rest of the evening they talked about their pasts, and how they had ended up where they were. Grit was enchanted to hear how Smith had given up trying to be a barrister because of his anarchic and flagrant left-wing inclinations. He told her about how, while reading law at the London School of Economics, his extreme views had almost got him kicked out. At the time, he was a member of the Socialist Party of Great Britain and, while he managed to get a pupillage, no chambers would accept him permanently once they found out who he was and what he had been up to. When he gave up on this, he went into education, but soon found his Socialist leanings coming to the fore, becoming involved in union activities.

Smith heard how Grit's father had died in peculiar circumstance when she was five and how her mother had raised her in a fashion, while Daniel, her younger brother, was adopted by grandparents. He was impressed to hear that, in spite of this, she had been the first in her family to go to university, scraping a 2:2 from York.

She told him about Mrs Robson and then Joan Fisher. Smith was even more impressed with her story about how she had got the crèche at West Durham College going.

'Are you going to start another crèche here?' he asked.

'I don't think so.'

'Is that because George goes to school now?'

'There is that, but it's more about the fact that you have to fight here and still get nothing done. Joan Fisher, she was principal at West Durham College, had my back from the start. She even fixed it so I could shorten my teaching hours while I was getting it going. I can't see them doing that here.'

'I just noticed something.'

'What?'

'We're back talking shop again, and I've finished my third bottle.'

'We don't want that, do we?'

'Actually, it's getting late. I should get back.'

They held each other's gaze for a few moments until Grit found herself moving towards Smith. Their lips made contact. He pulled away for a few seconds, but gave in. They embraced for a short while, but it seemed like an eternity, for Grit at least - an eternity she wished would last forev....Pulling herself up mentally, Grit realised she was more than happy with this tautology.

'Stop over if you like,' she said when the infinite couple of minutes had eased back to a sort of parallel reality.

'How many bedrooms are there?' Even during times of passion, Smith could be practically minded.

'Two.'

'No, it's fine then. I know what sleeping on the couch does to my back.'

'I wasn't thinking of the couch.'

Thirty One

Smith was someone who tried to avoid the attraction of other women by pretending it didn't exist, especially when he felt the same way, but now it was blatant where Grit was heading.

'I'm married.'

'Can't you be un-married; just for tonight?'

'I shouldn't. What'll I tell Helen?'

'Tell her you stayed on the couch. After all, we have had a lot to talk about.'

'If she didn't believe me, I don't know what she'd do.'

'Well, if you said you didn't want to, I would...' Grit loosened his kipper tie, continuing, '...not believe you!' as she whipped the article from around his neck.

It was no good trying to pretend, Smith had always wanted Grit: she was so direct and feisty. This was unlike any woman he'd got to know before. Until now, she hadn't tried to ensnare him with feminine charm, which was how he had experienced most women's advances - even Helen's to some extent, with hints and innuendo and little touches. Being approached so brazenly was refreshing. Even though it was wrong for her to do it, at that moment he wanted her more than he had any woman.

'I'll go upstairs and clean my teeth and you come up when you're ready. It's the second door on the right.' With that, she kissed him on the cheek.

'Which one's the bathroom?'

'First on the right.'

As Grit went upstairs, Smith drew himself a glass of water from the kitchen tap. As he sipped it slowly, the thought he was really doing the wrong thing went through his mind. And he was so much older than her. Now he knew about how her father had died, could it be that her attraction to him was rooted in this somehow? This train of thought made him baulk, so he left it downstairs.

As he entered Grit's bedroom, she was already in bed under the covers. 'They're in the drawer,' she said.

'What?'

'Blobs.'

'You certainly know how to woo a man, don't you?'

'Shut up, get stripped, and get it on.'

'I might not be ready.'

'Oh, you're ready. I can tell.'

'It might be a bit embarrassing, being undressed next to you.'

'Why, what do you think I'm wearing?'

'Two-piece pyjamas, probably button up ones with a collar.'

Grit flipped over the top of the duvet to reveal her small, pert breasts. 'Wrong!'

Smith dis-robed to the waist and got into bed. Grit jumped on him straight away and pulled quite violently at his underpants.

'Off, NOW!' she demanded.

Grit had a thin but feminine frame. Smith had never appreciated before just how delicately muscular she was. She was nearly all muscle, but it was soft muscle. He liked this. By now, she had wrestled his underpants to his knees, so he gave in and let her take them off altogether. Then she got on top of his chest, took his hands, and pulled them toward her breasts. He followed the cue and held them, gently. This made her nipples shoot out like lipsticks twisted at the base.

'It's been a long time,' she said, guiding his right hand slowly down her body. He followed, reaching a bit further and further until he was touching her more intimately, where he squeezed gently. Grit responded with a quick intake of breath, and leant backwards.

'You're ready aren't you?' she said.

'Yes, and no.'

'What do you mean?'

'I haven't put it on. I only just took my pants off.'

'Oh yeah, well get it on.' Grit leapt off Smith while he fumbled with the condom's packaging.

'Hurry up,' said Grit, 'I'm desperate for a ravaging.'

Once Smith had managed as best he could to get the thing on, Grit jumped back onto the bed next to him. 'Now I want you on top.' Smith duly obliged.

Having found his way into her, Smith was shocked by the power of her grip. *My god, can she squeeze it.* He'd never been with a woman whose body was as toned as hers, so his experience was new. He kissed her on the mouth, which made her squeeze even harder.

'Boobs. Now!' she whispered

As he began to feel her breasts with their hard, protruding nipples, Grit let out a cry.

'Are you alright?'

'Sorry,' she panted, 'I'd forgotten how good it is.'

They moved together under the covers and Grit let out a louder, longer cry, so failed to hear the pitter-patter of George's feet on the stairs. Smith soon felt himself ready to climax harder than he could ever remember having done before, when he lost consciousness.

Thirty Two

Now freed from the hand dryer, Morrell sat telephoning the secretary of the Tyne and Wear Chamber of Commerce to apologise for Boyle's absence that evening. She was forced to postpone the call, however, because of the screams coming from behind a closed curtain in a nearby bay.

'If it's painful, can I suggest some anaesthetic?' the registrar asked.

'Absolutely not! You'd cut my jumbo off and I wouldn't even know it.'

A reverberating metallic sound was followed by more cries. 'It would have been useful to have a diagram of the machine,' the registrar commented. 'I'll have to say it does seem well and truly lodged. Now if I try unscrewing this bit. Nurse, could you just hold on here...'

'JESUS FUCKING WEPT!'

'Yes, that's done it. Now I see what we're dealing with!'

'What?'

'These must be the elements. Now I don't know if you'd care to look down and you'll see what's happened.'

There was a short silence, 'Oh no! Oh God! OH CHRIST!'

'Not to worry, Mr Boyle. Your foreskin has cauterised and fused to the element, here.'

'You'd better not be chopping it off.'

'No, no. A standard circumcision should suffice.'

'Are you sure? I thought half of Jumbo was a goner there.'

'No, not at all. We'll get you prepped and down to theatre. Before you know it, you'll feel like a new man.'

'Pardon me, doctor, but that is not exactly a phrase I appreciate at the moment.'

'Why ever not?'

'I *was* starting to feel like a new man when... You know.'

Morrell couldn't help smirking. Dialling the number, a big part of her felt it served him right.

* * *

Morrell had always thought herself attractive, but while she could play men up to a point, none of them had wanted to settle down with her. Morrell wondered whether this was because she still lived with her mother. Now the wrong side of forty, she had decided that ship had sailed, but felt her career now demanded she looked the part.

When she got home, her mother told her that her hair looked the worse for wear. She peered tentatively at herself in the mirror.

'It's no good. I'll need another appointment.' She had managed not to have her hair cut crudely from the machine, but the ends were singed, something which looked incongruous next to the bleached almost-white remainder and there was nothing she could do about that.

This wasn't fair. Morrell had been Boyle's loyal lieutenant since she first joined Durham College as an office manager. Yes, she had a vice-principalship and a salary to go with it, but at what cost: tirades of abuse, a constant fear of being inauspicious, taking flack when things weren't going right? She had rescued Boyle from the backwash of numerous cases of constructive dismissal. She had lied to employment tribunals about what he had said to get him off the hook. She was currently at the sharp end of implementing the new contracts of employment. And what thanks had she got?

It was the same time and again. Morrell had only been trying to help Boyle by her efforts to free his jumbo from the hand dryer but, in return, had received several earfuls of complaint and a threat from the bad-tempered ingrate. Not to mention the toasted coiffure.

And as for calling it a jumbo... She had not actually seen Boyle's penis in all its glory, as its glans had been stuck inside the machine, but if the thing's girth had been anything to go by, well... No, all this certainly wasn't fair, and she was beginning to wonder for how much longer she could stand it.

Thirty Three

Boyle was still at the hospital, his operation complete. As the anaesthetic began to wear off, the true level of discomfort began to inflict itself upon him. His anger toward Villiers raged within.

He wrecks my car. He shows me up with the students. He probably ruined my reputation at College, and then there's what that diabolical machine's done to me. It's as if the bastard planned it all.

Boyle ached to put him on his termination list again, but regrettably Horace Villiers's self-termination had rendered this unfeasible. Had Villiers remained extant, Boyle would have been sorely tempted to appoint him to a position just so he could sack him again. As it was, the fact that his rage was in vain compounded itself in a cycle of impotence. Boyle usually knew how to draw a line under these things, but he was getting close to self-destruction in the knowledge that he was unable to avenge himself for what Villiers had done. *Or was he?*

Thirty Four

Regaining consciousness, Smith heard Grit shouting, 'I know you're protective of me, George, but you don't just come into my bedroom.'

'I thought he was hurting you,' George shouted back. 'What was I supposed to do?'

'He wasn't hurting me, we were... doing adult things. And you should have been asleep,' she added as if to justify her and Smith's actions while George had been in the next room.

'Are you going to have a baby?'

'Why would you think that?'

'Because if he wasn't hurting you, the only thing you could've been doing is what ladies and men do to have babies.'

'No I'm certainly not having another baby. You're quite enough to cope with.'

'So what were you doing?'

'As I said... we were doing *adult* things. Now I'll have to go back through to see if you've killed him.'

'Killed him?!'

'And let me tell you, son, you are in very serious trouble if he is dead. You might even have to go to prison.'

'No I won't. I'm below the age of criminal responsibility.'

'Not being criminally responsible doesn't mean they couldn't take you away. And they would do that, George, believe me!' Grit almost sounded as if this was something she would like to have happened.

This conversation did not quite make sense to Smith. As Grit returned to her bedroom, wearing a light coloured, billowing dressing gown, he asked, 'Did I pass out? Getting too old for it probably.'

'You did pass out...'

'Oh dear!'

'... because my darling son bashed you on the head with a frying pan.'

'That explains the headache. I thought maybe I'd had a stroke.'

'We were about to... Anyway, you might need to get that looked at in Casualty. I've had too much to drink; I'll call you a taxi, or do you think an ambulance?'

'Don't know. See how I feel in a minute.'

'He is still alive, isn't he?' George called from the landing.

Thirty Five

It was half past midnight when Smith arrived by taxi at Flassburn General Hospital. With a sore head, he sat down and waited to be triaged, wondering through his concussion whether he might be able to hide his injury from Helen and, if he could, how he would explain his absence that night. She would be expecting him home late, but not this late.

Seconds later, a large woman in her late fifties and wearing a loose-fitting dress and shiny, rubberised jacket carrying a bulging shopping bag stopped near the reception desk. She was accompanied by another, smaller woman, who may have been a little older. She said to her nervously, 'I'm sure this sort of thing has been going off and on for years, but I've never dared confront him about it.'

The smaller woman replied, 'Trust me, Vi, it's best out in the open.'

'But...'

'But what?'

'I don't know. It's just that, well I don't feel I can.'

'We've been here before, so what's stopping you? You're not afraid of him, are you?'

'No... Yes. Yes, I am afraid of him.'

'You're afraid of what he'll do to you?'

'He'd never hit me. I'd flatten him if he tried that, but Laurence has ways of making you feel bad. If I accused him of something, I just don't know what he'd do to get at me.' Tears welling up, she got her handkerchief out.

The smaller woman took her by her other hand. 'Honestly, Vi, it'll be okay. I'm here, and if he tries anything you just shout.'

The receptionist had got down as far as them.

'Can I help you?'

'I'm looking for someone,' said the larger woman, dabbing her face with the handkerchief.

'Name please?'

'BOYLE.'

'I'll just check for you. Are you a relative?'

'I'M HIS WIFE.'

'He's in Room Six,' the receptionist pointed across to one of the many doors that led from the waiting room.

'Thank you,' said the woman.

'Off you go now,' the smaller woman said quietly.

The larger woman, whose face was now very red, took a deep breath and strode over to the door the receptionist had pointed to. She knocked twice and went straight in.

'Here are your clothes,' she said brusquely. Smith then heard a voice he recognised instantly.

'And about time too. Where the hell have you been?' The door closed and for the first half a minute or so, Smith was unable to make out what was said. But then the woman began to raise her voice.

'...and Alison Morrell of all people. We had her to dinner. She was charming, wasn't she? All over you like a rash! I implored you to keep your distance, but what do I get from her tonight, eh? A phone call telling me about how she'd gone to hospital trapped in a hand dryer with you. Can that really be true, I thought.'

'It is true, but-'

'-What possible explanation could there be for that, I wonder? I knew you had a sadistic streak, Laurence, but I never realised you were a masochist as well. Frankly I thought you were too conventional in bed for any of that. It seems you've found your ideal partner now, doesn't it?'

'THAT IS SLANDER,' shouted Boyle, 'I don't know what Alison's told you, but you'll have got the wrong end of the stick. Not for the first time, either.' The savageness in his voice was followed by what sounded almost like a plea. 'Vi, love, you've got this all out of proportion. Nothing like that has happened.'

Right or wrong about this one, she wasn't to be deterred. 'It wouldn't be the first time, would it?' she snapped, 'And it's not just today. It's the fact that my husband, the man I've stood by all these years, ever since he worked for an estate agent. The man whose ambition I've always done my best to support would do something so publicly humiliating.'

'I told you NEVER to mention the estate agents. EVER!' Boyle's voice had a sinister quality to it even Smith found unnerving, 'And it won't become public. There are strings I can pull to make sure that doesn't happen.'

'Of course there are. But then there's the reason why you don't want me to mention the estate agents, isn't there?' Mrs Boyle went on, 'Perhaps I should mention the name of th-'

'-SHUT UP!' bellowed Boyle.

One of the nurses made her way towards it, but the door opened before she got there.

'Is everything alright?' she asked.

'Not really, but I'm going anyway, thank you,' Mrs Boyle answered, before turning back into the room.

'You've got your clothes, now I'm going to stay with Angela for a while. You can make your own way home.' With that she came out, shut the door, and walked quickly over to where the smaller woman was waiting.

'No wonder our daughter moved to Botswana,' she said, breathily.

'That can't have been easy, but he's had it coming a long time,' said the smaller woman.

'I know,' said Mrs Boyle, inhaling through her mouth. The tears were coming again as they left the building.

Thirty Six

Boyle opened the door and made his way gingerly over to reception.

'Can you call me a taxi?' His face looked like thunder.

'The phone in the corner's for that. You can telephone any of the local cab companies from there,' the receptionist replied.

'Really, pet? I thought that was supposed to be your job.'

On his way over to make the call, Boyle heard the receptionist's voice behind him. 'By the way, Mr Boyle. What did you want us to do with this?'

Boyle was not easily embarrassed, but any mortification he had felt so far that day was dwarfed next to his experience on turning around. The remains of the mordacious machine that had accompanied him and Morrell to hospital were resting on the desk, propped up by the receptionist.

'Nothing,' he spluttered. '...I mean I... I don't know what it is... I...' Boyle continued walking towards the phone, but backwards. He tripped over the end of a bank of chairs and rolled to the floor.

The bitch did that just to show me up.

He edged around to find someone sitting on the chairs was offering him a hand. Boyle took it and hauled himself slowly to his feet with the aid of it, unaware of the hand's owner.

On raising himself to his full height, or as near to it as someone with a partly-numbed groin could, he looked to see that the person seated in front of him, who had helped him to his feet, was none other than Bob Smith.

Boyle nodded at Smith, pretending he did not recognise him as anything other than a stranger who had helped him, let alone the poultice Smith was holding in his other hand. After all, he had never met the man before, not to speak to at least.

Although Smith gave no clear indication he had recognised him, there was no doubt the termite had done. What's more, he'd have heard the argument Boyle had just had with his wife. On the other hand, the head injury clearly meant something. Maybe a little investigation was called for...

* * *

As he made the call, the receptionist sniggered quietly in the corner. *Talk to me like as if I was shit on his shoe, would he?'*

Thirty Seven

Smith woke on Friday morning struggling to remember a connection he had made in his sleep. He had overheard the burly driver of the Transit van telling Grit he had been contracted to fit a new handrail. Yes, *that* was what he had been trying to recall! There was a handrail at the top of the tower. One person falling or, indeed, hauling himself over a handrail on a relatively new building should not damage it, so why on earth would it need replacing? There was only one likely answer to this. It had not been compliant with health and safety law. *Aha!*

College management would undoubtedly be intending to cover itself. They might well seek to replace the rail if it did not comply at the time Villiers had got to the wrong side of it and fallen. If a risk assessment had been required to show the Inquest that health and safety at the college was adequate, what would Boyle *et al.* be likely to do?

Now Smith was beginning to understand what had happened. Proving it posed a problem, though. If its height had been altered, was there a way to find out whether the old height had not been health and safety compliant?

The idea of locating more and less recent pictures of the building crossed his mind, but he decided his best bet was to locate someone who had worked on the Tower – ideally that builder who drove in during the picket.

This train of thought was interrupted by Helen bringing him a cup of coffee. 'Now Bob, darling...' She sat on the bed and ruffled his already unkempt hair, '...

When you have woken up I think some explanation would be in order.'

'Explanation for what?' Smith might have been lucid on the subject of Titas College, but as far as the previous night's events were concerned, he was still fast asleep.

'An explanation as to why you didn't get in until four o'clock this morning and what caused the massive bruise on your head.'

He pulled himself up the bed, causing his cranium to rub slightly against the headboard. With a sharp pain, the terrible reality began emerging. 'How did you know I had a bruise on my head?' He winced.

'You woke me up when you came in. I asked you what the matter was, and you said then that you had bashed it. Even if you'd said nothing, it was clear something was wrong with it.'

'I thought you had believed that to be the case for a long time.' Smith cautiously picked up the mug of coffee from the side table and sipped a little, before resting it on his chest, all the while attempting to keep the level of pressure on the back of his cranium at a constant minimum.

'I mean you said it hurt and you have never, to my knowledge, suffered from migraines.' Now sitting at the dressing table and brushing her hair, Helen continued. 'So what happened?'

This was the moment when there was no avoiding the subject. Either he would tell Helen that he had been bashed on the head by a nine year old with a frying pan, followed by the inevitable questions of circumstance. At some point he would either have to confess what he had been up to, or... 'I slipped and fell against a door.'

'Well it was a bit icy out last night, so that's not surprising. But why so late?'

'I was having a meeting which over-ran, particularly when the booze started flowing.'

'Was this the meeting you were having when you phoned me?'

'Yes.'

'It ran on a long time, didn't it? Where was it?'

'It started at the café at the Shops a Go-Go. We were discussing how to make health and safety as problematic as possible for Boyle.'

'Then where did you go?'

'To Grit's house. That's where I phoned you from. We were going to come here but she had to pick her son up from his friend's.' While revealing where he had been could cause some consternation, Smith was glad to include the bit about her son. After all, Helen would be less likely to suspect he and Grit had been up to what they had been up to if a child was present, wouldn't she? And the idea that they intended to go to Smith's house, especially with Helen there, would kick any further suspicions Helen might have begun formulating into touch, wouldn't it?

'I see. Okay darling. But the next time you spend half the night at a female colleague's house, it would be handy to let me know before-hand.' Was it just Smith, or did Helen's calm, reasonable and accepting tone harbour the tiniest hint of the aciculum?

'I know. I'm sorry. I did leave about eleven, though. It was just that I slipped and fell as I was leaving. I spent the next few hours in A&E. She was going to drive me there, but we'd had a bit too much to drink.' Smith felt a sickness at weaving truth and mendacity, but he couldn't bring himself to admit to Helen what he had done, could he?

Throughout the day, Smith was troubled by his lies but, he thought, maybe he would tell Helen what had actually happened later: make a clean breast of it. Would that ever be possible without severe consequences? After all, his first wife, Elizabeth had left him after discovering he was having an affair - and that wasn't his first.

Thirty Eight

Having understandably taken his first ever leave from Titas College on Friday, Boyle arrived at his parking space on Monday to find there was a paper bag over the sign.

Grrr! Some bastard's really got it in for me.

He got out of the car and lifted the bag off. At least the name plate had been replaced, but then he noticed something causing a renewed burst of fury, reminding him of something he needed to attend to. Seeing Smith in A&E with a head injury was definitely worth investigating. Any knowledge that could help him execute his *termination list* could be invaluable. He was going to fix Smith good and proper. Oh yes.

As he got to his office, he leant on the stanchion in the open doorway between his and his secretary's offices.

'Lisa, love?'

She looked up from her computer screen.

'Yes, Maestro?'

'Will you find something out for me? Ask around, like?'

'Mmhmm?'

'Find out what that Smith was doing last Thursday afternoon and evening.'

'Bob Smith? You want me to check his timetable? I can bring it up here if you like.'

'Yes, do that.'

While Lisa did this, Boyle loitered for a moment.

'Can I get you a cup of coffee?' he said to her, but it didn't penetrate; she was too busy pressing keys on the computer. He glared at her briefly and began trying to make coffee for himself.

'How does this thing work?' he asked.

At cross-purposes, Lisa had found Smith's timetable, 'In the afternoon he was taking law of contract. Nothing in the evening.

'Right, I see. I was asking you about the coff- '

'-Take a cartridge out the drawer and push it into the slot on the right.' Lisa said.

Boyle opened the drawer and picked out a cartridge of latté.

'That's not your usual sort,' she said. Boyle looked up, helpless and open-mouthed. Lisa got up, and selected his usual mocha.

'And then you put it in here.' she said before realising there were no paper cups. Noticing, Boyle went through to his office and returned with the Austrian beer mug from the windowsill, blowing into it, 'Okay if I use this?' he asked.

The mug only just fitted under the machine, 'If it's switched on, it'll come through automatically in a minute.' A slight white noise began to emanate from the device.

Boyle stood observing the proceedings, 'So it'll be ready in a minute, will it?'

'Yeah, about a minute.'

'Right, so I know Smith's timetable from last Thursday p.m. Can you do the same now for Margaret Bulmer?'

After a few presses of the keys, Lisa lifted her head, 'English Speakers of Foreign Languages from one till four. Nothing in the evening.'

'Good. Can you email me links to all these?'

'Of course.'

The coffee machine was now expressing a frothy looking liquid into the Austrian beer mug that Lisa had placed under it, 'Is this ready?' Boyle asked her.

'Just a few more seconds,' she said. He made his way over to the machine and, when it looked as if it had stopped, picked up the mug and raised it as if drinking a toast to Lisa, 'Wait a minute, that's Freddie Hayek, isn't it?' Noticing the design on the front of the mug, Boyle turned it around to face Lisa, 'I thought it was just a gargoyle,' she said.

'Not at all. A great man, F.J. Hayek. Comrade Termiteski would do well to study him. So now we know Smith and Bulmer were both free last Thursday afternoon,' Boyle stated as if putting in place the first piece of a puzzle, while wiping the froth away with the back of his hand.

'They were luckier than you then, Maestro.'

'Eh?'

'I was just thinking of the predicament you and Miss Morrell were in last Thursday afternoon.'

He glanced one of his frightening looks at her and she averted her gaze downwards. 'I can do without mon bots like that,' adding, to drive his point home, 'especially at the moment... By the way, after last Thursday, I think I'd prefer something less bloaty. Is there any coffee without so much bloody froth?'

'I thought you liked froth, Maestro.'

'Nothing wrong with a man changing his mind, is there?'

As Lisa tipped the mocha away and put an Americano cartridge in the machine, Boyle went to his briefcase and retrieved the paper bag which had been on the name plate, now in a crumpled state from his anger when finding it, and tossed it onto Lisa's desk. 'This was over the new sign at my parking space this morning and do you know what's been scratched on the plate?'

'Er, no.'

'Sir Ian MacGregor.'

'Ewan McGregor? I didn't think he had a knighthood,'

Boyle stared at Lisa as if she had misplaced her brain. 'You know, The Miners' Strike, nineteen eighty four?'

Lisa realised they were talking at cross-purposes and wasn't going to query Ewan McGregor's age, 'Don't remember it. I'd have been one year old.'

'I see.' Boyle smirked, 'Actually it's quite funny when I think about it. McGregor was a man I had a lot of time for.'

'Why do you mind it then?'

'Some bastard clearly knows I had a paper bag on my head last Thursday, and wants to taunt me about it. When I find out who it is, it'll be termination for him. Or her.'

'Did McGregor wear a paper bag on his head, then?'

'Don't be bloody funny. Once, he did. Only once, and the press had a fucking field day.'

'What if Smith or Bulmer aren't behind the defaced sign or the bag?'

Boyle went quiet for a moment. 'Get Myrtle on the blower, will you?'

He went through to his office with his coffee and shut the door. Presently, just as his use of the term "blower" struck him ruefully, the phone on his desk rang and, after the obligatory six rings, he picked it up.

'I've got Mrs Howard for you.'

'Fine, put her through. Hello, Myrtle, are you alright today?'

'Excellent, Maestro, couldn't be better.'

'Now that's what I like to hear,' Boyle chuckled in a creepy, low monotone.

Myrtle was always so positive. She also spoke in a deep purr which reminded him of one of Margaret Thatcher's stock voices. He found this extremely sexy.

'You remember a discussion we had about keeping a look-out?'

'Oh yes, Maestro, I certainly do.'

'Goood. Well I was wondering if you knew of anyone who could tell us the whereabouts of two of our less congenial members of staff. One used to be in your old department, I believe.'

'My old department?'

'I mean at Durham College, before you took over *Novum*.'

'Margaret Bulmer?'

'Exactly, Myrtle. You are on the ball, if I may say so.' Boyle's oiliness positively oozed down the line.

'Anything to oblige. I'll see what I can find out.' Howard returned with an even deeper, smoother purr.

'I'd be *most* grateful, Myrtle.'

On ending the call, Boyle was starting to go weak at the knees.

Only five minutes later, his phone rang. It was Howard calling back.

'A little bird tells me she left College with Bob Smith, and they went to Jan's Café at the *Shops a Go-Go,* before returning, getting into Bulmer's car, and leaving together.' Her reference to a "little bird" rose with a chirrup like a flash from the velvety undertones, Fenella Fielding-like.

The deep enjoyment Boyle felt spread to his loins briefly before being scotched by a sharp pain, 'Aagh!'

'Is everything alright, Maestro?'

The propitious delivery of the question brought on a repeat experience, 'Agh! Oh, yes indeed, very useful information, Myrtle.' said Boyle, 'How did you find out so quickly?'

'I have a few contacts. Apparently instructions for Smith and Bulmer to be monitored by the CCTV system were given some time ago.'

'I see. The thing I love about you, Myrtle, is that you come to me with solutions. The other vice-principals only bring problems.'

'Oh, any time!'

This was the first time he had been aware of experiencing any degree of penile arousal since the previous Thursday and the resulting pain was not pleasant. Through his discomfort Boyle began to remember that he had in fact given a verbal direction to his more trusted vice-principals to keep an eye open for what Smith, Bulmer, Ogle and a few others were up to. Would this be enough information to catch Smith on the hop? Boyle didn't know, but he guessed that Smith and

Grit were united by more than a common fervour for troublesome politics.

Heartened, Boyle went back through to tell Lisa, holding his crotch gently. 'It looks like Smith and Bulmer had an intimate meeting last Thursday night.'

'I see.' Lisa grinned, 'Is that why you wanted the information?' she asked, choosing not to notice Boyle's crude posture.

'Of course not. I just wanted to keep tabs on those flaming Bolsheviks. Anyway, the point is, I happen to know Smith is a married man. Now I am in a position to offer him a lousy retirement package.' Letting go of his crotch, Boyle shook his right trouser leg.

'How come?'

'Because he'll bloody well have to take it, or else his wife'll find out about his dirty little liaison.' He opened the dartboard and removed the three darts pinning a large photograph to it.

'Are you sure that's wise, Maestro? Mr Smith certainly knows the rules and regs.'

'And how' replied Boyle. He threw a dart, missing. 'I'll get him, don't you worry!'

'We don't actually know for certain they are having an affair, do we?' Lisa added.

'Look, he might be twenty years older than her, but I know my instincts on this. You couldn't find a couple more odiously matched.'

'He also has management experience.' said Lisa after a pause, 'And with Dr Fisher's recent retirement... Is that vacancy for V-P Humanities still open?'

Taking aim for the second shot, Boyle spluttered, incredulously, 'You can't be serious. No way! I can't believe I'm hearing this from a mere secretary.' The dart missed the board and fell to the floor.

'Something about keeping your friends close,' she smiled.

'Insiders close, outsiders closer? He may be no insider of mine, but I'm not having a troublemaker like that on my senior management team. The man's a bloody Trot, for God's sake!' His third shot lodged towards the edge of the board, missing the picture on it.

'Couldn't you make such an appointment conditional on giving up certain... pursuits?' Lisa pouted suggestively.

'Certainly not,' replied Boyle reprovingly, 'I don't do deals like that!' He pulled the darts out of the dartboard and, leaving the one which had fallen on the floor, threw again. Lisa noticed how his shirt was sticking to him. Boyle had sweaty days when his excitement level was raised.

Thirty Nine

Not considering protracted angst about his matrimonial situation a useful vessel for his time or energies, Smith returned after work to the matter of the handrail. He knew it was always a good idea to have friends in low places. This may have been why he was quite well acquainted with Fred Thompson. Trying not very hard to make the meeting seem coincidental, he went for a pint at The Butcher's Arms, a pub just off the front street he had seen Thompson go into after work, and waited.

An hour and two pints later, Thompson arrived looking a little the worse for wear, 'Alright Fred? Fancy seeing you here!'

'It's a miracle I got here at all; god I need a drink.' Thompson was flustered.

'Allow me,' said Smith.

'Very decent of you, I'll have a Rotgut if you don't mind.'

'Rotgut?'

'That,' Thompson pointed to a tap with a label saying, 'Richards Premium Pils 8.2%'

'Sure.'

Once served, Thompson downed about a third of it. 'I needed that,' he said, wiping his mouth with the back of his hand. 'What brings you here?'

'Oh, I just like to try the different pubs; see what they're like, you know.' Smith replied with practised nonchalance. 'And as it happens I live just up the road. It is fortuitous I bumped into you.'

'Oh aye, I hope it isn't work-related. I've had my fill of that place for one day.'

'As a matter of fact-' Smith started.

'-I don't want to know.' Thompson raised his left hand and made an outward cutting motion with it. Smith continued undeterred, 'Has the handrail on the tower been replaced recently?'

'I told you Bob. No!'

'Oh, never mind.'

'What for, like? Not ambulance chasers, surely. It's a bit late for that poor bugger anyway.'

'Do you mean Horace? The less you know the better, I think.'

Thompson seemed more concerned then, 'I don't think you should be making trouble. Confidentially, I'm afraid questions like that will make it even worse for poor Agnes.'

'Who's Agnes?'

'She's the cleaner who left the roof door open when he went up there. Used to peg her cleaning cloths out on the roof. A stool sitting next to the rail where he fell from, that was hers. There's been a proper witch-hunt to find out who left that door open.' Thompson looked down towards his feet. 'Oh God, I shouldn't have spoken.'

'Does she still work there?'

'Not for much longer, I reckon. She's that scared of what they'll do. Besides, Agnes is just about ready for retirement. Can I get you a Rotgut?'

'Well, actually I prefer the darker ales.'

Thompson eyed Smith suspiciously. 'Aye, you look the sort. Why don't you ask for a sample, then I'll get you what you want?'

'Sounds like a fair deal. Go on then.'

Smith tried the Rotgut, finding it even less palatable than he expected. It reminded him of the TNT Pils he had been encouraged to drink once when he had wound up in a working men's club in Seaham. 'Yeeees, I'll have another Ruby Red if you don't mind.'

'That's only four percent and it costs the same.'

'Well I had noticed they do have a generous range of malt whiskies behind the bar. I could probably manage a chaser… '

'On your bike!'

'Ruby Red it is, then.'

Thompson rolled his eyes and signalled. 'Joan, can I have another, please, and a Ruby Red for 'im.' He gestured, nodding his head sideways towards Smith.

They didn't talk until Thompson's second pint arrived. He took a swig and began to look thoughtful. 'I'll tell you who you might talk to.'

'You know me. Any information is treated confidentially and received gratefully.'

'Barry, er, whatsisname.'

'What *is* his name?'

'I can't remember, but he's a contractor. In fact, I believe he fitted a new handrail up the tower. Apparently they wanted it in as an emergency. I saw him this morning. He was working on the leaky roof at the students' entrance. Came in about eight. Was gone by dinner time.'

This revelation struck smith. 'A new handrail, just as I thought!'

'Eh?'

'Don't you see? They've had the handrail changed in case anyone from Horace's inquest came poking round. I'll bet you it wasn't compliant.'

Thompson looked directly at Smith. 'It wasn't. I can tell you that much.'

'In what way?'

'Too low. That was why the roof was supposed to be locked.'

'Bloody hell, Fred! Do you know by how much?'

'No. I just heard Waverley mention it.'

'Well what about the builder who put the new one in, then?'

'I'm sure he could tell you. He's got another job on across town he's working afternoons. There's more work to do here, I know that much. I suggest you come in for eight o clock and keep an eye open.'

'Eight o clock?' Smith's face fell.

Thompson shook his head. 'It's not early for those of us that have to work for our living.'

'Well, I'll have to say, Fred, I'm much obliged.'

'You can do the same for me some time. And there's another thing.'

'What?'

'I'm not telling you. I might when it's *blown* over,' Fred smirked. 'Careless talk and all that.'

'Is it about Boyle? I've seen the film of him embarrassing himself in front of a lot of students.'

Thompson changed the subject. 'By the way, and I don't want any of this repeating.'

'Oh yes, what, what?'

'I'd one hell of a job explaining to Ron Waverley how the CCTV recordings got wiped on the twenty fifth of September. That Morrell had been after him over them. He said she tried to force him to tell her who *accidentally* wiped the tapes. He gave me one almighty bollocking, but he's not one to go telling.'

'What recordings?'

'Your friend Grit. You know I found her in HR.'

Smith had come to believe he knew most of what there was to know about Grit. Perhaps this was a naïve notion.

'Anyway,' Thompson continued, 'I heard on the grapevine Morrell was out to get Grit over catching her in there, so when I had an evening shift monitoring the cameras, I *accidentally* dumped the file with her in there on it. My head was on the block too. I told Morrell I'd asked Grit in by mistake. I had to dump all the other files taken at the same time for the whole of College to make it look like a genuine mistake. I just hope to God nothing serious was going on at the time.'

'I see. Well we're grateful to you, Fred, even if it was to save your own skin!'

What on earth had Grit been up to?

'I'm not happy about it, mind. I've told you too much. And it's the second time I've pulled that one. The first was when they came looking to see who left the door to the roof open. If I'm not lucky I could be heading for the sack.'

'The end is justified if it leads to increasing the power of humanity over nature and to the abolition of the power of one person over another.'

'What're you on about now?'

'Karl Marx.'

Fred nodded cynically, 'That'd be right.'

'What would?'
'Well, you're one of them, aren't you?'

Forty

It was lunch time the next day. Smith had just finished teaching the first half of *Practical Law for Shop Stewards,* a day release course. He enjoyed teaching this programme because there was always plenty to get his students' teeth into with case law.

He had brought a packed lunch to stay back and eat while discussing any questions they had. Questions from his students answered, he mused on recent events concerning the handrail. He had done as Fred suggested and gone into work early, located the builder, Barry Carruthers, above the students' entrance, and asked him about the handrail, only to be told 'I've not got the time to worry myself about shit like that.' It also irked Smith that Carruthers had ordered him clear of the location, claiming he would be responsible if there was an accident.

* * *

Back in the present, Smith had become aware of a caretaker hanging around jangling keys. Expecting the person to try to evacuate them from the building, he turned to explain that they would be there all day and noticed it was Thompson.

'Hello Fred, come to kick us out?'

'Kick you out? No, but I've got a message for you.'

'Really, from whom?'

Fred looked over Smith's right shoulder as if concerned about the two students noshing on their sandwiches and crisps.

'Barry Carruthers,' he whispered.

'Any idea what it's about?'

'No, all I know is he found me in the caretakers' office and asked for you.'

From Thompson's uneasiness, Smith guessed he probably did know, but wasn't entirely happy about being identified as the messenger.

'Ah, did he say how I should get in contact with him? I don't want to have to traipse about in the middle of the night again.'

'Middle of the night? I expect you just loll about all day eating sandwiches and drinking tea.'

'It's an interesting course, Fred. I think you'd enjoy it.'

'I've no doubt, but come five o'clock I'm knackered.'

'We can arrange a day release for you.'

Again, Fred lowered his voice to a whisper, 'If it's all the same to you I'll leave it. I don't want to get a reputation as a trouble maker, particularly after all the CCTV business.'

'Never mind. How *do* I find Carruthers?'

'If you're here all day I'll tell him to come here. What time do you finish?'

'Class finishes at half past four. About a quarter to five, I suppose.'

'Right, I'll tell him to call in, then.'

* * *

A couple of minutes before quarter to five, the burly builder turned up. Smith was expecting an earful about something. He wasn't wrong, but it wasn't quite the sort of earful he imagined.

'I'm glad I found you,' said Carruthers almost meekly, holding his hand out.

'Oh?' Surprised, Smith shook it reluctantly.

'I've changed my mind.'

'Have you? What about?'

'About the old handrail. You asked how high it was.'

'I did.'

'It's ninety two centimetres,'

'I see, and can I ask why you fitted a new one?'

'Who said that was what I was doing?'

'You did.'

'Did I? I think you're mistaken there, mate.'

Smith looked at Carruthers, surprised to infer he was having a joke with him, 'Didn't you?'

'Alright, I might've done, but that was before I knew you were that trouble maker.'

'Okay, right. But now you know I'm *that trouble maker* as you put it, why tell me now?'

'I can't stand trouble makers, but when you're dealing with that bastard, I doubt there's any other way.'

Smith indicated his intention to leave the classroom and continue talking to Carruthers in the corridor. Carruthers followed.

'Which bastard?' Smith asked when safely out of the students' earshot.

'Whatsisname, the head master.'

Smith took a moment to cotton on, mouthing "head master" back to Carruthers.

'You know man,' Carruthers slapped Smith on the back, winding him in the process, 'the head honcho, the big cheese. I mean, what - a - wanker!'

Finally it dawned, 'I do hope you aren't speaking ill of Titas College's distinguished principal,' he said, relishing the dryness of his delivery.

'Principle? That reptile's got no principles! Last Thursday, he cut me up on the road outside in that four wheel drive thing he's got. Had to slam my brakes on. Just missed him. I didn't know it was, then.'

'Didn't you?'

'No. If I did, I wouldn't have told you to get lost when you came to see me. Anyway, yesterday morning, I spotted the car going into that car park with the barriers. I followed him in and the barrier came down on my van. I got out and confronted the bastard, but he just sat in his car and threatened to have me removed from the premises. "Do you know who I am?" he shouted at me through the closed window. It was only afterwards when I asked Fred who he was, I found out.'

While tempted to join in this diss-fest at The Maestro's expense, Smith thought it best to get back to practical matters. 'Thank you for that info. It really is appreciated. Can I ask, though, there isn't any possibility you might be willing to make a written statement as to the height of the old handrail, is there?'

'I don't see why not. I'll not be working at this place again, not as long as that shit house is here anyway.'

'Don't shoot yourself in the foot.'

'I've got more work than I can handle: don't think that's gonna be a problem.'

'Well, Mr Carruthers, all I can say is that I'm very much obliged.'

'No problem, mate, when do you want it?'

'The sooner the better.'

At this, Carruthers pulled a folded piece of paper headed with his company's name and something already written and signed. He plonked it on the desk in front of Smith, who picked it up and examined it, if only to see if it was some sort of a joke. It wasn't.

'Thank you. Really, thank you very much.'

'No problem, mate, and good luck with the rabble rousing,' Carruthers said with a conspiratorial smile and marched off down the corridor.

'Excellent,' thought Smith. 'This'll have Boyle properly on the hop.'

Forty One

Feeling even more perverse than usual, Boyle let his telephone ring ten times before answering it. On the other end was Mohammad Sadiq (V-P, H&S).

'What can I do for you?' asked Boyle, cynically.

'I thought I should let you know, Maestro – I've just heard from Mr Waverley that the contractor fixing the roof over the main entrance has walked off the job, so completing the replacement is going to take a little longer.

'Get another contractor then. As fast as you can.'

'We are doing our level best, Maestro, but I thought I should warn you.'

Suddenly it occurred to Boyle just who exactly the unpleasant exchange that morning had been with. 'That's noted, Mohammed. But as far as that contractor leaving the job is concerned, I'd say good riddance to the termite.'

'Very good, Maestro.'

The line went quiet for a minute. 'Well, Mohammed, much as I'd like to, I really can't stay chatting all day. Was there something else?'

'As a matter of fact there was, Maestro.'

'What?'

'We are having tsunami of paperwork here.'

'That's what you're there to deal with.'

'But it is too much.'

This really displeased Boyle. In his view, Health and Safety was supposed to take care of itself.

'What do you expect me to do about it?'

'I was hoping we could have a little more assistance here; or you could help draw up a plan.'

'I don't know what I can do. We're stripped to the marrow as it is, and I am especially busy.'

'I wondered perhaps if we could have an emergency meeting to decide what to do.'

Boyle was about to explode and tell V-P, H&S to go away and sort it himself, but then something occurred to him. 'You couldn't perhaps enlighten me as to the source – or sources – of all this paperwork?'

'It comprises almost entirely requests for risk assessments.'

'AAAh. Then squirrel them away; send a standard letter out and bury... Look you know what to do, Sadiq, work it out for yourself.'

'But Maestro, I really think we need to decide what to do: I am responsible, but need to have the-'

'-Rest assured, Sadiq, ninety nine percent of these requests are just FUCA stirring up trouble. You needn't waste your time on spurious crap like that. Use your head, man.'

'Okay, I'll do what you say, Maestro, but I'll summarise our discussion in an email and would be very grateful if you would acknowledge-'

'-Yeah, yeah, yeah,' Boyle interrupted. 'You do that, Sadiq,' before hanging up. *Some people think I've nothing better to do than worry about minutiae.*

***

What with the handrail and the risk assessments, and that truculent tradesman, as well as the fact that he couldn't help thinking somehow Smith had a hand in Margaret Bulmer managing to keep her job, Boyle was feeling hounded. There was no evidence for this latter concern and he knew it, but he just had to do something about Smith, if only to alleviate his own paranoid suspicions.

The trouble was that Smith was very clever, exceptionally knowledgeable, and rather too well connected. Terminating Smith by whatever means could easily cause more problems than it solved. He did, however, have suspicions of an extra-marital relationship between Smith and Bulmer. Then again, Smith was probably also witness to the row he had with his wife in Flassburn General Hospital, not to mention the blasted hand dryer. The details of this had the potential to make him even more of a laughing stock than he already was following the "mini-puke" incident. Then there were questions that could arise from what Smith would have overheard from his argument with his wife.

Oh God, no! Nobody else must know about the estate agent's!

Boyle could probably use what he knew to make Smith do what he wanted, but doubted it would be enough to scare him into place longer-term. There was, however, the possibility of providing an incentive to make Smith a generous offer with strings attached. Boyle felt such a decision excruciating, but could some sort of *Détentes* really be the way to go? He felt a sharp pain in his belly: whether this was caused the realisation of what he now knew he had to do, or trapped wind from the curry he had eaten the night before at the *Raj*, he was unsure.

Forty Two

Meeting at Jan's café after work seemed to be becoming a habit for both Grit and Smith. Today was no exception, but Grit was wondering how Smith would seem to her now. Would their intimate encounter last Thursday night have changed things at all? Part of her wanted to tell him to leave Helen and marry her instead, but she was sure he wouldn't. Besides, if he was prepared to cheat on Helen, would it be different if it were Grit who was married to him? She doubted it. He was bound to stray sooner or later.

Grit sat with her espresso, pushing a large mug of coffee across the table to Smith as he arrived.

'Thank you. I'm pleased to report that the management is now inundated with paperwork, and I've now been given a report from the builder stating that the handrail was below the regulation height,' Smith sounded triumphant.

'That's good. Bob. Would you marry me?'

'That's a difficult question, particularly at the moment.'

'I thought it might be. Never mind.'

'No, I didn't say that. It's just there's so much going on... and I am married already.'

She sighed ruefully, 'Yes, I know.'

'Had you considered you were missing a father figure rather than me?'

Grit felt the ache that had gone entirely since their night together returning. 'I don't know, but thanks for that!'

Smith took a couple of sips of his coffee and began talking to her in a lowered voice, making her a confidante. 'You'll never guess what?'

'No Bob, I don't suppose I will, but if you've got to tell me I can hardly stop you.'

'You know I got the taxi to hospital when I left yours last Thursday? While I was waiting to be seen, I saw Boyle's wife go through the waiting area into a side-room and heard them have a blazing row. I didn't know it at the time, but he was in there already.'

Grit smiled, whatever the concerns regarding her relationship with Smith, the idea of Boyle in a compromising position was sure to provide some amusement, 'Go on?'

'Mrs Boyle described him caught up in a hand dryer with Morrell and made it sound like they'd been indulging in a bit of the old S&M.'

'Well if they were, that's their business, isn't it?' Grit lowered her own voice, 'Just as if we do...'

Grit put her hands on his. Smith held them and then let go.

'...Anyway,' he continued, 'it all sounded most bizarre.'

Grit looked into the distance, thinking. 'Maybe she just got the wrong end of the stick.'

'Perhaps. After she had gone Boyle came out and asked the receptionist for a taxi.'

'So what?'

'She told him to use a phone at the other side of the waiting room, picked up what could have been the remains of some contraption, and asked him what he wanted done with it.'

'Really?'

'Yes, and he wasn't at all happy to see it. In fact he almost ran away from it and tripped over on the chairs near where I was sitting. I helped him up, in fact.'

Grit smiled 'Always out to help others. Even arseholes like him.'

After a pause, Smith became more sober in tone. 'What's this about you sneaking around in Human Resources?'

Grit gasped: 'Who's been talking? I didn't think anyone knew about that.'

'Never mind who told me. Is it true?'

'Oh it's true, but it was back at the end of September.'

'Would you mind if I asked what you were doing there?'

'It's private. I really don't want to talk about it.'

'You know you narrowly avoided quite a scrape there, don't you?'

'That's true. Fred the caretaker found me, and when Morrell appeared he told her he had mistaken me for the person who reported the light and invited me through to show him.'

'I see. Do you know what happened after that?'

'Yes, I got interviewed for my own job and got it. Hurrah!' The flatness of Grit's tone of voice was at odds with her exclamation.

'Had you thought about the CCTV?'

Grit's spine shuddered. 'Yes, but that was before the event, not after. Besides, nobody's got back to me, so I don't think it was camera'd where I went. Or nobody's looked at the footage. And even if it was, it gets over-written after a while, doesn't it?'

'It is camera'd.'

'Oh... Shit!'

'And Morrell tried to find the footage.'

'Has she found it?'

'No. It was destroyed "by accident".'

'When you say, "by accident", you mean...?'

'...to make sure Morrell couldn't see it.'

'By whom?'

'All I can say to you, Grit, is that you're lucky to have such good friends.'

'I didn't know I had.'

'Changing the subject slightly, what were you trying to find out?'

Having heard these details from Smith, Grit felt she could not hold out any longer. 'I wanted to look at my file.'

'And you couldn't trust them to forward it to you without cleaning it up?' Smith understood her wave-length.

'Precisely. And I was right about that.'

'How do you know?'

'They had written, "Do not re-employ" on it.'

'And this was before you were interviewed?'

'Yes, just. It was full of rubbish about my conduct in board meetings.'

'Interesting. I could be wrong, but it would seem to me that they are afraid of what you might have found out, so didn't dare get rid of you. Plenty of ammunition for constructive dismissal. Did you take photographs?'

'I did of mine. There was no time to do it with Horace's.'

Damn!

Smith's eyebrows rose, 'You looked at Horace's file?'

'Well, er...'

He leant back in his chair, smiling. 'Ever since I heard you'd been there I suspected you were trying to find out about Horace.'

'He had, "Do not re-employ" written on his file as well.'

'Yes, but I doubt if he did anything as stupid as making unsanctioned visits to look at his record.'

Grit paused, 'There's an answer to that, but I'm sure you know as well as I do that to give it would not be in the best of taste.'

'Yes, there is. But still. Maybe it's just not my way of doing things, that's all.'

'Do you know who Wilfred Garnier is, by any chance?'

'Never heard of him. Who is he?'

'The name of someone mentioned by Horace in a letter apparently signed by him in nineteen eighty five at some engineering company. I think the one they talked about at his funeral.'

'Cholmondeleys?'

'That was it.'

'Yes, Horace was a director. What did the letter say about this person?'

'It raised concerns about Garnier's accounting.'

'So the question we should ask is who would have an interest in keeping that letter in Horace's file?'

'It is a puzzle. But you're far better at this sort of thing than I am.'

'I'd guess it'd be someone with access to the filing system. Morrell, or maybe someone lower down, perhaps Tracey Millicent.'

'Why would anyone lower down have reason to keep it? Besides, Morrell had Horace's file.'

'How do you know?'

'When I first looked I couldn't find it... She walked up to the files, and I hid while I watched her put a file in the drawer. After she went I opened the cabinet. The file was there.'

'That's interesting. It is possible she was putting something into the file, or looking at another part of it, but wasn't aware the letter was there.'

'But if Morrell did see it, and hadn't put it there, wouldn't she have wondered why it was there?'

'I suppose she might.'

'So, given that it was there after she had been at the file, might it be fair to suppose that Morrell placed the letter there?'

'It seems likely.'

'Why would she do that?'

'I don't know.' Grit thought about Smith's question for a moment. 'Insurance of some kind, maybe?'

Smith smiled, 'That's exactly what I was thinking.'

'We're closing now,' Jan called across from behind the counter. 'Do you want anything else before I shut the till down?'

Forty Three

It was Friday. Smith had been summoned by Boyle for two o'clock. Sitting in Boyle's secretary's office, he surveyed the scene. No wonder Boyle had employed Lisa, he thought. She really was quite beautiful, with a soft mouth, high cheekbones and dreamy eyes. She was also tall, at 5'11, a good three inches taller than Boyle.

His eyes roved to a bookcase. The writing on most of them was too small to make out, so he leant forwards and sideways to see if he could. Then he scanned his way to a file with "Philanthropists' prudential / RFZ" written on it. Why would there be such a file in Boyle's secretary's office?

As the clock on the wall hit 2.20pm Boyle could be heard on the intercom, 'You can send the termite in now.' Lisa smiled at Smith.

He heaved himself up from his sunken position and went through, but the principal's office seemed empty. Where on earth was Boyle?

Smith thought this could have been another ruse. He wasn't wrong. The room was full of towels. A pile of the things was stacked on a table by the door. Another was strewn over the back of Boyle's chair and yet another hung on a door knob. Curious, he opened a couple more doors, which proved to be cupboards. Then, for a split second thought he had happened upon a mirror,

'Must do something about those blackheads,' Smith thought, before his conscious mind told him what he had found.

Forty Four

Bob Smith's own face stared back at him, pock-marked with dart-holes. He had stumbled across *The Dartboard.* His prediction that his own picture would be on it was true. He took out his mobile and fumbled with it, trying to take a photograph, but as gadgets were never his strong point, Smith didn't know if it had worked. Being certain to make sure he had taken a picture could have cost his being caught in the act. Not really worth it.

He pocketed his phone and closed the doors to the dartboard quietly. Could he use what he had seen later when he had the time, if not the proof? What happened next gave him a start.

'Bob? Where are you? I'm on the toilet,' said the distant but familiar voice and a door he hadn't investigated opened slightly.

'Now then, Bob. I want to talk to you about the job that's come up.'

Why the "Bob" all of a sudden? Smith was tempted to point out the reference made to him across the intercom, but managed not to.

'You aren't leaving us, are you Principal?' He tried to eradicate any hopefulness from his tone.

'No, I am not. It's a job for you I was talking about.'

'Really? So was I.'

'Teuch! If I were leaving, you wouldn't be getting my job.'

Smith immediately had an inkling of what was going on. 'Really, what job?'

'Vice-principal in charge of Humanities.'

His suspicions confirmed, he played along, 'Why, Principal? Humanities are hardly my subject.'

'Anyone can manage humanities, Bob. It hardly requires any special expertise.' Boyle sounded as if he was pushing on the word *expertise*. A number of ripe-sounding echoes followed.

You make me a proposal sitting on the loo and I'm supposed to take it seriously? was what Smith managed not to say. 'So you want me to apply for the position?'

'Do you think I'd waste my time inviting you here to talk about the weather?' growled Boyle as the en-suite door opened fully, exposing what had sounded like a small trickle as the toilet flushing. 'What you lot don't appreciate is that you won't find a man more earnest than The Maestro.' He emerged wiping his hands with yet another towel as the peppery scent of Insignia aftershave proved thin disguise to the waft from hell which followed, 'Blimey, you should try the fal at the Raj.'

He dropped the towel on a chair, 'Not all that hot in your mouth, but by heck, watch out for what happens at the other end.'

Not wanting to be drawn on the merits of local Indian restaurants, Smith got back to the point. 'Thank you for your generous invitation, Principal, but I'll stay as I am if you don't mind.' Smith took a handkerchief from his breast pocket and pretended to wipe his nose, trying in vain to shield his olfactory function from the miasma which, thankfully, was beginning to lose potency.

Expecting Smith to resist initially, Boyle put a hand on his shoulder, 'Got a family have you, Bob?'

'They are separate from work. I prefer not to talk about them.'

Boyle backed away, showing the palms of his spread hands. 'The thing is, Bob, I've heard things.' He forced a smile.

'Have you, indeed?'

A flash of suspicion interrupted Boyle's attempted *bonhomie*. 'Why, what've you heard?'

'Something about hand dryers. I'm sure it isn't important.'

Smith could picture Boyle back in A&E. He was pleased to see him shudder.

'What are you talking about, Bob?'

'Just that thing I saw you running away from in the hospital last Thursday night. It couldn't have been a, what do you call it... a HAND DRYER by any chance?'

'I never run away from anything, Bob, but I'd be obliged if you kept quiet about that. Anyway, I want to know why you won't apply for the job?'

'Because my notion of a well-run college clearly differs so much from yours.'

'I run a tight ship here. What do you mean?'

Smith took the opportunity to roll off a number of faults in the way the college was managed. 'I've heard that Titas is losing badly over the offender learning contracts because of its inadvisedly low bids.

Boyle looked at him disdainfully. 'If you understood business, you would not make such an asinine comment.'

Smith shook his head once before continuing. 'I've heard about the non-compliant handrail which may have contributed to Horace Villiers's death.'

'That's a lie. I've got records to prove it.'

'But I can prove you had a new one put in before the inquest had a chance to inspect it.'

This seemed to have wrong-footed Boyle slightly. 'Whatever you might *think*, Bob-'

Smith was on a roll now. '-Moving on, I know about bullying of some of the staff which will undoubtedly have been sanctioned by you. For example, the rolling programme of forcing staff to apply for their own jobs at reduced rates of pay and worse conditions, which is illegal by the way.'

'No it fucking isn't. Do you want to see this place go down the tubes?'

In spite of Boyle's assertiveness, Smith was not to be diverted. 'I've also heard about registers marking absent students present presumably because, if they didn't, funding would be cut.'

'Bob will you just shut the fuck up-'

'-I've also heard about taking substantial government funding now being used to keep students with learning difficulties trapped studying basic skills. Few, if any, will progress to learning a trade, but hey-ho, most colleges are doing this now, *aren't they*?

'Look here. If you had the slightest idea what I-'

'-But I have. And while we're about it, let's not forget about students' grants from the benevolent fund remaining mysteriously unpaid. You want me to go on?' Smith observed Boyle was calmer now than when the hand dryer was mentioned.

Boyle was now sitting on the corner of his desk. With arms folded and one leg swinging, he smiled with surprising benevolence. 'All of which I will make sure is investigated. I've got nothing to hide, believe me... But maybe, Bob, you can tell me what your position would be on SEXUAL relationships between members of staff in

College.' As Boyle put undue emphasis on the word "sexual", it seemed to Smith that, as he had feared, his spies had been on the job.

'I don't see anything wrong with it, as long as it doesn't interfere with their work.'

Boyle had moved around to his chair. Now sitting down, he reclined while nodding up and down quickly. 'My feelings exactly. What would your position be if one *or other* of the said members of staff was married to someone else?'

'I would say that was a private matter,' said Smith stiffly. The fact that his first marriage had ended, because of his philandering, gate-crashed his thoughts. Helen knew about this. Helen had also threatened him with a fate worse than death if she ever discovered he had done anything like that to her. Then there was the fact that, since he had been married to Helen, Grit had been one of a select group of three. The other two were women he had met while staying away from home to attend conferences. The chances of Helen finding out about either were slim, but there were still times when he lay awake at night worrying about it.

'Oh, yes, an entirely private matter.' agreed Boyle, beginning to smirk this time.

Smith had the unwelcome feeling his thoughts had just been read.

'The question is,' Boyle continued, 'whether the spouse of one of the said parties got to hear about the said relationship. What do you think she - or he - would do if he - or she - heard?'

'I don't know. You tell me.' Smith wasn't going to demean himself by asking what the point of the questions was. He knew already. The power of his physical attraction to Grit made it even worse. But he did not want to leave Helen. Could he bring himself to make a clean breast of it to Her? Not likely. Not ever. Good Captain Clack had made his bed.

Boyle had found Smith's Achilles Heel, even if he couldn't *prove* Smith and Grit had been on terms of intimacy.

'I couldn't generalise,' Smith answered, 'but if you were expecting me to give the example of a particular set of individuals, I-'

'-Oh no, Bob, what do you take me for?' Boyle had heaved himself up again and was now touching Smith's elbow. 'Son of the second Mrs Smith at Lyon's School, is he? A good little school is that, better than the local juniors at any rate. But the fees will cost a pretty penny. Have you checked what this job pays? Am I right in thinking you could do with a bit more? Extra wonga, worth having?'

Boyle rubbed the thumb and fingers of his right hand together. His softened vocal tone caused the polyps to flap in his throat, producing a gargling sound as he spoke.

'With respect, Principal, my personal finances are none of your business. I have always liked helping people improve the terms and conditions of their employment, so I wouldn't want the job. Besides, I would have thought I was the last person you would want in your coterie of acolytes.'

Boyle spoke slowly with widened vowels as if talking to someone with difficulty hearing. 'Your family situation means you're not likely to take early retirement. You'll double your salary if you take the job, and you've successfully made my life a fucking nightmare for the last few years.'

'But I've only worked here for seven weeks.'

'That's right, Bob, but then there's what you've written in the *Draguian Educational!* Surely you weren't so stupid as to think I didn't know about that? To cut the crap, if I've got to have you at all, I'd rather have you pissing out than in.'

'I take it that my acceptance of the position means I'd have to relinquish my union activities, and support for colleagues engaged in tribunals against this college?' queried Smith, knowing that he earned almost as much from his article-writing and advocacy work as from his current lecturing position.

'What the hell do you think?' Boyle was now starting to shout with incredulity, 'Have you ever heard of a vice-principal being a shop steward?'

He had now backed away and was standing leaning on his chair, with his hands on the back. 'And while we're about it, is there any chance you might be able to rein in that little friend of yours?'

'What little friend?'

'Margaret Bulmer. We can really do without her making trouble at board meetings.'

Already under extreme pressure from the latest developments, the idea he would be expected to control Grit made Smith feel crushed, 'I hope you're not suggesting I have any hold over her.'

'I am. What we need now is not to have people like her upsetting the apple cart. Your wife, Helen, a lovely lady, I understand...'

Smith felt a shiver down his spine.

'...One of those perambulant violin teachers, isn't she?'

'What has that to do with anything?'

'Oh nothing much. It's just I happen to know the county music co-ordinator. A fellow Worshipful Brewer, you know. I was just thinking how your lady wife might feel if he happened to let slip to her about your various adventures with that little friend of yours.

Not exactly subtle in the final analysis, Boyle looked smugger than ever. Smith began entertaining a fantasy of crucifying Boyle at his dartboard by ramming the points of the darts through his hands into the opening blackboards at either side, his portly body writhing ineptly as Smith struggled to pin him down through so much wobble.

'You have put some very serious points to me, Principal,' he said after a pause. 'Perhaps you can give me some time to think them over?'

'Of course' said Boyle, oilily. 'You can submit your application along with the others. Closing date's in a week, so you'll have to get your skates on.' He smiled and placed his left hand on an envelope on his desk. 'By the way,'

'Yes?'

'These are the questions you could be asked at interview and what answers we'll be looking for. You're a bit weak on the managerial front, so you'd do well to learn those by heart.'

'You want me to take it?'

'No, but if you happened to walk off with it, I wouldn't happen to notice.'

'That's corruption Principal and I'm having no part in it.'

'How plausible do you think you'll be if you don't?'

'If you want me to have this job, principal, taking me as I am comes as part of the package.'

Boyle laughed, 'You self-righteous idiot. You know I've got you over the barrel.'

'How would it look if I reported you for this?'

Boyle's expression changed suddenly to one of menace. 'Try it and see what happens. And by the way...'

'What?'

'If I hear you've so much as whisper anything about handrails to the local coroner, your wife will hear exactly what you have been up to. You follow me?'

Smith was cornered. This was something he was neither used to nor felt able to tolerate. 'If this is a taste of things to come, principal, then maybe I should stay where I am and take the consequences.' As soon as he said it, Smith realised how foolhardy this would be.

'You think about it anyway. If you stay as you are, I'll see you regret it. There's something you should know for the record.' He added, taking the top off his trusty Faber-Castell ball-point.

'Yes?'

He pointed at Smith with the pen. 'You should know by now that people address me as Maestro. I see no reason why you should be an exception.'

Smith smiled back and nodded, displaying no obvious sign of the colossal inner rage he felt.

As Smith made for the door, Boyle added for good measure, 'I am the maestro. Me. Not you,' pointing to himself as he said it.

* * *

Leaving the office with a moderate perma-grin painted on his face, Smith managed to make his way back to his workspace and, although his work was slower for the rest of the day, also managed to leave work quite calmly, drive to The Butcher's Arms and down three treble malt whiskies in succession. This was the beginning of an evening which continued in a similar vein.

* * *

Boyle opened his dartboard and threw the three darts. They all landed comfortably on Smith's photograph.

Then he pressed the intercom, 'Lisa, love?'

'Yes Maestro?'

'Can you come through and turn the smoke alarm off?'

'I don't think that's in my contract, Maestro.'

'Well get some caretaker or other bugger to do it then.'

'I'll try, Maestro.'

Ten minutes later, the device attended to, he lit a large Havana cigar.

'I didn't know you smoked, Maestro,' she commented.

'Only sometimes,' he replied as he picked at the cut in the cigar, 'on very special occasions.' Boyle leant back in his seat, feeling much as if he had just conquered a significant part of North Africa.

Forty Five

Wearing a brown suit with a waistcoat and a gold watch chain, Cyril Richards rocked slowly along the corridor with his walking stick and knocked on the outer door to the Principal's suite. Lisa answered it.

'I'm sorry, Mr Boyle's in a meeting. Is it about the board meeting next week?'

'No, lass. I know where Mr Boyle is. It were you I'd come to see. If you've got a minute or two.'

Forty Six

Ten days had passed, and the end of term was approaching. Boyle would not normally have countenanced the idea of playing Santa-Claus to a load of kids. Indeed, he had refused to do so initially. But after receiving an early Christmas present in the form of Smith's application for the position of Vice-Principal (Humanities) Boyle had been in a celebratory mood. In addition, he would always play to the gallery when publicity for himself or Titas College was involved. A Christmas party for the children of students and staff would be just the ticket to arouse positive interest from the media. This was much needed after the debacle of the vigil/strike.

Of course, it was only when Lisa had a very quiet word in the ear of the college's vice principal in charge of marketing, Mr. Azuma, every effort was made to ensure the TV cameras would be there.

Seiji Azuma had had worked very hard indeed since he was first employed at Titas College. Formerly an officer in the Japanese navy, he was fastidious in his preparation for everything, so had obtained Boyle's suit measurements from Lisa, who had happened to have them from a recent occasion, when she had measured him and sent them to a tailor. This time, it was to ensure Boyle looked the part in a state-of-the-art outfit, made with special fibre-optics, which could appear any colour at the flick of a switch.

As nobody from the media was due yet, Boyle rolled up rather grumpily. 'Right, whaddo you want me to do?'

he said. Celebratory mood or not, his reluctance to participate might have been considered an understatement.

'Ah, most delighted to see you Maestro,' said Azuma, bowing low before Boyle, 'Would you be so kind as to try this on for size?'

'Is this a suit? It's the wrong bloody colour, isn't it?'

'It isn't switched on yet, Maestro.'

What the fuck? 'Don't tell me it's *electric*.'

'Only a little bit electric.' Azuma gestured a small gap between his thumb and forefinger.

'For fuck's sake.'

The only thing that saved Boyle from walking out at this point was the fact that Azuma had worked very efficiently in his role, and he was Japanese. After all, the Japanese were good with electrical things, weren't they? Nothing like that dead termite Horace Villiers. As Boyle put the suit on in a curmudgeonly fashion, Azuma pressed a remote control and the whole thing lit up in red, giving Boyle a start in the process.

'Without getting into details, I'm not best pleased with trying out electrical things at the moment. There'd better not be anything going wrong. Where's my beard and hat?'

Azuma went away for a few seconds and returned with a false beard and a ladder, which he placed in the corner of the Grotto.

'And what am I meant to do with this? I've got to interview someone for the post of Vice-Principal in charge of Humanities in twenty minutes.'

'All is well, Maestro. If you could come back at six o'clock it would be most appreciated. We will have a most splendid hat ready for you then.'

'A splendid hat, eh?'

'*Most* splendid. Only the best for you, Maestro.'

Boyle unplugged his electric suit but walked off still wearing it. He didn't want to have to undergo a second fitting, did he?

Forty Seven

'Do come in, Mr Smith.' Morrell was standing by the Board Room entrance, gesturing with her bracelets dangling.

Adjusting to the darkness, it took Smith a few moments to recognise the man who, dressed in a white beard and apparently wearing some sort of extended string vest. Even through the beard, the smugness Boyle had exuded in spades at their private meeting ten days previously had not deserted him entirely. This was exacerbated somehow by the bald head glistening above the outfit. Smith couldn't see anybody who looked like another potential candidate for the job, but still wondered if part of the "test" presented by the interview had something to do with Boyle's attire. These management types were always after some cutting-edge ruse or mantra to illustrate a practical metaphor, analogy or system weren't they? Smith smiled wryly to himself.

What load of shine will they come up with today?

'Now then, Bob,' Boyle gestured to the "lavatory" seat which in board meetings was occupied by the chairperson. Smith sat down in it reluctantly, peering down on the other two vessels in the semi-darkness, 'Can you summarise for us as concisely as possible what you can bring to the position of vice-principal in charge of humanities?'

'Indeed, I have a considerable knowledge of the further education sector as a whole, as well as cooperating constructively with colleagues and students. My practice and teaching of law are similar in terms of their discursive and cognitive approach to subjects covered by the department of humanities-'

Clearly far too busy to devote the time for a full interview, Boyle nodded impatiently, folding his arms. '-Would you say you were good at helicoptering?'

Smith refused to deign the expression as part of any management lexicon, so played ignorant. Leaning forward slightly, he said in dessicated tones, 'I'm sorry, I regret I did not realise the duties included piloting a helicopter.'

Boyle sneered through the false beard, 'It means taking a wider view of the situation. You know, hovering above, as if you were in a helicopter. But of course you knew that.' Santa nodded up and down in an exaggerated fashion and Smith copied the movement.

'Can you give us an example of when you have done this?' Even if the job was in the bag for Smith, and Boyle not inclined to a whole interview, this clearly didn't stop him from making things uncomfortable.

Smith remembered the threat of Boyle making sure Helen knew about his little liaison with Grit and how making a disaster of this interview could, in turn, have terminal consequences for his marriage. He tried to use this unpleasant thought as a spur to focus his mind but could think only of answers relating to his anti-college management positions, 'Indeed, following so much negative publicity about many F.E. colleges.'

'Like this one.' Boyle twisted the knife,

'Including this one, yes, and its predecessor, Durham College, I could see gagging clauses would be incorporated into contracts and was one of the first to warn about the folly of colleges going down that route because of their effect on staff morale and employment culture in my column. But that might be described more accurately as foresight. Of course I have never mentioned Titas College specifically in my column since I took up my current position.'

'Rest assured, I would know about it if you had.' The voice emanating from behind the beard showed its sinister edge.

On reflection, Smith wondered whether there was ever a justification for this concept of helicoptering and was frustrated he couldn't think of any examples more palatable to The Maestro.

'Yes, well, it is one form of helicoptering, I suppose,' Boyle replied, apparently reasonably satisfied if not exactly delighted with the answer. Distracted suddenly, he ejaculated, 'What the? The bastard isn't even plugged in. Grrrr!'

The fibre-optic suit had lit up suddenly without warning and began flashing red and green alternately. 'Fucking Azuma! He's for it now. I'm done,' he said, 'I can just see him bowing down in shame, but that isn't going to cut any ice with me.'

Smith suspected that Boyle would have loved to have continued throwing awkward questions but, it seemed, the distraction led him to call it a day, 'Have you any questions, Alison?' he asked one of the other vessels, shaking his head sideways.

'None, Maestro.'

'Right, well we'll leave it there. We'll let you know our decision aysap. Christ, I feel as if I'm hawking Ready Brek here. And I'm supposed to give out parcels to the little brats looking like this! The things I do for this place.' With that, he struggled free of the enormous executive chair and, once he had got his breath back, headed off to face the music, singing, Eddie Grant's *Electric Avenue*.

Surprised by Boyle's apparent self-deprecation, Smith was curious how, or indeed whether, Azuma's renowned diplomatic abilities would assuage the impending tirade, but he wasn't going to waste time going to see Sanstro in his grotto in the hope of finding out. What Smith did not know was that Boyle's unexpected self-deprecation was probably a consequence of the charm-offensive he had embarked on very recently following Violet's return to the matrimonial home.

Forty Eight

Term was over. A strong cold snap had brought snow with it. Grit's mother, Evelyn, whom she hardly saw the rest of the year had invited herself and Grit's younger brother, Daniel, for Christmas dinner. Grit had also felt obliged, as ever, to invite Conor, George's father, a bankrupt Irish poet who, when he wasn't indulging his extreme relationship with alcohol, worked sporadically as a merchant seaman. Grit couldn't help still liking Conor, but there was no way she could live with him.

In fact she had sent him the DVD of *Zombie Expunger Two* with his Christmas card and a note to bring it with him. He wouldn't have known what to give George anyway. Last year it had been a *Bushmills* track suit. The year before it was *Beamish* pyjamas, which Grit thought looked good on George and, unusually, an appropriate present, believing Beamish to have meant smiling and happy. When he came into the sitting room wearing them, she would call, 'Come to my arms thou Beamish boy,' to which he would cower 'Muuum'. The alternative was that it referred to an historically themed open-air museum, which was also fine. She wasn't having him grow up to be an alcoholic, like his father.

On Christmas morning, Conor had turned up at five thirty, allegedly having hitched his way from North Shields. He smiled at Grit as she opened the door, 'I guess I'm just in time to see our son open his presents.'

Feet thundered downstairs. Grit looked on as George put his arms around his bear of a father, whose right palm almost covered the top of his head, 'Steady on, son; your dad's frozen solid.'

'Would you like some coffee?' Grit asked, wondering whether the fact that Villiers had been a similar shape and size to her ex-partner had anything to do with how annoying she had found him.

'I wouldn't mind an Irish coffee,' he replied, producing a bottle of whiskey from one of the many pockets of his woollen coat.

Grit sighed, 'It's half past five in the bloody morning, Conor. I'm sure you're more than capable of doing your own Irishing.'

'Please Margaret, I wish you wouldn't take the Lord's name in vain.'

'Bloody is an adjective describing something as endowed with blood. And I think that's a fair allegory for this morning.'

Conor sighed towards George, 'Sure you have a clever English lecturer for a mother.'

'Can we open our presents now?' asked George, jumping up and down.

Grit nodded towards Conor. He stared back, baffled, but then nodded and brought out two bottle-shaped parcels from his carrier bag.

Grit shook her head, 'Can I have a word, in the kitchen?'

He followed her through, 'Margaret, love, I'm afraid I forgot to bring the thing you sent me for George.'

She nodded, unsurprised, went back into the sitting room and announced, 'Yes, darlings, why don't we open our presents? After all, it is nearly six o'clock, and time and tide wait for no man.'

'Yay,' called George.

His father handed him one of the bottles, 'No Conor!' said Grit, 'He's not having alcohol.'

'Relax Margaret, you'll see what it is.' George opened it to reveal it was what looked like a bottle of *Jameson.* Grit was aghast as Conor handed George a pound coin, 'Put that in the top, son.'

George put the coin in and the bottle lit up and played, *Whiskey in the jar*, 'Cool. Thanks Dad.' He then embarked upon opening his various other presents, which included a sledge.

'Ah, he's a chip off the old block, aren't you son?' Conor chuckled.

Margaret shook her head again and peered at Conor, waiting for the point at which George would realise there was no *Zombie Expunger Two* amongst his presents, 'Your eyeballs are looking a bit yellow again.'

'I'm fine, Margaret. I know when to stop. That's why my younger brother is dead. The bottle ruled him, so it did. Poor Shaughan!'

Grit remained silent as her reply could well have alarmed George, and handed Conor his present of a cashmere scarf. Conor gave Margaret her present. It was a bottle of Jameson's. A real one this time, 'Have one with me, why don't you?' she said, dryly.

'On no, it's a present for you. I wouldn't dream of it.'

Then the dreaded words came, 'I thought I was getting *Zombie Expunger Two,* mam!'

'Oh, yes, well I'm really sorry, George. It's been held up, I'm afraid.'

'So I won't be getting it today, then?'

'No.'

For a moment, George looked as if he might have a tantrum and blame everyone for ruining his Christmas. But then he asked quietly if he could go out and play on the sledge that was amongst his presents.

This had Grit worried. She was afraid his mood was unbalanced, and he might do something daft like picking a fight with some dangerous youth. How many of her students carried flick knives? She shuddered at the idea. Grit was about to reply in the negative when his father said, 'Of course you can, son. But it's freezing fuar outside, so put all your warm clothes on.'

'But Conor, it's pitch black out there.'

'There are plenty of lights on out at the brewery there. Besides, nobody's about at this time. Here,' he continued, 'Put this scarf on from your mother.'

'Mam, can I have some carrots and a cabbage?' George asked through the scarf.

'Yeah go and get them. Don't take the *whole* cabbage, though.'

'OK,' He pulled some leaves from the outside of the cabbage, placed them on his sledge with the carrots and pulled it out of the door.

When George had gone, Grit gave Conor an earful about undermining her. He replied with a limerick:

'*There was once a young boy in cotton wool*
Whose apron strings his mother would pull
One night he went out
Ignoring her shout
And ne'er returned to his belly-ful'

Grit shook her head, 'That wasn't one of your better ones.'

An hour or so later, she had been busying away in the kitchen while Conor sat immersed in something or other by Charles Dickens. As the first reluctant glimmer of light appeared in the sky, George returned, 'Come and see what I've done,' he said excitedly.

'Maybe later, son. I'm still barely thawed out after my journey.'

'Aw! Will you come, Mam?'

'I've prepped the veg, prepped the duck and the Yorkshire pudding mix is in the fridge, so why not? I've got time on my hands until I've have to go and pick mother up. Of course I'd prefer to go back to bed, but...'

'No, come on, Mam,'

When she'd got her coat and gloves on, George led his mother out of the house to the far side of the brewery, where at the bottom of the bank a giant snow monster could be seen clearly in the brewery's security lighting. It had pebbles for eyes, carrots for a nose and ears and a wrinkly cabbage leaf for a mouth.

'It's a Roberts zombie,' said George with glee.

Now although she had communicated with her via email and spoken to her on the telephone once, Grit had never actually seen George's class teacher, Miss Roberts, but recognised the effigy immediately.

'So it is!' she said, shocked by its similarity in appearance to the chair of Titas College's governors, Councillor Mrs Phyllis Roberts. Only the over-elaborate, horn-rimmed glasses were missing. So there it was, Miss Roberts was probably her daughter. Intelligence, or a lack of it, was also something they seemed to have in common, thought Grit. How else would Miss Roberts be able to gain a post in a North Wear Education Authority school apart from through having her mother as a councillor?

'Now look,' said George proudly as he pulled his sledge to the top of the bank, got on it and started off down. It was too late before Grit realised that he was heading straight for the Roberts monster.

'Stop!' she shouted in vain as George ploughed his sledge into the thing of which, following a considerable initial impact, the head seemed to collapse on top of him quite slowly.

Grit rushed over to find George with a burst lip which, by the powerful lighting from the Brewery, was bleeding into the white of the snow. In spite of this, he seemed delighted, 'See Mam, I well expunged Roberts.'

'You could say that.' Grit wondered if she might be doing the right thing trying to get George seen by a child psychologist.

When they got back inside, Conor noticed the burst lip straight away and also the fact that George seemed completely sanguine, 'You haven't been letting him get into fights, have you Margaret?'

'No I have not. I would've said it was an accident, but to be honest I don't think so,' she said as she went to the first aid cupboard and got some witch hazel and a couple of cotton wool buds, 'Come here.'

'What've you been up to in front of your mother, son?'

'I made a Roberts zombie and crashed my sledge into it. I well-expunged her, Dad,' George replied grandly as Grit tipped some witch hazel onto one of the buds.

'What ever is a Roberts zombie? Is this a new game he's been playing?'

Grit sighed, as she held George's face, trying to dab the bud onto his bottom lip, 'Miss Roberts is his teacher.'

Conor was shocked, 'You mean you've been letting him get away with demonising his teacher? Margaret, I thought you of all people would understand how important it is to teach children to respect their teachers.'

'But Dad, she's a bitch!' said George, pulling away from his mother.

'I will not tolerate that kind of language. Go to your room.'

'Hey, that's not fair.'

'Your mother might be prepared to put up with your blasphemy, but I am not. Now go.'

'I don't have to go to my room. It's Christmas.'

'Can I have a word about this, please Conor?' Grit tried to interject.

'No. Mam, tell him.'

'George, will you go to your room, please?'

'But-'

'-I need a word with your father.'

George stomped upstairs, slamming his bedroom door.

'I'm sorry Margaret, but I'm not having him behave so disrespectfully. I'm still his father and-'

'Just one minute, Conor,' said Grit as she put the buds in the bin and the bottle of witch hazel back in the drawer, 'You haven't seen your son for five months. I'm the one who has had to cope with him and his problems at school. You know nothing about those, do you? Have you any idea how excited he's been to see you and how disappointed he is that he didn't get the game I sent you to bring? And on top of this, I've got to cook dinner for my bloody mother and my brother while trying to keep a lid on everything. And what do you do to help, eh? "Go to your room, George!"'

Conor said nothing. As Grit called George back downstairs, he went to his coat, got a flask out of it and poured it into the coffee from two hours earlier which by now was stone cold.

Upon descending the stairs, George stared at his father pouring, 'Is that whiskey?'

'So it is, son. Look, George, while you have no excuse for disrespecting your teacher, your mother's just explained to me that I've missed quite a lot going on with you while I've been away. I'm sorry if I've jumped to conclusions about things.' As he took a large swig of his Irish frappé, Grit looked at him in acceptance.

'That's alright Dad. The thing was, one of the zombies on this computer game I like to play does look like Miss Roberts. Because I didn't get the game I wanted, I made a statue of her out of snow and then expunged her by crashing into it.'

'I see. This game you're talking about wouldn't be *Zombie Expunger Two,* would it?'

'Yeah, Dad, that's the one. It's awesome. Have you played it?' There were ways the child did not know his father.

'No, I can't say I have.' He looked accusingly at Grit, 'And I've an apology to make to you. The reason you didn't get the game for Christmas is because your Mum sent it to me, and I forgot to bring it.'

'Aw, Dad!'

'And I was going to say I'm very, very sorry. But now you've given me some idea what the game involves, I think perhaps serendipity played her hand.' He turned to Grit, 'If he knows so much about what the game involves, where has he been playing it?'

'At his friend's house.'

'Well, George, I don't think you should go round there again. Not if they've got you playing games like that.'

'Conor, that would be difficult. It's his friend's mam who baby sits George when I'm still at work.'

'Oh, well then I think there's a problem,'

'I share your worries about this game, Conor, but all his friends have got it.'

'*There was a boy from Abercrombie*
Who went out and killed a green zombie
He pulled out his mace
And smashed in its face
Sure now he's weaving the baskets with Bombie.
I'm just slightly concerned, Margaret.'
'Well you're not the only one.'

Forty Nine

It was half-past ten. Grit had set out to pick up her mother and brother, who lived twelve miles away in Hylton in Sunderland. The return journey took almost two hours, much of which was from trying to coax the car up the hill when they got back. It wasn't until Grit had got them back to her house, and her mother spotted that the presents had already been opened, that she was reminded why she avoided her mother whenever she could.

Evelyn had been pleasant enough opening the front door, amenable as she handed Grit her bags to go in the back of the car and positively cheerful as she hobbled down the path, aided by her walking stick, in her massive overcoat, her red bouffant springing out in front of her hood, even if Grit thought her limp was perhaps a trifle exaggerated.

She spoke nicely about Daniel, Grit's brother, even before they had got to his house - how he was doing alright and asked about George as the walking stick flopped down over the car's gear stick and Grit helped her with the seatbelt.

When Evelyn surveyed Grit's front room, the trickle of malaise began, 'I have to say I am extremely disappointed,'

'Why, Mam?'

'The presents have been opened, haven't they? It isn't much to ask that we all open our presents together as a family, is it? But oh no, you can't possibly wait until your mother gets here, can you? *She* won't mind. *She* doesn't matter.'

'Mam, you can't expect a nine year old to wait till almost lunch time to open his presents.'

'Perhaps you should have invited me to stay over, then. Seeing my grandson open his Christmas presents is one of the few pleasures I still have to look forward to.'

'Sorry, Mam.'

'Never mind. Just remember that for next year. If I'm still here, that is.'

'But Mam, I've only got two beds.'

'I don't mind having yours. It wouldn't hurt you to sleep on the couch for once. Anyway, if you've got such a good job, I don't know why you can't afford somewhere bigger.'

'I've told you before, Mam; I bought at the wrong time. My mortgage is more than the house is worth.'

'Typical! I told you before people everywhere are living beyond their means. The banks were lending too much, and the housing market was going to take a tumble, but would you listen to me?'

'I don't remember you saying that.'

'Perhaps you didn't. But listening was never exactly your thing, was it Margaret, dear?'

This went on and on. When dinner came, the vegetables were undercooked and Conor was a layabout, and why were they having roast duck instead of turkey? When it came to clearing the dishes away, Grit took the scarf she had given as a present to Conor, wrapped its ends around her hands, held it taught and approached her mother from behind slowly as she rummaged in her handbag. Conor, by this time thoroughly oiled, made a parrying gesture with both his hands, and began reciting another limerick,

'There was an old gorgon called Evelyn
To her daughter was constantly peevin'
Until the worm turned
And bridges were burned
She's alone now on Christmas evenin''

'I might have expected that from a lazy drunkard like you,' retorted Grit's mother.

This time, it was Daniel who tried to intervene, 'You have had quite a bit to drink, Conor,' he said.

Conor burst out laughing, 'If you think that's bad, try this for size,

In the graveyard we had to withdraw
because of the zombie we saw
It was so terrifying
There's no way I'm lying
But found 'twas the mother-in-law.'

Grit's mother was becoming incensed. 'That's disgusting, especially with your nine year old son here, and I should point out you and Margaret were never married. You know what that makes him, through no fault of his own?' Evelyn was clearly doing her best to seem aghast.

'Oh, oh yes that's right, sorry George. We weren't married, were we?' Conor butted in again. 'Well try this one for size,' he said, spilling drink down the front of his shirt.

'*One time I was able to score*

Bonny Margaret; she was my draw
I was going to marry her
but for a great barrier
Who'd have been my mother in law!

'I don't have to stay here and be insulted. Margaret, throw him out.'

'I'm not going to do that, Mam. And just for the record I was about to strangle you a few minutes ago, but Conor stopped me.'

'Very well. I know when I'm not wanted. George, here's your present. If your mother won't let me watch you open your other presents, at least I can see you open mine. After which I'd be obliged, Margaret, if you took me home. Another Christmas ruined!' she sighed.

'So she *will* be alone on Christmas evenin'' laughed Conor in a state of drunken hysteria. Evelyn gave him the most poisonous look possible as she handed a parcel from the bag to George.

Temporarily at least, Grit abandoned her plans to murder her mother. 'What have you got him?' Besides, if she was going to do it, it was probably not such a good idea to have an audience – especially this one.

George had already torn off the wrapper, transfixed by its contents. It was a box with *Zombie Expunger 2* written on the side.

'What do you say to your Gran, George?'

'Wow, thanks Nana; you're the best.'

Yeah, George would think that, Grit thought to herself. *Far be it for me to disillusion him about his grandmother.*

Fifty

Smith was keeping the news he had received on Christmas Eve until dinner. The whole process had been so weird. How else could he tell his family about it?

As they sat around the table on Christmas day, he announced to Helen, Toby, and Emily, who had brought her friend Pam, that he had been appointed as Vice-Principal in charge of Humanities.

Toby chomped on his goose, 'Well done, Dad. You're a high-flying pajero, now!'

'Thank you for that, Toby. Can I have some goose as well, darling?'

'If you have to; it needs eating up, I suppose.' She put a piece of vegan wreath in her mouth and chewed on it thoughtfully, 'I don't remember your even telling me you were going to apply for this job.'

'Yes, it was all rather sudden. It even surprised me.'

'Hang on, Bob. What happened *rather suddenly* to precipitate this?' Helen took a cake slice and helped herself to some hazelnut quiche. 'If I remember rightly you were dead set on an ordinary lecturing position so you could continue your other activities, like your column, relatively unhindered.'

'Can I have goose gravy as well?' Asking an unrelated question gave Smith a little think-time.

'If you must. I only made enough for three. Have you all had all you want?'

'Shall we be kind to Dad?' Toby asked Emily.

'Yes.'

'You're a Daddy's girl.'

Pam glared furiously at Toby as if she was about to treat him to some severe form of torture, 'Don't you talk to Emily like that.'

'Why not? She's only my stupid half-sister.'

Pam intimated punching her left hand with her right fist, causing her bosom to sway inside its sports bra, noticeable through the shirt and suit she was wearing, 'When you're on your own, you and I are having words!'

'That's enough!' Helen said into the ether, somewhat bemused at the apparent aggression displayed by Emily's chosen companion. Emily and Pam looked like total opposites as Emily was a delicately built blond, while Pam was thick-set and dark-haired with a side-parting. 'It looks like you're in luck over the gravy, darling, but you aren't getting away with not answering what I asked.'

Smith took the gravy and poured the last of it, while pretending to look thoughtful.

'There was a bit of a problem there. The principal didn't like what I was doing so he promoted me. That's basically what's happened.'

'Promoted you on the condition you didn't make life difficult for him?'

'Yes, there was something of that.'

'Funny. That sort of thing never bothered you before, did it?'

'Not really.'

'So why should it bother you *rather suddenly* now?'

Smith was cornered. There was no way out, so he just tried to accentuate the positive, 'He said I can keep my column.'

'On the condition you write only what they let you.'

'That has always been the case. I have never written one word specifically against Titas College since I started working there.'

'But you have against what some colleges are doing and that often happens to include yours, doesn't it?'

'Well yes, but-'

'-And you'll be reining that in now, will you?'

'Not if I think there is something to be said. I'll just have to word it a bit more carefully, that's all.'

'Hmm. What will you be making with this new job?'

'Seventy five thousand and a pension to match if I can hack it up to retirement. So you see, it really is in our interests.'

'That's something I suppose. But you'll have less time to do your legal moonlighting.'

'It'll still be worth our while. Honestly it will.'

'Hmm.'

Smith could plead with Helen as much as he wanted. He knew she mistrusted what he had said and wondered for how much longer he could keep from her what had happened with Grit.

Fifty One

The spring term had begun. Grit was worried. The first matter of her concern was that she had been told by Maria Hetherington, that Wesley Johnson had been permanently excluded from the college. She was instructed to continue to mark him in the register as an "Explained Absence" until at least the end of the spring term. Suspecting Wesley's removal from the college had something to do with the fuss he had made about his grant not being paid, Grit had not agreed to this. But given her current lack of trust in all but her closest colleagues, she was not about to question why.

Then there were "Basic Skills" classes she had been looking forward to teaching like a dose of gout. At least most of her GCSE students, like Wesley, had been interested in her lessons. A lot of low-scoring, teenagers probably wouldn't want to be there by choice. And they would probably remain forever if the Government and Boyle had their way. What were the chances she could convey her love of language to them?

Another thing that was troubling her was the fact that she had not received a reply from the internal auditor to the letter she had sent about non-payments by the Students' Benevolent fund back in November.

Apart from this, she had many confusing feelings about her relationship with Smith. Had sleeping with him actually meant anything? Was it just a one-night stand? Part of her had fallen hook, line and sinker for him, but why was it only part? What was preventing her from shouting her love for Smith from the roof-tops? It was only on considering this question that Helen came into her mind.

Smith had been prepared to cheat on Helen with her. Did this mean he might be prepared to leave Helen for her? Did she want this anyway? And how would she feel about Smith if Helen ended her marriage – perhaps on the basis of what Grit and Smith had done? How much would she have wanted him then?

* * *

Titas College had been closed for the first week of term because of the weather. Having made her way in on the Monday of the second week, Grit was dogged by questions like this, as well as with Smith's lack of contact with her. Had she become too reliant on him for support, particularly over her worries about what was happening at the college? There was the contract the union still hadn't agreed to, resulting in varied, on-going industrial action. Second were the various cases involving staff. Third, was the question of health and safety issues. What had Smith decided to do about his proof that the hand rail had not been legal? What was the progress with the various risk assessments? She needed to speak to Smith badly, but he was nowhere to be found.

Bill Ogle did not smoke, but during the summer often frequented Smokers' Corner. These appearances tended to diminish once the weather turned and autumn set in. Grit was surprised, then, to find him there in the freezing cold, barely visible through his attire.

Grit had already taken her cigarettes and lighter out as she approached him in Smokers' Corner.

'Have you ever thought of trying e-cigarettes, Grit?

'I have, but I love my ciggies too much.'

'E-cigarettes aren't supposed to be as bad for you.'

'I'm not going to be drawn, Bill. How are things going with you at the moment?' she asked, changing the subject.

What was visible of Ogle looked even more dour than usual. 'Not good, Grit. Not good at all.'

'What's wrong this time?'

'Not much, it's just that Maria Hetherington has been on at me not to fill registers in when students are absent. I've found out what Bill Kay means when he says he's "sacked" his students, and then there's something else, now what was it…?'

'What does Bill Kay really mean when he says he's sacked his students?'

'This is delicate, Grit, and of course he's your colleague more than mine.'

'What, Tom? What's he been doing?'

'Have you seen his Entry Three pass rates for English Literacy?'

'No.'

'Well I'd just start there. I was talking to a mutual student, Terry Nicholson. A right tearaway. Bill said he'd sacked him, but Terry told me he'd passed the course.'

'So he didn't sack them, er, put him off the course, then? It's possible Terry could be lying.'

'It could be, but Grit, am I right in saying that Entry Level students are allowed support in examinations?'

She put her lighter out before its flame could touch the tab in her mouth. 'He's making them pass by doing the work for them so that he can get rid of them?'

'It looks like it. Happy New Year, by the way.'

'Happy New Year. I could check his registers and their papers, or I could ask him about it.'

'Well yes, Grit, but be careful.'

Lighting up finally, Grit thought how, compared with her sojourn into Human Resources, checking the registers of classes in her department should be easy. 'By the way Tom, have you seen Bob? He's not answering his phone. No surprise about that. He's probably lost it, but he hasn't replied to email either, and I need to talk to him urgently... Well... quite urgently.'

Ogle seemed to recoil in slow motion. 'Ah, well. That was the other thing... I thought you'd have known.'

'Known what?'

'He's our new boss. Didn't you know?'

'Who?'

'Bob is.'

'Is he?'

'Yes, he's the new vice-principal in charge of humanities.'

It took a while for Grit to digest this bombshell. Her first thought was that it was marvellous. Bob Smith a vice-principal! That would soon lick the likes of Boyle into shape, wouldn't it? Something was preventing her from jumping for joy.

'What does that mean, Bill?' she asked, eventually.

'Ooh, Grit, I don't think I can answer that one honestly.' He took off his glasses, and looked at Grit blindly as he began cleaning them. Grit thought how glasses are usually seen as a barrier. Ogle looked vulnerable without his, but his lack of ability to focus without them was tangible, even more of a barrier than when they rested in front of his eyes.

'Answer it dishonestly, then,' she said at last.

'In that case it's great. More power to Bob's elbow.'

'Why the misgivings?'

'Boyle hates Bob, so why would he appoint him?'

'Because he's extremely capable and very good at his job.'

'Do you really think that would be reason enough for Boyle to promote Bob? After all, he has made quite a bit of trouble for The Maestro; *look at what he's written in his column.*'

'I have always read his column, even before I qualified. He has a way of getting straight to the point. No messing. But he never anything specifically about this college since he started working here.'

Grit looked away and took a draw on her cigarette. 'You know I worshipped him because of his writing. That was before I met him, I suppose.'

Ogle returned to the reasons why Smith should not, in normal circumstances, have been offered, let alone accepted, the post. 'It's not just that, Grit; look at everything else he's been doing. Boyle's bound to know he's behind the health and safety campaign, for example.'

'That does seem strange. I'll have to talk to him, look...' Then the explanation struck her. Grit's face fell. 'Are you saying he's been bought off? That wouldn't work with Bob, he isn't int-'

'-Perhaps not. But a little bird told me you and he...'

Grit took her cigarette in her hand and lowered it angrily. 'What's that got to do with this?'

'But Grit, he's married.'

'Again, I know, but-'

'-Just put it this way, I don't think any tactics would be below The Maestro.' Ogle pulled his hood backwards so his face could be seen and then mouthed "blackmail". Grit felt her face flush red. She was about to punch Ogle for suggesting this but stopped herself in time. She had a sinking feeling he could be right.

* * *

Grit went out to lunch feeling numb. Her normal cynical self would have reasoned that Boyle was playing Smith. But she had started to idolise Smith as someone who knew how to get the upper hand over the Powers-That-Be. Thanks to Smith, the industrial action had been taken without repercussion beyond a lot of empty threats. Unlike her, most members of staff still had their hours stated in their contracts.

She also believed deeply that Smith had principles. More than this, Grit had begun to accord Smith an almost super-human status, even if he was just as susceptible to the base of a frying pan as the next man.

But she was also used to being disappointed. Men were certainly no exception. Now she began to suspect that, during their liaison, Smith had known he was going to abandon his various seditious pursuits. This was over a month ago, now. Could Smith have betrayed her, if only by omission? Men who did that sort of thing to Grit were ejected from her life by a very large catapult. And Smith had already showed he was capable of betrayal. And he was married after all. Who the hell did he think he was? The rat! As her ire rose, Grit found herself unable to finish her sandwich.

Fifty Two

'Where on earth is my mobile?' Smith said to himself as he cleared his desk ready for his move upstairs. Even though she had retired, he had been hoping to hear from Dr Fisher. He had left her a couple of messages in the forlorn hope she might set him straight on a few things. After all, who would know the job better than his predecessor? *I thought I'd be glad to be getting my own office*, he thought.

But he wasn't. Smith felt mildly sick, for which he could partly have had his hangover to thank. He also felt dirty - even more so than when on discovering he was having an affair, Elizabeth, his first wife, had left him. He thought of the half dozen members of staff he had been supporting. They had been engaged in various types of dispute with the college. Some of them had undoubtedly been discriminated against. Smith was looking forward to their cases. He loved doing that sort of thing.

Not my problem now.

A hardening urge to leave the building for several hairs of the dog was interrupted by draft of air to the back of his neck. He didn't have to wait long to determine its origin.

'And what is this?' snapped Grit.

'It's a pencil,' replied Smith as he glanced momentarily down at the freshly-sharpened HB Grit was holding threateningly towards him.

This was no time for laconism. 'It's only my herculean will preventing me from using this to gouge your eyes out.'

'Oh God,' sighed Smith. He had been wondering how to explain away what had happened to a number of people, not least Grit, but couldn't help thinking the register of her latest utterance reminded him of Horace Villiers.

'Oh God?' repeated Grit, 'Is that all you can say?'

'Apparently not. It's a long story.'

'A *long* story, is it? Just what the hell do you think you're playing at?'

'I didn't know. I can explain if only...'

'A lot of people have trusted you. You have been their rock in this quagmire. Like it or not, that's a privileged position you've just abused.'

'I know, look.'

'So you admit it?'

'Yes. No. Yes,' His head pounded. Why did she have to shout so? 'You can't see my mobile anywhere here, can you?'

'I'm furious with you! Do you think I'd give a flying flick about your phone?'

'I know, it's just I can't find it.'

'I'm not interested. It's no good, Bob.' Grit brandished the pencil again as if to stab it upwards into the underneath of his chin. 'If I don't go now, I will use this, so help me.'

With that, she stormed off.

* * *

Half an hour later, Grit was still shaking. She checked her phone for messages. There were five from Smith, with a number suggesting they were made from a telephone in the college.

'Bloody Judas,' she muttered to herself, skipping over them each time his voice could be heard.

Later, though, she began to reflect on all Smith had done, and also what she had done to him. Grit had known Smith was married when she cajoled him into bed, when she yanked his knickers down to his knees and held his hands to her naked body.

And then there was Helen. Having thought about this, Grit had only just realised she loathed the woman in whose presence she felt like a...The only word she could think of was "guttersnipe" even though it was arcane. Helen had done nothing to her. Not on purpose, anyway. It was just that Helen represented something Mrs Robson had encouraged Grit to aspire to; but for Grit's appreciation and knowledge of, literature, Helen was a cut above - clearly schooled in some sort of Bohemian academia from birth. Could this have been why she had led Helen's husband to adultery?

No, it wasn't. Grit remembered her feelings for Smith. Deep feelings. Feelings which recently, until her current reflection, had been over-written by anger and painful disappointment that he was not all she had imagined him to be.

Her painful train of thought was interrupted by the phone. She was glad of the distraction.

Fifty Three

For the first time in a while, Boyle felt as if things were looking up. Sitting quietly in his office, he began to get the glowing thrill of being on top again.

He pressed the button on the intercom, 'Lisa, love. Can you get me a coffee?'

'Are you still taking Americanos, Maestro?'

'Indeed I am. There is no way I'm risking that frothy stuff again. Not after what happened in October.'

One source of joy was that he had received an offer that very morning of an OBE.

He remembered his wife talking to him about the prized contents of the envelope at breakfast. She had peered over her tea cup before taking a slurp.'But do you think you should accept it, Laurence?'

He had looked back at her, baffled. 'What do you think, Vi?'

Mrs Boyle had adopted a straight face as she buttered the toast. 'It was just all you said about how lollipop ladies were getting MBEs and hereditary titles not being quite the thing in a meritocracy.'

Boyle had begun to get annoyed. 'Sometimes, Vi, just sometimes, I could swear you were taking the mickey.'

Mrs Boyle placed his toast in front of him, already buttered and with marmalade. 'Really, love? Now why would you think that?'

He shook his head. 'I've worked bloody hard to get where I am. Don't you think I deserve it?'

'Oh, I know you *do*, love. And you've suffered too. You and Miss Morrell.'

'Absolutely. I, I mean, we, have. Hang on, what exactly do you mean by that?'

'Well, you getting trapped with her in that hand dryer only because you were testing it. I mean, the things you've done over and above the course of your duty. Or should I say *duties*, there being two of you involved?'

'For God's sake, we've been through this a hundred times since you came back from Angela's. Nothing happened between me and Alison.'

Mrs Boyle put a hand on his, laughing. 'I believe you, love. I just thought it was funny the adversity you've had to suffer-'

'-Can we change the subject, Vi? I need to get to work and would prefer to be in a better frame of mind than when I'm thinking about that pillocking machine.'

'Of course, dear.'

'Right, now where is my briefcase?'

Back in the present, Boyle smarted at how irritating his wife could be. That did not detract, however, from the idea of getting an OBE. Neither did it do so from his thoughts about Bob Smith.

Now he's exactly where I want him.

Without Smith advising Bulmer, FUCA, or the rest of those termites, It gave him the greatest pleasure to think that, should Smith cause any problems for him, Boyle would be on the blower to the county music adviser, and Bang would go Smith's marriage. Oh yes, Boyle understood these things, and a damned good job too.

Fifty Four

'Is that Margaret Bulmer?' A softly spoken voice she didn't recognise came down the line. An earnestness which made her feel that the caller was not trying to solicit, sell or otherwise con her prevented her from hanging up, 'Yes.'

'I see. This is Marion Villiers. You gave me a note at my husband's funeral asking if I'd get in touch with you.'

Grit's handing a note to Mrs Villiers with an invitation to contact her had been a shot in the dark and forgotten. As someone who was basically quite practically minded, and who had encountered grief at such an early age, Grit had little appreciation of the time so many who experience bereavement take to be ready to face the matters it raises. Her own father's death when she was nine had been dreadful, but she had little memory of the timeline surrounding it.

'Yes, I did,' she remembered, 'I just didn't expect to hear from you now.'

'Well if you're not interested...' Mrs Villiers sounded as if Grit had just slapped her across the face.

'No, no. I'm very interested. Sorry. I'm just distracted at the moment, that's all. Obviously I'm at work most days, but if you'd like to suggest a time at the weekend. Thursday afternoons are clear as well.'

'That's fine. Any time will do really. I had to give up work six months ago. How about Saturday morning?'

'Let me get my diary out.'

'I would really like to talk to you as one of Horace's colleagues from College. You see, I didn't really know anyone from there and, well, I'd like to try to piece things together for myself now.

Grit remembered that she took George to his taekwondo on Saturday mornings. Or was it kickboxing? She could hardly keep up with the extent to which her son dabbled in the martial arts. But this, she thought, was important.

'Yes, that's fine, except...'

'What's the problem?'

'I can do Saturday morning if you really want, but after lunch would be a bit easier.'

'That's fine by me. I'm usually pottering in the garden, but the forecast isn't great anyway.'

'Okay, one thirty?'

'I wasn't really one of Horace's colleagues, you know.'

'Oh, so you didn't know him, then?'

'I knew him. Actually we were what you might call sparring partners. I'm the staff governor at Titas College, you see.'

'I remember your saying so at Horace's funeral.' Mrs Villiers's voice went downwards on the second two syllables of the word "funeral".

Grit took note of this and considered her next utterance, 'Are you afraid I'm playing the tune of Boyle and the management?'

'Yes.'

'Oh nooo! There's so much wrong and I'm trying, with little success maybe, but attempting nonetheless, to get to the bottom of it. Um, does that mean you feel angry towards them or...?' Grit wanted to ask whether Mrs Villiers had felt that "the management" more particularly “The Maestro” was responsible for Horace’s death. She was glad she hadn’t asked it in the moment, but still wanted to know.

‘I don’t think I feel angry towards them. It’s more I couldn’t trust them. You know, there’s the sense that something I said could be misconstrued, perhaps used against me.’

‘I know the feeling, believe me!’

‘I thought you might.’

‘Would I be right in thinking we’re both trying to piece things together, then?’

‘Yes, I think perhaps we are.’

‘Where shall we meet? Would you like to come to mine? We can have coffee or tea or something?’

Fifty Five

Grit had stood outside for nearly a minute in the freezing cold before the plump, red-faced lady she had seen at Villiers's funeral answered the door looking bemused.

'Hello, pleased to meet you.' Grit offered a numb right hand.

Mrs Villiers looked up at Grit. 'Are you? Why?'

'Um, I'm glad you contacted me and agreed to talk about Horace and the college.'

'Did I?'

'You are Marion Villiers?'

'Yes.'

'I'm Margaret Bulmer.'

'You're Marg... Oh I am sorry. It slipped my mind entirely. I haven't been myself lately. Keep forgetting. Come in, come in, you must be frozen!'

As Grit entered, she thought that this was just the sort of house she would have liked to live in. It just looked like a large semi-detached on the outside, but patterned tiles on the hall floor, together with oak panelled walls and a faux gothic staircase set off a very spacious home indeed. Through its open door, Grit could see that the living room was enormous, with what looked like rather valuable, heavily framed paintings on the walls, a huge Indian rug sitting in the middle of a pastel green carpet and what looked like Victorian antique furniture.

She followed Mrs Villiers past another couple of expansive rooms through to what seemed little more than a cupboard at the back of the house.

Noticing a cooker on one wall and a sink crammed in the corner next to the kettle, Grit wanted to ask why such a big house would have a kitchen considerably smaller than her own, but bit her tongue.

'I normally stop and make a pot of tea at about this time,' said Mrs Villiers, 'or would you prefer coffee?'

'Well yes, actually I would. I don't drink tea.'

Mrs Villiers got a jar out of the cupboard.

'I never know how strong to make coffee,' said Mrs Villiers, as she picked up an ornate silver spoon from the drawer, 'so tell me how much?'

'One and a half of those, heaped,' said Grit, 'I like it nice and strong.'

Mrs Villiers did as she was told, excavating the instructed quantity of semi-congealed granules, and put everything tea-break related onto a tray. 'I think we'll go through here,' she said, heading into a room with shelves and shelves of books, but just two high-backed chairs facing each other over a coffee table and next to the large fireplace, which had a spray of dried flowers in the grate.

'We always called this Horace's room,' remarked Mrs Villiers as Grit took her first mouthful of coffee, regretting it straight away.

'He spent most of his evenings here reading and writing.' Grit noticed a desk and chair in front of the window. 'He read a great deal, you know. I still haven't got all the books back from his flat.'

This came as a surprise. 'He had a flat?'

'Yes, on the main road, next to the college.'

'I had no idea,' replied Grit, the bitter taste of strong, instant coffee still throttling her tongue. She decided to hold onto what was left in the mug to get the last of the chill out of her fingers.

'We weren't living together when he died, you see.'

While the inquest had reached an open verdict with regard to exactly *how* Villiers had fallen, Grit had come to imagine him as a sort of martyr, throwing himself off the tower in protest of his and other members of staff's treatment - treatment she had been unable to prevent. She had not considered whether Villiers had problems at home.

'I didn't come here to tread on any toes, but can I ask why?'

Mrs Villiers went on to explain that she had suffered a heart attack and how his presence in the house had been stressful for her. When she told him this he had decided to move out, 'It seems funny looking back on it. I was already up a height because he was late coming in, and his dinner - beef wellington - was ruined. He was irate because of something or other the principal had done. I'd had shooting pains in my left arm all afternoon, but my chest got so tight I keeled forward, and do you know what Horace said?'

'No.'

'He told me to take some Tramadol and put on some Burt Bacharach. He thought I was just stressed - or overcome with emotion. As if I made a habit of being overcome with emotion! He was beside himself when he realised.'

'I can imagine that. I hope you don't mind.' Grit was about to tell Mrs Villiers about how she had used to refer to him as a pompous twat, catching herself just in time.

'Lord, no. Horace was *insufferable.*' Mrs Villiers took a tissue from a box on the hearth and dabbed her face with it. 'You had to put him in his place or he'd drive you to distraction.

'Anyway, the consultant told me I had to avoid stress at all costs. Horace took it on himself that he was my sole source of stress.'

'Wasn't he?'

Mrs Villiers smiled, 'No, perhaps my single biggest source, but by no means the only one. I had told him that if he carried on as he had been it could kill me, so he decided he couldn't trust himself to regulate his moods and moving out was what he had to do – for the time being at least. It wasn't meant to be permanent, at least as far as I was concerned.'

'Do you think he thought it was?'

'He might have. One thing about Horace is that on reflection he would always do what's best for me and the children – apart from when he was having one of his tantrums.'

All through this conversation Grit was niggled by thoughts about the document she had read surreptitiously in Villiers's file in HR, which referred to his bi-polar disorder. She wondered what Mrs Villiers would think if she knew what she had done. Grit's mind skipped to the other letter she had seen in Villiers's file: the one from nineteen eighty five about an employee at Cholmondeleys' Engineering.

What did that mean? For God's sake, don't mention anything about what was in his file.

'Horace wasn't always a teacher, was he?'

'Heavens, no. He was an engineer. In fact he was a partner and chief engineer at Cholmondeleys'. It's down near Darlington. Do you know it?'

'I've heard of it.'

'Yes, it's a fair sized company and he was there a long time, but he had to take early retirement because his, well his...'

'-Yes.'

'...were getting the better of him. In fact he was in a psychiatric hospital for six months. It took him a few years after that really to recover. He went into teaching when he was asked to give a talk about careers in engineering to the local Workers' Educational Society. Horace always did like the sound of his own voice, but they were such an appreciative audience.'

Grit couldn't help but titter.

Pouring herself some more tea, Mrs Villiers pressed her lips together. 'You obviously know what he was like.'

'Maybe, but I thought he'd always been that way.'

Mrs Villiers paused knowingly before answering eventually, 'I think it's fair to say he got a lot worse when he went into teaching. I'm a history teacher myself. I only did it part-time since the children started at school. That was nearly twenty years ago. Gave it up when I had the heart attack. But I used to keep telling Horace that teachers didn't have to hold the stage as he liked to. He'd say, "You're a teacher, but I'm a lecturer. Teaching is more difficult. Unlike you I've got a captive audience which *is* there by choice." Then he'd usually do his annoying grin. You know the one?'

'Oh, do I not!' Grit thought about how she had enjoyed her job when it mostly entailed lecturing, but her recent experience trying to teach "Basic Skills", not to mention "Foundation Skills", to students who didn't have much choice in the matter, was teaching at its most toilsome, and that was before even thinking about "Vocational Studies".

Mrs Villiers went on to tell Grit how, when he started as Durham College, Villiers had thought of his job as a retirement occupation, but soon came to see it as a second career. Before long, he felt things were blighted by management decisions, and got worse when the new principal at Durham College, Laurence Boyle, was appointed principal at Titas. Boyle might have achieved financial solvency for Durham College, but at the cost of a frightened, angry and disillusioned staff. Then there was how Horace had always enjoyed projects. He felt strongly how processes used in training at College should reflect those in a real company developing marketing and selling products. 'I don't know if you heard about the hand dryer.'

'I know the college was developing one and that the principal was going to do product testing in his bathroom there.'

'So I understand. But I think this might've been what drove him over the edge.'

'Drove Horace over the edge?'

'Yes. Did you know he had a heavier work allocation than the other course leaders in the department?'

'No.'

'This started about a year before the amalgamation with West Durham College. He had about thirty contact hours a week. To think the job was meant as a retirement therapy for Horace. It's all so *stupid.*' Mrs Villiers's voice quivered.

Grit said nothing for the moment. Not really knowing the woman she had come to see, she did not know how to respond. After a pause, which Grit hoped would have given Mrs Villiers the space to add anything if she wanted to, before commenting, 'I wonder what - or who - was behind the heavier workload.'

'I think we can both guess the answer to that one.'

'Maestro.'

'Quite, but that wasn't all.'

'What else did he do?'

'Horace used to come home really depressed sometimes because of what someone had said to him.'

'Uh-oh! That was probably me.'

Mrs Villiers looked at Grit. 'I very much doubt it.'

'I called him some quite colourful things, you know. Um, "obnoxious old bore" was one, "conversation gate-crasher"; "failed Shakespearean actor"; "domineering dickhead"; "Brian Blessed nuisance."'

Mrs Villiers laughed, 'Oh, Margaret, you obviously didn't know him very well. That sort of thing wouldn't have bothered Horace in the least. He knew when he'd asked for it, and I've no doubt he did with you. No, from what Horace told me, Boyle would corner him when nobody else was in earshot, and tell him that he was like a depressive illness, a loser, asked him why he didn't resign. I told him not to take any notice of it, but you could hardly blame him if he did.

'But with Boyle, I don't think it was so much what he said. It was more the underhanded way he did it that upset Horace.' Mrs Villiers looked across at Grit, 'Going back to what I was saying, through comes this order to develop a hygienic hand dryer. It's a long story, but I don't know if you'd heard about blown-air dryers in loos re-circulating faecal matter?'

'No. I can't say I have.'

'Well, Horace saw that developing one that didn't do this was an opportunity for his students.

'I heard he liked to keep things practical.'

'But there's a sting in the tail here and Horace was a bit naughty. You see he thought he would put the principal in a position where he would have to test the dryer or look bad, by putting out press releases when it was almost ready. That was his way of protesting. He was really grateful to the brewery man, Richard was it?'

'Cyril Richards. He's on the board.'

'Horace felt it would be pay-back for the way he'd been treated. Boyle would have to agree to it being installed in his office or be seen not to in the public eye. Not a good choice for him, especially as he always wanted to appear virtuous to the public. You know, "*I'm a hands-on principal: I like to get down and dirty with the weeds...*"' Mrs Villiers scoffed.

As Mrs Villiers had done her best to imitate Boyle in her last sentence, Grit's smile turned to laughter.

With a slight smirk, Mrs Villiers poured herself some more tea, cutting some sponge cake this time offering it to Grit, who declined with thanks, and then devouring it herself.

'Were staff being re-appointed by any chance?' asked Mrs Villiers once her mouth was clear.

'Re-appointed?'

'Having to apply for their own jobs.'

'Yes. I think it's disgusting. I've had to take a twenty percent pay cut. But that's only one of the things I'm furious about. The governors delegated the power to do this when Titas was first set up, apparently. And apparently this is usual. Not being the most experienced in politics, I found it hard to understand.'

'I see, because I'm wondering if he had lost his job but hadn't told anyone. I've written in to request his records under Freedom of Information, but as I said, I've not been very clear in my mind.'

This struck Grit like a bolt of lightning. 'Did you know that there was a large protest by students at the college because of how they thought Horace had been treated?'

'No.'

Grit was shocked. Could Mrs Villiers have been confused through bereavement or was she holding something back? 'It was kept out of the news, but I can't believe nobody told you.'

'A few I didn't recognise spoke to me there, you included. Who was the mature sort of man: what used to be called, "tall, dark and handsome"?'

Grit felt her heart leap. 'That would be Bob Smith. He *is* going a little grey.'

'Just a little, yes. It was his question that made me wonder if new contracts were being forced on staff.'

'He did mention that to me, but refused to say any more when I pressed him. Look, I don't want to lumber you with too much, but can I have your Wi-Fi key?'

With the key code typed into Grit's tablet, she played the film on *Candid* of Boyle talking to the students, and getting sick from a projectile, before retreating angrily from the scene.

'Well I never!' said Mrs Villiers, 'So he *was* getting rid of Horace and even told a crowd of students. I hadn't a clue!'

'He wasn't that specific, but it does make it a possibility.'

'A probability! I don't normally like to swear about people, but...!'

'I can't disagree with that.'

The meeting had ended on a friendly note and they agreed to keep in touch. But Grit couldn't very well have admitted she had seen "DO NOT RE-EMPLOY" scrawled on Villiers's file, or asked about the letter she had seen about Wilfred Garnier. Either could have forced her to reveal to Mrs Villiers that she had been surreptitiously looking at Horace's file. Grit couldn't risk losing Mrs Villiers's trust.

While she now knew a good deal more than when she had arrived, some questions were still unanswered. Who *was* Wilfred Garnier? And what of the accounting misdemeanours all those years ago? Could the letter have had anything to do with more recent events?

Fifty Six

It was the January meeting of the Board of Governors, The Maestro began in magnanimous form. 'I am delighted to inform everyone here that I have been offered an OBE and intend to accept it. I do not intend to do so for me, but because we are one big team here at Titas College and all those who buy into our vision are equally deserving of this honour.'

'I agree the principal is right to recognise the contribution of staff, students and governors,' said Grit.

'Thank you, Miss Bulmer. I am touched,' replied Boyle, trying his best to keep the sarcasm iceberg submerged.

Knowing that bitch there'll be a sting in the tail.

'I concur with what you say, because we all know what the three letters, 'O-B-E' are understood to stand for in the vernacular: Other Buggers' Efforts.'

What a fucking nerve! Boyle glared lividly at her, his face and neck glowing in the gloaming.

'I think you should apologise to the principal and everyone present for those repercussions,' the Chair said eventually.

Grit looked around her and sighed. 'If I have offended anyone by what I just said then I retract it and apologise unreservedly. Will – that – do?'

'We'll leave it on the bookcase, shall we?' said the Chair.

Before the meeting was the intention to withdraw from the Sutton Coldfield and region prison contract. As the most recently appointed vice-principal, Smith was the first to offer a jibe. 'We've made our bed. Why shouldn't we sleep in it?'

Having his OBE denigrated on one flank by Bulmer, and his prison policy questioned on another by Smith, Boyle was feeling that, somewhere down the line, he must have been far nicer than either of them deserved.

'I can answer that one if you like,' drawled Myrtle Howard in her honeyed tones.

Myrtle's taking the guns. Thank God!

'Because the penalty for early release from the contract is roughly two point four million,' she purred, 'which is about the same as the amount we are projected to lose by the end of the contract.'

Oh yes, who else could make a bailiwick answer sound so sexy?

'And how much did we bid?' asked Grit.

'Twenty one million,' said Howard. 'Of course, the true costs of fulfilling our obligations could not be foreseen befor-'

'-But they were foreseen, weren't they?' said Smith, taking over Grit's line of questioning from the outer circle. 'Mr Richards pointed this out. I refer you to the minutes of Wednesday the fourteenth of September. It is clear from these that you had made a decision to dominate the offender learning scene regardless of the costs.'

For a few moments all that could be heard was the sound of the coffee machine gurgling in the corner.

The bastards are ganging up on me. But I'll have his head. Oh yes!

'That's past,' Boyle asseverated, with a dismissive gesture. 'What possible benefit is there in digging up old disagreements? It's to satisfy old grudges. And naturally you don't have any of those, do you Bob?' He did his best in the dusk to look threateningly at Smith.

'Of course not, *Maestro.* I'm just trying to establish an accurate picture of the background to things.'

'You thought you'd take that upon yourself, did you? Well, just remember where you are now.'

'I'm only saying that the reason was a political one because if there isn't much difference in the cost, why don't we just serve the remainder of the contract?'

Morrell waded in, 'It's about supply and demand. If we withdraw from the contract, we will be lowering demand for prison education contracts.'

Boyle banged the desk in front of him. 'NOT NOW ALISON!' he barked. *Oh God. Trust her to put her foot in it!*

'Sounds a bit like insider trading to me,' quipped Smith into a silence that continued for several moments.

Exactly! Boyle was clouding over, ready to thunder the termites back into their leaf mould, but knew he had to be calm. 'Bob's jibes aside, it is acknowledged by Prolapse, we have provided the best value to the prison service. That's why we got the contracts.'

'Have you any appenduous questions, Mr Smith?' asked Roberts, warily.

'No. Nothing further for now.'

The cunning shit, thought Boyle. *He knows exactly when to stop!*

Boyle folded his arms. 'If you want to discuss the fine details of the prison education plans, Bob, my door is open. Nice hairdo, by the way, Alison,' for all he could see of it.

* * *

For a split second Morrell actually believed Boyle had paid her a compliment, but his sneer as he delivered it took her back to that dreadful day with the hand dryer and the state of her hair afterwards. An intense mortification and a new found anger towards him followed. Although she did her best to hide the fact, this was the second Alison Morrell came to a decision.

* * *

Smith now suspected something was afoot between Morrell and Boyle. It was hardly surprising following the hand dryer incident, not to mention Morrell's role bringing in the new contracts of employment. Taking note of it, he was not going to rock the boat more than he could get away with. For now, anyway.

'If we are to withdraw from the Sutton Coldfield contract,' warned Tom Scruton (V-P Finance), 'we would need to think long and hard before jumping in with both feet again.'

'If the efficacy of the finances regarding future contracts concerns you, Tom, I think we need to have a private meeting later.'

During Boyle's reply, a sound a bit like his own voice came from the coats hooked up on a hanger in the corner of the room. 'Those are the answers you'll have to learn by heart. Should you happen to walk off with it, I wouldn't happen to notice,' were spoken to a distorted noise in the background. This repeated twice and then went silent.

'I do wish people would turn their phones off when coming to meetings,' said the Chair. Boyle's face changed colour again, this time from puce to almost-white, appearing a paler grey, as Richards fiddled with his hearing aid, causing it to whistle. The Chair closed the meeting.

Smith would wait to see when the minutes became available. As he left he got his coat, noticing something in its pocket. His mobile phone, which he had missed for some time, was in it. He turned it on. "1 missed call" was recorded from a number he did not recognise off-hand.

Fifty Seven

Grit was at her "workstation" marking students' essays. The task she had set was to write an effective letter of complaint. Generally nonplussed by the results, she looked up at the picture she had on the wall behind her desk of George when he was five. While she felt a deep maternal endearment towards him, she had to admit he could never have been described as a "sweet" child. Was everything she did at work in his interests? Perhaps not, but as long as it did not interfere with her being a good mother, why should that matter? Then there were the staff she felt she had let down.

Am I just wasting my time on that board of zombies?

Whether by free will or imperative, Smith seemed to have gone off to massage his own career. This did not encompass the scheming that had been his penchant hitherto, in spite of his palpable ability to toy with Boyle in the meeting. Was there any point in that sort of thing anyway? She was coming to doubt it.

Grit returned her attention to the work she was marking. Nicholson, T. had produced a reasonably compelling letter stating why football practice should not take place after lunch hour, albeit with appalling punctuation and spelling, while Duxbury, S. had been quite persuasive about the lack of practical work in product design - something she commented had been almost absent since Horace Villiers's demise.

Then Grit turned to a piece of work by Wesley Johnson, an essay she guessed must have gone missing. It was an appraisal of the importance of good administration in an organisation – a highfalutin topic, but the sort of thing he had always liked to tackle. Grammar aside, Wesley had spelt out extremely cogently about his grant not having been paid and the way he had suffered as a result. Its subject explained why it had been mixed up with the other, more recent, pieces of work, because they were letters of complaint. She formed the impression that he had been kicked out of the college before the matter had been resolved. A coincidence? Perhaps, but there was something about it that stank to high heaven.

Having resolved to check this as a priority, Grit heard her phone ring. It was Smith. She thought twice before answering.

'You've found your phone, then!'

'Hello Grit. It's Bob.'

'I know it's you. I haven't wiped you from my directory yet.'

'Oh, I see. Um... I know I have a lot of explaining to do.'

'You have, but you know what?'

'What?'

'I don't want to hear it.'

'Okay, fair enough. Look for all that's happened there is something else I think you are entitled to know about, particularly seeing as you are on the board of governors.'

Grit couldn't help feeling intrigued. 'All right then. I'll give you two minutes.'

'You know the meeting yesterday?'

'Yes. You put up a surprisingly good fight considering how you've sold out.'

'I haven't sold out. Can I tell you what happened?'

'One and a half minutes and counting.'

'Ah, well, to cut a long story short, Boyle forced me to apply for the job of Vice-Principal Humanities because he wants me under his thumb.'

'So why didn't you just refuse it?'

'He threatened to let Helen know about us if I did.'

Grit was speechless for a moment, shocked at the implication of what Boyle evidently knew. Ogle's wild speculation had just been confirmed.

'You weren't prepared for your wife to know about us, then?

'Well... no.'

'Perhaps I should tell her about it myself.'

'You wouldn't!'

'Oh, wouldn't I?' Grit was beginning to enjoy making her fallen idol squirm. 'You know, Bob, I would have loved if you'd left her for me...'

'Oh nooo!'

'...But as far as I'm concerned now she can keep you.'

'Did I really mean that much to you?'

'Yes, but you've well and truly blown it. Not that I stood much of a chance anyway.'

'You put a stake in my heart.'

'So you aren't a zombie, then. You're a vampire.'

'Don't, Grit. Please don't.'

'One minute and still counting.'

Grit felt a sudden, unexpected, swell of sympathy towards Smith, followed by a twinge of guilt for thinking he had sold out. Even so, there was no way he would find his way back onto the pedestal he used to occupy.

'There was something else.' He added.

Grit sighed. 'Alright, what?'

'Do you remember telling me about the website used at Student Services being the Philanthropists' Prudential, when it should have been Philanthropists' Provident?'

'Yes.'

'I should have let you know before. Boyle wanted to see me about taking this job under the threat of...'

'Right.'

'Well... I was waiting in his secretary's office and noticed a file with "Philanthropists' Prudential" stroke "RFZ" written on it.'

'Not Philanthropists' Provident?'

'No. Prudential. Definitely.'

'The pretend bank from Student Services?'

'Exactly.'

'Bloody hell!'

Grit heard the faint but familiar click-click of footsteps before the door into the office opened some fifteen yards away.

'There's someone coming. I have to go.'

'Alright. I just thought I should let you know.'

'Thanks, I appreciate it.' As Grit hung up, she had done her best to sound business-like in Morrell's earshot, carefully avoiding addressing him by name.

* * *

'Could I have a moment of your valuable time please, Margaret?'

Grit sighed, 'I suppose so. I'll need to pick my son up from school soon, though.'

'I'll try to be succinct. I can't prove it, but I know you were looking at confidential letters in HR on the twenty fifth of September last year.'

'As you accused me of at my job interview. I see no reason to admit to it.'

'You don't have to.' Morrell placed a creased piece of A4 in front of Grit.

'From the board meeting before that, you tried to get them to discuss Horace Villiers's death...'

Grit studied the paper. Headed, "RE: WILFRED GARNIER", it was the letter had found in Villiers's file when she went looking through it. She had been terrified of being found out for her discovery of this before, but knowing she had been didn't seem to bother her now. After all, Morrell had just admitted she couldn't *prove* anything. Nevertheless, whatever Morrell was up to, Grit needed to tread very carefully indeed.

'What is it you want?'

Morrell pointed at the letter. 'I want to know who Wilfred Garnier is.'

Grit studied it for a few moments under the vague pretence that it was for the first time. 'Can't help you there.'

'You know that this was in Dr Villiers's file in my department, don't you?'

'I'd take your word for it, of course,' Grit said, knowing fine will it had been, 'How did it get there if it is from nineteen eighty five?'

'I'm going to have to take you into my confidence. Can I trust you, Margaret?'

Grit felt a shiver down her spine. 'It depends what it's about.'

Morrell wheeled a chair across from a neighbouring, unoccupied desk and sat on it, bending so she was close, Grit thought uncomfortably so, to her, and spoke almost in a whisper, forcing Grit to inhale her rather sour breath, over the powerful dose of *Black Opium.* 'I retrieved this original from the bin in Maestro's office. I put the photocopy of it in his file.'

'Good for you, but I really don't see-'

'-The question is how did Maestro come by it? Why would he have kept it and why would he have wanted to dispose of it in September?'

'I don't know. Maybe this Garnier was a friend of the principal's and Mr Boyle had a grudge against Villiers for writing it. But surely you don't need me to suggest possible reasons for-'

'-I'm not going to spell it out to you, Margaret, but if you were able to shed any light on it, I'd be extremely grateful. The plate tectonics are moving and I don't intend to fall through the cracks. That's all I have to say.' With that, Morrell turned and strutted out of the office.

This certainly put a new slant on things. Why would Morrell want to know who this Garnier was? And why would she be prepared to demonstrate to Grit that she was being less than loyal to Boyle? After all, Grit was a known adversary of the college's management, wasn't she? Did it indicate a change in Morrell's position as one of his supplicants? Why was it apparently so important to her?

What Grit thought far more important was getting to the bottom of the non-payments from the Students'

Benevolent Fund. Nothing had been heard from the Internal Auditor. Had he done anything about it?

It took her a while to process two intrigues in quick succession. Once again, she found herself simmering at the thought of Smith accepting the promotion. Grit wasn't sure whether the threat of her relationship with him being revealed to Helen ought to assuage her anger towards him. It was just a one-night-stand when all was said and done, whatever her feelings might have been. Grit couldn't help thinking it was only fair to cut him some slack, given that he had updated her on what had been going on, albeit belatedly.

That aside, she resolved it did not matter that Wesley was no longer a student. She should still find out whether he did finally receive his grant, and also contact the Internal Auditor, Stuart Singleton. He should be reminded that concerned parties were looking for an answer. Grit thought it likely that Boyle had something to do with the phishing site and non-payments. If he did, and it was proven, would this raise the possibility of bringing him down? That could only be a good thing, couldn't it?

Grit had supposed it idle curiosity bringing her back to Morrell's question, but there was something common to both things wasn't there? Financial mismanagement and predatory pricing were not too far removed, come to think of it. Perhaps Morrell's question was worth looking for an answer to after all.

Fifty Eight

Dr Fisher always liked to give her furniture at least an annual polish and wax. It was mid-morning and she was doing some spring cleaning when her telephone rang. It was Grit. 'I have an odd question.'

'Really dear, and what might that be?'

'It's a question Alison Morrell asked me, so that might give it some context, I don't know...'

'Well the only way you can find that out is to ask it.'

Grit took a breath before asking, 'Have you heard of someone called Wilfred Garnier?'

The line went quiet.

'Are you still there?'

Dr Fisher croaked, 'Umm, yes dear. I think I have.'

'Who is he?'

'It was all such a long time ago... The last time we spoke...'

'Really? Was it anything to do with Cholmondeleys Engineering?'

'No. What does that do?'

'Develops wind tunnels or somesuch. The reason I ask is because the name cropped up in a letter from nineteen eighty five. Apparently there were concerns about Garnier's accounting brought by Horace Villiers, who apparently worked there at the time.'

'Horace Villiers, I see. Look I don't think I can remember at the moment, dear but the cogs are definitely turning. I'll call you back when I remember something, but Margaret...'

'Yes.'

'Keep your head down. I know how you can go into things with both feet. This, I suspect, requires discretion.'

'So you think I am impetuous, then!'

'Sometimes, yes. It's not meant as a criticism, dear, but I wouldn't want you to land yourself in any trouble.'

'Oh, alright!'

Fifty Nine

Back to her polishing, Dr Fisher found her mind transporting itself to 1976, the last year of her doctorate at Durham. She was sitting alone on the grass behind the St. Cuthbert's Society. Having just split up with her first boyfriend, she was feeling miserable. It was a swelteringly hot day, and the shadow of the old building was very welcome. Perhaps less so was the barrage of problems her friend, Marjorie Bates, was confronting her with.

'Wilfie says that if he doesn't put the money back and they find out about it, he'll get kicked out.'

That was what she said! I remember now, it was the Students' Society. He got in debt over his digs and was the treasurer. He took money from the account and in the end he was. Now... what else did Marjorie say?

'I'm sorry about that, Marjorie,' said Dr Fisher back in 1976, 'and I shouldn't think I can be of much help to you. I have no money to spare.'

'Oh, that's alright. It might be over between us anyway. I think he's seeing someone else.'

'Please don't take this the wrong way, but it wouldn't surprise me in the least.'

'Of course, you never liked him, did you? But he's such a dish.'

'To each to his own. That's what I say...'

* * *

Dr Fisher reached for her phone book but didn't hold great hope of it bearing fruit. She and Marjorie had drifted apart gradually, their lives taking different courses. Dr Fisher doubted whether they had spoken in fifteen years.

Still, I'll give it a shot.

She dialled the number. The phone rang just a couple of times.

'Hello-ho,' a voice at the other end sang out loudly and piercingly. Dr Fisher began to recall why she had not worked harder to keep in contact with Marjorie.

'Hello, um Marjorie, dear, it's Joan Fisher. Is this a bad time to call?'

'Joan? Which Joan?'

'I'm sorry if I've got the wrong number,' said Dr Fisher, knowing to her regret that she had not. 'I was hoping to speak to Marjorie Bates.'

'Speaking,' the voice adopted its sing-song tone again.

'This is Joan Fisher. We were at Durham together.'

'Jooooan, what a surprise. I haven't heard from you in aaaaages!' Dr Fisher moved the receiver to a safe distance from her right ear, 'Remember when we were young Mary's Fairies together, hmmm? Oh it seems like it was yesterday, but it must have been ooh, twenty-odd years.'

'Nearer forty, dear, and I didn't go to St. Mary's. I was at Cuthbert's.'

'How extraordinary, I'm sure you did.'

'No, dear.'

'Well how on earth did we meet?'

Choosing to ignore Marjorie's question, Dr Fisher got down to the matter in hand, 'Actually, dear I wanted to ask if you remembered someone from our student days.'

'Really, dear, how intriguing! Who?'

'Wilf or Wilfred. I think he had a French sounding surname, Gardet, Gaudin, something like that.'

'Oooh, Wilfie, Wilfie Garnier! How could I forget? I had quite a thing for him if you remember. We went out for a while until I found out he was two-timing me, the rat. Then he got thrown out. Something to do with the misappropriation of funds while he was Students' Society treasurer. I cried for a week.'

Dr Fisher was beginning to remember the full odiousness of Garnier. 'Did you, dear? I thought he was revolting.'

'Thaaat's right, Joanie, but then you were never really one for the boys, were you darling?' Marjorie tittered, before going for the jugular. 'We really should meet up soon, Joanie.'

Oh no! 'Yes, that would be wonderful. The sooner the better.' *Let's get it over with.* Oh dear, was she leading poor Marjorie on? Perhaps, but her ulterior motive was an important one. Then something occurred to her. 'An ex-colleague has been asking me about someone called Garnier. We wondered if it was one and the same.'

'Really, whatever for?'

'It's all a bit complicated. I was wondering if you'd mind my passing your number on to her,'

'I'm not sure. Do you know her alma-mater?'

'Really, Marjorie dear, I can't see that's of any importance.'

'I don't want just anyone phoning me. I have too many cold calls as it is.'

'I believe she went to York.'

'The odour of red brick dust ascends the nostrils. Oh well, at least it wasn't one of those ex-polytechnics. I mean you can practically get a degree from the local chip shop nowadays, can't you? What *class* of degree did she get?'

'Heavens, Marjorie dear. I didn't realise you were such a snob.'

'Yes, well, one has one's standards.'

'I thought you got a third.'

'How dare you, I got a two-two in English and the Classics from Durham. That is equal to a two-one at least from just about anywhere else.'

'That's as maybe, Marjorie, but would you mind if she contacted you?'

'Oh...Oh, well I don't suppose I'd mind. But we must still meet and catch up.'

'Of course!'

Sixty

Still enraged by Grit and Smith's remarks at the board meeting, Boyle's hand hovered over the receiver. He felt so close to calling the county music advisor, but had resolved to play that particular card only if Smith did something heinous. With that bomb dropped, what ammunition would he have left?

Resolved to send Smith a threatening email, reminding him of the card in question, Boyle twitched as the telephone began ringing. *One, Two, Three, Four, Five, Six…*

'Laurence Boyle speaking.'

It was Stuart Singleton, the college's internal auditor.

Time for a charm offensive.

'Good to hear from you, Stuart. What can I do for you?'

The news from the other end of the line was not encouraging.

'WHAT?'

Singleton explained about having received a request to investigate the non-payments by the Students' Benevolent Fund.

'IT'S GOT NOTHING TO DO WITH ME. TALK TO SCRUTON. HE'S THE FINANCE.'

There goes my campaign of flattery. Damn!

He wound himself down. 'Oh, I see, you're telling me as a courtesy. I understand. But I don't know what I can do about it. So you will speak to Tom Scruton? You have already, then. That's good... By the way, Stuart, you couldn't enlighten me as to the source of this letter, could you?

'WHO?'

'Well thanks for that. Another termite I'll have to deal with. Cheers, Tom.'

Margaret Bastard Bulmer, thought Boyle. *There has to be another way to kick her into touch.*

Sixty One

A little later, Grit had a call from Dr Fisher. 'Margaret, dear, I have the number of a contemporary of mine at Durham. She dated a Wilfred Garnier for a while. He was thrown out of the university for financial irregularities with the Students' Society. She said I could pass her details onto you. But just so you know dear, she is a little... eccentric.

Thrown out of the Students' Society for financial irregularities. And the same name as the person Villiers had reported accounting concerns over. This couldn't be a coincidence, could it?

Having taken the number, Grit found herself agreeing to meet Marjorie in Durham for lunch on the following Friday, which just happened to be the spring half-term, in the Three Tuns Hotel. Marjorie was so sure of the locale, it seemed unnecessary to check the detail. Then she remembered that staff were now supposed to work during these shorter holidays. Also, could she risk taking George with her? Perhaps not. She phoned Brandon's mother, Rita, to try to arrange for him to stay with her. The result was rather the opposite and she found herself agreeing to drive the four of them for a day out in Durham.

* * *

Grit hoped the trip might help to solve a few riddles. She had Googled articles relating to "Wilfred Garnier", "financial" and "Durham University Students Society", but to no avail. Apart from the possibility Marjorie might be able to tell her about Garnier, perhaps she could also visit Durham Records Office to see if any newspaper articles had reported what went on over the "financial irregularities" or find out if Clayport Library held copies from back then. Failing that, maybe the Students' Society had records of what had happened, but that would probably be for another day.

Grit didn't get to sleep until about a quarter to five the next morning. Her head was a gearbox. Was she becoming obsessed by the question Alison Morrell had asked her, when her priority should be students not being paid by the Students' Benevolent Fund?

When finally she did fall asleep, Grit dreamed of Myrtle Howard as a prison guard pointing a machine gun towards junior colleagues who appeared to be inmates in some sort of secure institution. Howard said to her, 'A happy workforce is all well and good, but there's only one way to teach these people compliance. So, for want of a better solution I will continue to use this cane.' The voice had risen above its normal velvety tones to full 1980 Conservative conference flow.

The teachers were now all dressed in prison togs. Howard brandished a long cane, with a large label dangling from it with the word "unemployment" written on it. She instructed the prisoner that was Bill Ogle to bend over, took a dozen steps back, and ran towards the miscreant's backside, raising the cane above her head, her nun's robes flailing.

Grit ran towards Howard and, grabbing the middle of the flogging stick, shouted, 'Cease this grotesque exhibition!' but tripped over and landed inelegantly in a soft armchair very similar to the one in Boyle's secretary's office. The armchair then removed her from the scene as if by ghost train to her own sitting room, where the television was on, apparently showing a continuation of the flogging from which she was now removed. After about half a dozen thrashings, the punishees began filing into her sitting room.

One lifted his shirt and asked another 'Is it bleeding?' The one who was looking said 'Yes. Just a bit. Now you do me.'

'It's just like being back as school. I was thrashed as a boy and then they banned corporal punishment, so I never got my turn to take it out on the little bastards. Now we've been thrashed as adults. Does the humiliation to which they subject us have no limit?'

'Humiliation be damned,' howled another. 'It's the pain. Oooh, the paaain.'

'Thirty years I've been teaching and I knew things were getting bad, but I never thought I'd see the day it would come to this,' said one. 'I've never been so insulted in all my life,' said another – a phrase she often used.

'This will *definitely* be raised with the union' said Ogle, removing a hand briefly from clutching his backside to adjust his spectacles. 'This time they've gone too far!'

'Union be damned,' said the first one, 'They didn't help us when bullying was reported before, nor when the college was tearing up the contracts, and they've only just balloted about taking action on the redundancies. And the students just get worse; think they can do what they like. I tell you, if some of them had the thrashing we've just had, the world would be a better place.'

'I can't stand it anymore, I'll resign,' wailed the third.

Not for the first time, Grit was drowning in a cacophony of displeasure. She bellowed, 'Shut up the lot of you. You are always complaining. I've tried to keep you happy and shelter you from this evil, not that it did much good, but I did my best. And what have I got in return? Moan groan grumble nag whine whinge gripe. I've had it with the lot of you! Don't you realize you're grown adults? Now you know what it's really like in the big bad world and you will damn well have to fend for yourselves.'

'See, even you don't care,' said one, folding her arms.

Another moaned 'Now we haven't even got someone to carp on at. It's not fair. I *hate* you!' She stomped her foot on the words *not* and *fair*, pushing her bottom lip out.

The phone rang. One of the teachers answered it and threw the receiver through the TV screen to Grit. She put it to her ear, hearing, 'Just look at what he's done to my car! Do you know what this is going to do to my insurance premiums? Do you honestly think I'll be able to afford them on what I make?'

She then realized who it was. 'I know who you are. Don't you try and fool me, Mr Garnier!' Laughter came along the line as she realized she was in a dungeon with a copy of *the Witton-le-Cone Chronicle.* The article at the side of the page had the headline, 'Sad ending for much loved local man.' One of the warders, who looked very much like Horace Villiers, came in with a tray that had a bottle of Pol-Roger champagne and a plastic mug on it, saying knowingly, 'You're in your own prison now, dear lady.' She looked out of the small gap in the open cell window. It showed a panoramic view, much as that from the top of the tower at "The Cathedral".

On the ground, people were gathering around the bust of Earl Grey, which appeared to have fallen onto a giant pocket watch. Scruton, Titas College's V-P (Finance), dressed in a flamboyant floral skirt, started picking up a dog turd from the remains of the watch and a Pekingese dog wearing spectacles came out yelling at everyone, 'It can't have been Wilf. He's too sexy.'

Then Bob Smith appeared as a giant and lifted her gently out of the window of the tower. He had a benevolent expression on his face. Grit shook her fist at him shouting, 'You're still in my bad books!'

'Why?' asked the giant Smith, looking genuinely baffled.

'You bloody well know why: a man of principle, you? You're more interested in licking the principal's brogues.'

There came no reply as Grit thought he was placing her carefully on the ground, before realising that her gradual descent was in fact caused by his fairly rapid deflation, and that he had become a wrinkly midget.

Sixty Two

Friday morning was a trial. Grit had arranged to meet Marjorie at the Three Tuns Hotel for lunch at one o'clock. It was a couple of years since she had been to Durham City, and she had never met Marjorie before, so felt rather flustered. A very red sunrise in the morning was followed by a strangely lurid sky.

At least George seemed excited to go, which was a relief. Grit had expected a tsunami of negativity, but no, he had pestered her to get up since half past seven. When they finally left to pick Brandon and his mum up at ten, George seemed positively euphoric, at least until she told him that Rita would be travelling in the front. He pled with her, but Grit insisted. 'Adults go in front,' which had led to her thinking about Smith again.

How dare he interrupt her day out? Grit had to remind herself that this was Smith as he was in her mind, not necessarily the reality, and her opinion of him had run somewhat hot and cold lately.

On the journey to Durham, about eight miles, she discussed the itinerary with Rita. They would have a look around the Oriental Museum first and then split, meeting at three in the café on Palace Green. It was only when that matter was sorted that Grit gained an idea as to why George seemed so happy about going to Durham.

'Rose West's in the jail in Durham...'

'Who's Rose West?' asked Brandon.

'She's the serial killer I was telling you about. Her husband was as well, but he hung himself so he never went to trial,'

'Wow, are we going to see her?'

'Mam, are we going to the Jail?'

'Certainly not! Why would you want to go there?'

'It would be cool, wouldn't it? I bet when you meet her she's nicer than Miss Roberts.'

'Everyone's nicer than Miss Roberts. Do you think Miss Roberts is a murderer?'

'Er, just a minute. How do you know about Rose West?' Grit interrupted the conversation.

'I read a bit about it in an old Draguian you left lying around.'

'I didn't know you read my newspapers!'

'I don't usually, but I saw a headline "Serial Killer" and it looked cool, so I read some of it. The paper said she was in Durham Jail.'

'And so you would like to go to see her, then?'

'Not half!'

'Not likely! And George, love, while I would encourage your reading, there is the question of whether my newspaper is necessarily the best material for you to be practising your skills on.'

'Aw!' George stuck his bottom lip out.

Then Brandon blurted, 'Mam, do you know what rape is?'

Grit and Rita looked at each other with a sense of dread. About to swerve into a lorry she was overtaking, Grit focused quickly back on the road ahead.

'Yes,' said Rita, 'The question is, do *you* know what it is?'

'No. That's why I was asking.'

'I just wondered because I remember now. George said the article said her husband raped and killed young girls, and she sort of joined in with some of them, or told him to do it. I'm not sure.'

'Now I see where it has come from!' Grit intruded, 'If it said that in the article, why didn't you say so?'

'I thought you'd tell me off for it. I don't know what it is, but it doesn't sound very nice.'

'You're right. It isn't nice at all. And can we leave the discussion there?'

'Is rape the name for what Mr Smith was-'

'-That's quite enough of that. I'll talk to you about it another time!'

'Okay, I'll be quiet if you take us to the outside of the jail,' said George.

'Oh, well I expect we can drive past it – if it'll shut you up.'

Aware of Rita looking quizzically at her during the latest exchange, Grit felt compelled to say something, 'I'll tell you about it when we've both had a few drinks.'

'Don't worry about it. Your business is your business, Grit.'

* * *

Having visited the Oriental Museum and parked up in the Prince Bishops car park, the party split: Rita took George and Brandon up toward the Cathedral, and Grit looking for the Three Tuns to meet Marjorie.

Grit found what appeared to be the place, but was dismayed to find the place boarded up. Her anxiety was worsened by her kicking herself for not checking this detail before-hand, but Marjorie had seemed so certain!

On the other hand, Dr Fisher *had* warned her about Marjorie.

What to do now? Grit looked around to see if there was anywhere convenient in an easy line of sight that looked as if it served tea and coffee and perhaps a light meal. The Half Moon Inn was just along the road on the opposite side. The pub next door was closer, but it looked as if it had been shut for some time. Tempted by the idea of libations, Grit baulked at the fact she had to drive home later. On the other hand, this was by far the best place where one could sit down and keep an eye on anyone outside the Tuns or the police station, for that matter, so she crossed the road at the traffic lights and tried to order a pot of coffee, but discovered the place served only cold drinks. With some irritation, she ordered a Coke and sat in the window.

At about a quarter past one, Grit saw an over-dressed woman getting out of a taxi. The woman was carrying a tiny suitcase in one hand and a small, animate, furry object in the other. In spite of the windows being boarded up, the woman, undeterred, tried the door and appeared most disgruntled at it being locked. Grit went out and waved. The woman didn't notice, but continued looking annoyed, so she went out to meet her.

'I didn't expect this,' she said to Grit, annoyedly. 'I've arranged to meet someone in there.'

'Well, assuming you can't go in, what would you do?' Grit played along.

The woman sighed, 'What a stupid place to meet!'

She turned to face Grit, 'But I suppose that is what one expects from these redbrick graduates.'

Lost on the significance of being a "redbrick graduate" for the moment, Grit decided to quiz the woman, 'Do you know the person you were intending to meet?'

'No, dear. An old friend put me in touch with her. Wanted to know something about an ex-boyfriend of mine. But she clearly hasn't the courtesy to turn up on time, so I expect I'll go elsewhere for lunch. Besides, there's plenty to do now that I'm here.'

'I am affronted by your aspersions, for I am she.'

'You're Margaret Bulmer?'

'None other.'

At this assertion, Marjorie embraced Grit, pecking her on the cheek, 'Darling, I'm soo pleased to meet you!'

Afraid that the small, furry creature would be asphyxiated or otherwise bare whatever destructive tools it possessed, Grit pulled away slightly. In spite of this, her fear was confirmed when a surprisingly deep growling sound emanated from somewhere around Marjorie's bosom.

'Oh, don't mind Hercules,' said Marjorie, 'he's a softie really. I say, where should we go?'

'I'm in the pub over the road. They only do cold drinks.'

'That sounds like a capital idea. Joanie is a bit of a teetotaller, so I never expected to go in a pub.' The gold filling on one of Marjorie's teeth flashed at Grit, 'I remember when I swore I'd get her into the bar at Cuthbert's and she wouldn't. Managed it in the end, though.'

'Did you?' Grit did not want her image of Dr Fisher corrupted by what Marjorie may – or may not – have led her into during the distant past, so she changed the subject, 'Are you staying in Durham?' she regarded the diminutive nature of what was no bigger than an average handbag.

'Yes darling, I like to travel light. Just think of me as Grace Kelly in *Rear Window*.' Grit tried to picture Marjorie without about thirty years and five stones. To her surprise, it seemed this claim may not have been all that wide of the mark.

'I hope you weren't planning to stay in the Tuns.'

'No dear, I'm going to a friend's in South Street.'

They made their way back over to the Half Moon, Marjorie ordering a bitter lemon. After a little while telling each other about themselves, it was Marjorie who finally broached the subject of Wilf Garnier, but it was from discussion about their sons.

'Rupert's doing ever so well; I'm very proud of him. You know he's got a posting with the diplomatic service in Kenya. And he's just got engaged.' She brought out a picture. It showed a tall, thin man who looked like a camel, with a lop-sided face and a full head of hair.

'That does sound interesting. How old is he now?'

'Thirty eight,' Marjorie followed up with one of her rare moments of insight. 'And you thought I might have known more about sexy Wilfie because he was Rupert's father?' Marjorie banged the table and laughed voluminously, making the man behind the bar drop the glass he was polishing, causing it to shatter.

'I did, rather, but not after seeing that!'

'Oh? Are you saying my Rupert's not sexy like Wilfie?' Marjorie seemed genuinely affronted as the sound of the sweeping of glass carried across to them.

'No, *no*; I don't know if I have ever seen Wilfred Garnier. He could be who I think he might be, but then he might not. All I can say is that, from his picture, your son looks nothing like the person I think Garnier might be. Completely different. Actually, quite attractive, I'd say.'

'Er, Margaret, darling, didn't you have something to tell me about sexy Wilfie?'

'More to ask you; I was wondering what you knew about him generally.'

'You know we went out for a while. Gosh I *adored* him. He had such a rakish charm. And my goodness was he randy. That of course is perhaps what led to my discovering he was two-timing me, the rat. Such a dishy rat, though. He got thrown out of Durham if I remember. Something to do with fiddling funds in the Students' Society. He was from Carlisle - went back there and worked in an estate agent's, I believe. I really don't know what else I can remember about him. Oh yes, apparently his name changed: Garnier was only his stepfather's name.'

'Did you know what it was before?'

'No, um ...It might come to me in a minute... Boyd... No. Boyle! And he went by the name of Laurence: Wilfred was his middle name, actually.'

'LAURENCE BOYLE? He is the principal of Titas College.' exclaimed Grit, 'Did you know that?'

'As a matter of fact I didn't, dear,' said Marjorie, 'Joan used to be principal of West Durham College, but that was the last time I spoke to her, which was a few years ago. When she phoned me the other day we didn't really have a chance to catch up properly.'

Grit noted the disappointment in Marjorie's voice, 'My old college. It was merged to form Titas College. I don't think she liked that this had happened: not that Dr Fisher was all that bothered about not being principal any more. It was more that she didn't like big colleges. That's what she told me, anyway.'

'Joanie always stuck by her own principles, nobody else's.'

'I would say so, but if Wilfred Garnier was called Laurence Boyle before, could they be one and the same? And if they are, why would he change his name *back* to Boyle?' The idea that Boyle was sexy beggared Grit's belief. The man was repulsive, but then there was the secretary, and Morrell, perhaps. And people do change as they get older, don't they?

'Maybe he wanted to blot out his past,' said Marjorie.

'Why would he want to do that?'

'It's obvious, isn't it? If he left Durham under a cloud, a name change would seem in order, wouldn't it?'

'I suppose it would.' Grit was struck suddenly by Marjorie's perspicacity, 'If you met him again, do you think you would be able to tell if he was...' She stole herself, '...Sexy Wilfie?'

'I expect so,' Marjorie leant towards Grit and spoke quietly, as if taking her into her confidence, 'Tell me, is he still gorgeous?'

Grit sniggered, 'I don't think so!' recovering her sincerity as quickly as she could, 'I have to admit I have sometimes found myself attracted to older men, but in his case I'd say he was the opposite of gorgeous.'

'A pity. Still, it comes to all of us in the end, I suppose.'

'Or maybe the principal is a different Laurence Boyle after all.'

'It's possible, dear, but I would think unlikely. While neither name is especially rare, the name "Laurence" is of Roman origin and, while "Boyle" descends from "de Beauville", which is Norman; the pronunciation "Boyle" is exclusively Scottish. Further, he was training as a teacher and went into business. Of course I don't know, but something you need to know about me, dear: Marjie has a sixth sense for this type of thing...'

Grit was struck by Marjorie's knowledge of etymology, 'How did you know all that?'

'I might be a humble English teacher, dear, but I have always had a keen interest in where words come from. Helps with doing crosswords.'

'I see. Of course if we introduced you after all this time...'

Marjorie retracted visibly, 'I'll do what I can to help you get to the bottom of whatever it is you're trying to find out, but meeting sexy Wilfie after all this time, especially after what you've told me...'

'It's only my opinion.'

'Perhaps, but... sometimes it is better to remember people as they were.'

You mean cheating rats? Grit thought about what Smith had done to Helen, even if he was encouraged.

'Yes, but he was irresistible, Margaret. If he's as you suggest now, you have no idea...' Marjorie seemed to be imploring Grit to appreciate the allure this creature once had.

'I'll try to take your word for it.'

Marjorie wrote her email address down on a piece of pink, headed note paper and handed it to Grit, who observed the heading on the note paper. It said, "Marjorie Ann Bates-Mordue M.A. Dunelm" – *Hyphenated,* Grit thought to herself!

'Is, er, Mr Mordue your current husband?'

'Justin? Good grief no. He was the last but one. With the most recent two, I refused, absolutely, to take their names. Having been married three times before that, I reached the conclusion that any man who wants you to take his name is determined you should take his rammel. At least that's how I look at it. And I do not intend to put up with any more of that, especially from Mr Boyle, née Garnier!'

As she said this, Marjorie handed Grit a twenty pound note. 'Would you mind, darling? I don't want to disturb Hercules. It's his afternoon nap time, you know.'

'Of course.'

Grit was about to go to the bar to order more coke and another bitter lemon.

'Mine's a double vodka and tonic. Ice and a slice. You have whatever you'd like.' Marjorie smiled, shrugged, and then stretched back in the seat, her lower legs in the air, the stiletto-heeled shoes hanging from her toes. Grit regretted that she had to drive everyone back to Witton-le-Cone. She could have done with a real drink. Having foregone lunch at the Tuns, she was getting hungry as well.

* * *

After Grit bade Marjorie goodbye, she got herself a pasty, went back to the car, and looked up Durham Record

Office on her phone. She had never been there before and was rather frustrated it was in County Hall, which seemed to be the best part of a mile in the direction of home. She texted Rita to tell her where she was going in case they got back to the car early.

'Everything's fine,' Rita replied by text, 'Theyre having gr8 time.'

Grit then had a couple of hurdles to overcome. The first was finding County Hall. The second was getting into the record office. Apparently you were supposed to have an appointment, although the absence of existing appointments for that time of day meant she was able to have one then and there.

It took until about half past two for her to find the article, but there it was in the Northern Echo, Wednesday, 11th August, 1976: *Students' Society Treasurer stole £800.* The article described how Wilfred Garnier had been found guilty at Durham magistrates of embezzling its funds.

OF COURSE! BOYLE IS STEALING FROM THE STUDENTS' BENEVOLENT FUND.

She suspected Boyle had been called Sexy Wilfie at the time and looked to see if a "Laurence" might have been featured. No luck. The article identified the thief only as "Wilfred Garnier". Perhaps he wasn't Boyle after all.

She arranged to pick up Rita, George, and Brandon from the Prince Bishops car park. 'I'm sorry I was so late getting back,' Grit supplicated.

'Oh they've been fine,' said Rita, 'We went up the Cathedral tower. Were there a couple of hours. Quite a trek up, though, three hundred and twenty eight steps to the top.'

'Three hundred and thirty two,' George asserted.

'How many did you think it was?' Grit asked Brandon.'

'Dunno,' he replied, 'bout three hundred. That's all I know, but guess what?'

'What?'

'You can see right down into the prison from up there!'

'Oh yes, I was supposed to drive past it. I'm not going back now, sorry.'

Grit's car, which had behaved itself remarkably well recently, began to produce a new grating sound from the back near-side. 'That's okay,' said George, 'We got to see more than we ever would going past it!'

'Glad to hear it. Did you wave to Rose?'

Sixty Three

After a trip to Witton-le-Cone library the next day and a longish chat with a librarian there, Grit had managed to ascertain that, if Boyle had changed his name, such a change would be held in the National Archives. At least if it wasn't because he'd married. That was different problem. She needed first to search something called *The Gazette*.

Having paid to get a result, Grit now had the answer to the crucial question. She telephoned Stuart Singleton, the Internal Auditor. To her surprise, she was put through to him directly. Thinking on her feet, Grit wondered how to convey what she had to say without seeming belligerent.

'Without wishing to stir up unnecessary trouble, I haven't heard anything back over the matter of the money missing from the Students' Benevolent Fund at Titas College. I wrote to you about it back in November.'

Singleton became irritated straight away. 'Internal audit is not a weapon for you to work over your pet grudges.'

'But have you got anywhere with it?'

'I have been in touch with Student Services at the college, and they do not know-'

'-Then it is for you to find out, surely.'

'Now look here, Titas College is a large and complex body. You can't possibly find answers to questions like yours overnight.'

'Then that suggests robust systems of monitoring are not in place, doesn't it?'

'Okay, so what if they aren't? As you will know, the external auditors have resigned. And I'm perfectly aware of why.'

'If it's so arduous, then why don't you resign as well?'

At this, Singleton's agitation took a sinister turn. 'I have my reasons. But I must warn you of something.'

'What?'

'With big organisations like Titas College, it is never in anyone's interest to attack them.'

'Why not?'

'Because they have so much power. I advise you, now, to drop the matter. Leave it well alone.'

'If you are telling me that, what confidence can anyone have that you are going to ask the difficult questions?'

'The confidence of Titas College...'

'But...'

'-I perform auditing services for the college, not against it. If you follow me...'

'Go on.'

'Report them and you will be dealing with dark forces.'

'It sounds to me like you are too afraid to scrutinize them. That doesn't inspire confidence.'

'Since when have I needed *your* confidence?'

'There *is* a professional body I can report you to.'

'I'm not here to respond to threats.'

'Fair enough, but before I go, I need to tell you about evidence that Laurence Boyle has committed financial theft under a different name back in nineteen seventy six.'

Singleton was suddenly apoplectic, 'You expect my company to investigate something from over thirty years ago simply in order to pour dirt on the highly respected principal of Titas College just because he has upset you and a few of your spiteful coterie?'

'Eh?'

'You just don't appreciate that all Laurence is doing is what is needed to keep Titas College plc. solvent, and you and your ungrateful colleagues in employment.'

Grit heard Tom Petty echoing in her ears. Having come this far, she was unfazed by Singleton's little outburst. Now was no time to back down.

'That's fine, but just to let you know, I will be summarising our discussion in the report I shall be making to the Fraud Squad, which I will be submitting together with copies of all the evidence I have.'

'On your own head be it!'

Having hung up, Grit had the same feeling she had when asking the Board questions about Horace Villiers. She had clearly rattled the internal auditor's cage, but still didn't seem to have got anywhere.

As things stood, there was only one thing to do.

Sixty Four

'This is a fine mess you've got us into,' ranted Boyle at Howard and Scruton, as they stood like limpets stuck to the floor at the far side of his desk. 'Why didn't anyone tell me this could be illegal?'

'In my case, nobody asked.' A quiet voice emerged from an unobtrusive man seated in the corner.

'I suppose I should introduce you. This is the college's solicitor, Nigel Cockburn,' said Boyle.

'We know each other already,' said Scruton.

Howard turned stiffly towards him, purring 'So pleased to meet you.'

Cockburn returned a nod.

'Right,' said Boyle, sitting down and pointing the tip of his paper knife towards Howard and Scruton, waving it slightly sideways, 'Has either of you the slightest idea why I have summoned you?'

As the chairs from the far side of Boyle's desk had been removed, Scruton and Howard continued to stand awkwardly. They had no idea whatsoever.

Boyle picked up the letter, headed, "Smellie Higginbottom LLP" and turned it around to face them. Scruton picked it up stiffly and examined it before showing it to Morrell, 'Jaywick College have reported us to the Authority for Fair Trading.'

The following silence was interrupted only by the sound of Boyle tapping the handle of his trusty letter-opener on the desk as he glared up towards the limpets. 'If you recall, they held the North West contract before we were awarded it.'

Eventually Scruton spoke, 'I'd just like to say in my, and particularly in Myrtle's defence, that you were the main protagonist when it came to-'

'-That is totally irrelevant!' shouted Boyle. 'You have overall responsibility for the finances and Myrtle is responsible for the offender learning bids.' Boyle's anger trailed off in his reference to Howard. Ruthless as he was, he just could not bring himself to crush a kitten. 'The point is that neither of you bothered to find out what we were doing could be illegal.'

'I understand where you are coming from, Maestro, and of course I take full responsibility-'

Doing her best to purr in a contrite fashion, Howard was interrupted by Scruton. '-Don't do that, Myrtle; I appreciate it wasn't an official strategy for obvious reasons, but I remember clearly it was Laurence who wanted Titas College to dominate the offender learning sector more than anyone else.'

'And who the fuck are you to know what I did or didn't want?' said Boyle, quietly this time, but oozing derision.

'From what you said at several meetings I was present at when we decided to knock fifteen percent off the bid. We knew we would make a loss and I advised you of this at the time.'

'Really Tom? Do you have a record of having advised me of that?'

'Yes.'

Boyle was taken aback. 'Where?'

'I wrote it in my diary in case such a situation arose.'

Boyle sneered, 'In that case it is your word against mine. As far as I'm concerned you never even mentioned the subject. It was perfectly possible to make savings through revised contracts and reduced staff sickness rates.'

'But we've struggled to make a two percent saving over what Jaywick spent.'

'That's by the by.' Boyle began to smirk. 'Besides, if it was in your notes, why didn't you question the minutes?'

Holding his file tightly, Scruton sighed. It wasn't the first time he had been up against Boyle this way. He was not someone to look for trouble even when he knew it was there, but if accusations were made of him, he would stand his ground. 'What would have happened if I had questioned them?'

'I'd have made sure you were put right on the matter, as I am doing now!'

Scruton made an open-armed gesture, his file still in his right hand, knocking Howard on the nose. 'Principal, I thought you had decided to go ahead with the bids on these terms with your eyes wide open. Besides, I can't be expected to micro-manage the accounts for the Offender Mana-'

'-Shut up!' jeered Boyle, stabbing the point of his letter opener into the writing pad in front of him. 'I think we all know where we stand,' he said eventually. 'If the shit hits the fan, it's every man for himself, and rest assured, it won't be my head that rolls.'

'When you say that, Maestro, do you mean if the Authority for Fair Trading finds against us?'

'Yes Myrtle, that is exactly what I mean,' Boyle said gently, his delivery affected by a combination of the sense that he was addressing an imbecile, tempered with the regard in which he had, up until then, held her.

He leant back in his seat, 'I can't honestly see them finding against us. Isn't that right, Nigel?'

'It seems far-fetched, although there aren't really any similar cases to go by,' came the voice from the corner.

'But surely, if there was a concern about predatory pricing, it would have been for Prolapse to determine when they assessed the bids.' Howard purred a stab in the dark.

'If a dominant airline is selling artificially cheap air travel, its passengers are under no obligation to report it,' was Cockburn's succinct answer.

'Anyway,' continued Boyle, 'I think I know who the termite is behind this. Whatever happens, I'll make sure he regrets his actions. Have you any idea how hard it's going to be to stop this being a chuffing embarrassment? I'm going to be a laughing stock with Cyril bloody Richards.'

'But surely that is a risk entailed by this (ahem) unwritten policy,' said Scruton.

'WHEN I WANT YOU TO POINT OUT THE PILLOCKING OBVIOUS, I'LL TELL YOU,' bellowed Boyle belligerently. '

There was a knock at the door.

'WHAT?'

Lisa put her head around the door. 'I've got Margaret Bulmer here. She wants to see you about the predatory pricing.'

'NO SHE CANNOT SEE ME ABOUT PREDATORY PRICING! -OR ANYTHING ELSE. THE ONLY TIME I EVER EXPECT TO

ENCOUNTER THAT TERMITE IS IN BOARD MEETINGS AND HOPEFULLY NOT FOR MUCH LONGER.'

'Okay Maestro. I'll let her know.' Lisa spoke from a pool of calm.

Boyle was fed up with all the hassle he was getting. It was all completely uncalled in his view, but he would sort it. After all, he'd been through worse.

On the departure of Howard, and Cockburn from his office, Boyle pointed to Scruton. 'I want a word with you.'

'Yes, principal?'

Boyle grimaced, 'What's all this about grants missing from the Students' Benevolent Fund?'

'I know nothing about that.'

'Really? You are the finance, so *you* will be the proverbial fan when the shit hits it.'

'That is worrying, principal. But I don't know anything about it. Is there anything you can tell me?'

'Not a lot. It's just that some students haven't had their grants paid, but our records say they have.'

'Oh... That is a concern.'

'That is one way of putting it. I'm just warning you that it'll be coming that way unless someone gets to the bottom of it.'

'Yes, well. I'll go and ask Student Services about it.'

'You do that, Tom, but remember it was me who warned you about what was coming.'

'Of course.'

As Scruton left, Boyle picked up the telephone to the county music adviser.

Time to deal with those Bolshevik termites.

Sixty Five

Grit sat on a bench by the reception desk at the new police station up in Stanley, feeling as though she had been sent to see the head teacher at school. Hugging the evidence in her arms, she'd managed to compile everything she was aware of. Five cases of students not being paid by the benevolent fund. She knew there would be a lot more if it was looked for, but that would take time. Grit also had the evidence of the crime that Boyle, under the name Wilfred Garnier, had committed from the Durham University Students' Society back in nineteen seventy six. But did that matter? Indeed, would anything she had to show to the fraud division be taken seriously? Then there were the other documents she had brought, which caused her some angst.

A tall man with white hair and a tweed jacket with brown leather patches on the elbows emerged from somewhere. 'I gather you need to see me,' he said in gruff, Yorkshire tones.

'I'm not sure if *need* is the correct verb,' Grit replied.

The man released a deep, booming laugh.

'Let's see what you've brought,' he said

Grit handed over the dossier she had compiled. 'It isn't comprehensive, but I thought I should let you have what I've got.'

'Come through to my office and we'll interrogate you.'

'Eh?'

'Sorry, I meant we'll go through what you've brought.'

'Of course. I'll help as much as I can.'

'In case you were wondering, I'm Detective Inspector Smirthwaite.'

'If I can trust you I don't care what your name or title might be.'

He let out another laugh. 'I'm always up for a new challenge,' he said as they went along the corridor to an office with no outside windows.

'Are you partial to chocolate biscuits?'

'Not really. I wouldn't mind a coffee, though.'

* * *

As he perused the documents brought by Grit, Smirthwaite seemed more interested in her job, her son, her ex-partner, and her reasons for going into teaching than the matter in hand, until the coffee and biscuits arrived. After the fourth chocolate digestive, he finally got down to business. 'What you are reporting to us is the money going missing from the Students' Benevolent Fund, then?'

'Yes. I suspect there is some sort of phishing website Student Services is using, perhaps inadvertently, to divert the grants to another account. It was labelled "Philanthropists' Prudential" when it should have been "Philanthropists' Provident".'

'That's good detective work. On my first glance at things, one particular question does strike me.'

'What's that?'

'How did the money reach this RFZ Sparbuch account from the Students' Benevolent Fund?

'I'm not sure. A simple bank transfer?'

'That isn't possible with that type of account.'

'I was hoping you might fill in the gaps.'

'I see,' Smirthwaite frowned wryly, 'Another question also strikes me.'

'What?'

'Why didn't you go to the college's auditors?'

'I did. The internal auditor tried to warn me off, but the external auditors have resigned.'

'I'll admit it doesn't look good. It's not *proof* of illegality, of course.

Grit played what she considered her best card. 'Perhaps not, but if you look at the documents I've brought, you'll find that financial theft has been committed by the principal under a different name.'

Smirthwaite's ears pricked up. Once Grit had explained that side of things, Smirthwaite looked much as a dog that had been thrown a bone. 'I certainly think we can investigate this, Miss Bulmer. To be honest, when I saw you I thought you were someone trying to use us to exercise a personal grudge.'

Grit thought for a moment. 'Personal grudge, me? Never!'

Smirthwaite leant back in his chair, taking another chocolate biscuit from the plate on his desk. 'We often get that. Occasionally, and I do mean occasionally, they can end up being our best leads. Usually it's just wasting our time, but from what you have brought me today, there is definitely something that could do with a bit of poking into. Besides,' he smiled, 'the matter has already been brought to my attention by somebody else.'

'I'm glad, but who was that?'

Smirthwaite looked smugly mysterious. 'On that I am sworn to secrecy. Besides, they certainly did not furnish me with anything like this document. By what means did you manage to acquire it... if you don't mind my asking?'

Grit was perturbed to see the inspector holding a yellow and black passbook that had been in the file she had brought. 'I should have told you about that,' she said, sheepishly.

'Oh yes?' He leant forward.

'Well, you see, I sort of, um...'

'What?'

'...stole it.'

Smirthwaite waved his head from side to side in a floating motion. 'Now why would you go and do a daft thing like that?'

'To bring it to the police. My colleague, Robert Smith, told me he had seen the file I brought you in Boyle's secretary's office, labelled Philanthropists' Prudential – the false name given on the website at Student Services. Then, when the internal auditor tried to warn me off, I thought there was only one thing for it. I asked the principal's secretary if I could see Boyle about something. He was shouting at some of his vice-principals, so his secretary went in to ask him rather than using the intercom. Anyway, it gave me the chance to spirit it away. Actually it was under her desk, not in the bookcase as my colleague had said.'

'We can get warrants for that sort of thing, you know.'

'I didn't think you would believe me if I didn't bring some hard evidence.'

'Leave it with me. I'll see if we can find a way round it.'

Uneasy about what she had just admitted, Grit left the police station feeling drained. In spite of the inspector's assertions, she doubted it would have much impact. Further, she wasn't comfortable about admitting how she had obtained the evidence. But who else had gone to the police about the matter?

Sixty Six

Detective Inspector Emeric Smirthwaite had telephoned Boyle in advance and Boyle had been charming. His inquiries revealed Boyle's professional status. While Smirthwaite always tried to kowtow to authority, he never let it stop him when he got the scent of illegal activity.

* * *

Ever since Mrs Boyle's return from her exile from him, which commenced at the end of his *Deum Horriblis*, Boyle had been on a charm-offensive towards her. He had hated telling cleaners to clean, gardeners to garden, and while he enjoyed his meals out at the *Raj*, having take-away curries every night had become jaded. And not having anybody to cook his breakfast in the morning was beyond the pale. Bossing people about at the college was one of the perks of the job, but at home it was infinitely preferable to have someone who knew his quirks and entertained them, even if it was with occasional mordacity.

Mrs Boyle answered the front door to find Inspector Smirthwaite standing, his white hair blowing around. Gathering that this was the visitor he had been expecting, Boyle heaved himself out of his reclining chair in the surprisingly cramped living room of their executive detached, to greet the inspector. He invited him through into the dining room. While they sat at the table, Mrs Boyle offered tea and coffee and cakes, which were gratefully accepted.

Believing Smirthwaite to be from the Authority for Fair Trading, Boyle implied a degree of bonhomie.

'I assume you are investigating the completely unfounded case of predatory pricing by Titas College, of which I am principal and chief executive.'

'We are in fact investigating the disappearance of monies allegedly taken from Titas College's student benevolent fund. Was this something of which you were not unaware?'

Boyle felt himself jolt, reassuring himself with the notion the matter should not concern him unduly. 'I was shocked and saddened to hear about it. We are very proud of the students' benevolent fund at College and all of those it has helped. Cyril Richards, who donated a substantial sum to set up the fund, isn't very well at the moment, bless him. He would be most distressed to hear about what has happened. I hesitate to tell him because of what it could do to someone in his condition.'

'I see.' Smirthwaite paused, apparently reluctant to say something. 'Documents have come into our possession, sir, which indicate at least some of these funds have ended up in an account bearing your name.'

Boyle suddenly felt himself bricking it. His shoulders hunched; his neck stiffened. 'What documents, inspector?'

'An RFZ passbook in your name. It's an Austrian bank. Stands for Rothffeisen Zentralbank.'

'Yes, inspector. I am aware of what it stands for.'

Smirthwaite checked his notes. 'It has also come to our attention that the computer in Student Services at the college had a record of directing payments from the fund to a deposit account with details that match those of your own.'

'That's ridiculous. I know nothing about-'

'-Were you aware of these sums being paid into and withdrawn from your deposit account?'

'Not at all, Inspector.'

Smirthwaite looked at Boyle gravely. 'Are you sure?'

'I remember some odd payments for computer services appearing on my bank statement. Wondered if Vi was up to something, but she won't admit to it. As for any payments, I know nothing.' Boyle looked puzzled. 'I think I'm due a statement soon, though.'

'A pity, sir; we were really hoping you could help us with that one. What about the RFZ passbook?'

'I don't hold any such account. It's possible my wife could...' Boyle called through to the kitchen, 'Vi, love. You don't have a passbook with RFZ in Austria, do you?'

'RFZ?' she answered, slowly, 'No, I don't have any accounts in Austria, Laurence.'

Smirthwaite nodded. '-It's just that a passbook from that bank, allegedly taken from your office, holds payments totalling exactly the amounts withdrawn from your own deposit account at the Philanthropists' prudential'. But don't worry, sir. The lack of identity required for that sort of bank account means that it could belong to anyone who holds Austrian citizenship. You don't hold Austrian citizenship by any chance, do you Mr Boyle?'

'No, Inspector, I do not.'

'Nor your wife?'

'Well as a matter of fact she does, but as she just told you, she doesn't have any bank accounts there. As far as it having been taken from my office is concerned, I have no knowledge the damned thing was ever there in the first place.'

Smirthwaite made a note, muttering, 'knowledge...'

There's always some termite bound to be jealous of my success.

'Can I ask you, Inspector, how do you know that money in this bank account I know nothing about came from the Students' Benevolent Fund?'

'The amounts paid into the account were in cash, so we are trying to trace that, but regrettably without success. Of course we aren't accusing you. We are only making inquiries at this stage, but I was wondering if you had any ideas on how this came to be.'

'None at all, inspector. It could be a frame-up, of course.'

'A frame-up?'

'Jealous types. Believe you me, there are plenty who'd like to see me had up for something I didn't do. I wouldn't be surprised if the whole thing were concocted entirely for my distraint. Which branch are you actually from, then?'

'Fraud, sir. We used to be where Titas College is now, but were moved out to Stanley when our offices were demolished to make way for it.'

Someone had to be stitching him up. 'What led you to investigate this, then?'

'Regrettably, I am not at liberty to say how we came by the information, but the theft from the Durham University Students' Society in nineteen seventy six of eight hundred pounds could be related to it. Of course this was a long time ago, and I'm sure it's nothing to worry about.'

'I know nothing about that, inspector. And, frankly, if you continue to take that line with me, I'm going to have my solicitor present, so if you'll excuse me?'.

'I do appreciate it was a long time ago, but would have thought it would be in your interests to get to the bottom of the matter.'

'Indeed it would. It's just that I don't appreciate my good character being dragged through the mire in the process.'

'Well we'll leave it at that then, sir, thanks for the tea it was much appreciated.'

'Right you are.'

Boyle was now smarting at the thought of how much Smirthwaite actually knew about him. After all, such knowledge could land him in serious trouble, thus lifting so much ripe fruit from his reach.

Oh how those outsiders would love that.

The inspector headed for the front door with Boyle following. He opened it and was about to step outside when he stopped and turned to face Boyle.

'There was one other thing. When you were a student at Durham, did you know anyone by the name of Wilfred Garnier?'

Boyle gaped for a moment. 'No, er, inspector, I can't say I did.'

'Very good, sir.'

As the inspector left, Boyle felt a tightness in his chest, accompanied by something like acid indigestion.

Oh no! Oh God!

He knew. Of course Smirthwaite knew. He must. And if he knew who Wilfred Garnier was, which he almost certainly did, asking him was a ruse. A FUCKING RUSE. *What a bastard!*

As far as Boyle knew, there was nobody called Laurence Boyle on the register of students during his time at Durham, but there was a Wilfred Garnier. Where else would Smirthwaite have got the name from? It would only be a matter of time before Smirthwaite realised about the Durham Students' Society. Damn it, he probably knew already, didn't he?

Sixty Seven

It was going to be an interesting meeting, Grit thought. Without Boyle or most of the band of vice principals, and the chosen location a classroom with much better light than the dreaded Board Room, it would certainly be different. And she had been asked to take the minutes, which was unexpected.

As she sat, Grit heard the familiar *click-click* of heels approaching, followed by a waft of *Black Opium*. She felt a hand on her left shoulder and a voice, speaking more quietly than usual, 'Thank you. Thank you for everything you've done,' before its owner went and sat next to the Chair. It took a moment for Grit to realise why Morrell should be grateful to her and the thought left her feeling soiled.

Flanked by Morrell on one side and a male bookend Grit did not recognise on the other, the chair opened the meeting with a thick spreading of portent.

'I've called you here today because certain documentaries have come into my possession in relation to our steamed principal, Laurence Boyle. I regret I have not shared them with you in advance of the meeting because of their...' Roberts frowned, '...delectable nature.'

Nobody spluttered as various copies and a few originals of what had been sent to Roberts were circulated.

'Excuse me, Chair?' asked Grit. 'I am not clear why we have all been called to take a decision on the suspension of the principal. Wouldn't that be down to the HR committee?'

'That's a fair point, Miss Bulmer.' Roberts affected surprise. 'The reason is that no quorum of the Human Resources committee would be available for at least a month.' Grit nodded.

* * *

Cyril Richards raised a hand, 'Excuse me, Chair, but can I ask where the Internal Auditor, Stuart Singleton is? Surely it would be proper for him to be in attendance now.

Roberts nodded this time, flourishing a handwritten note, she read out, 'I regret I will not be able to attend the meeting as I have an unavoidable appointment in Shangri-la.'

'Shangri-what?' asked Richards.

'Shangri-la,' replied Roberts.

'That's what I thought you said. Can I see the note?'

'I don't see why.'

'It seems a strange place, so peculiar excuse for his absence.'

Roberts handed the note across without a word. Richards put on his reading glasses. 'Yes, Shangri-la. That is what it appears to say. If you'll forgive my explaining, Chair, I thought it was one of your malarkey-propisms.'

Roberts glared at Richards, who continued, 'I propose we write to Mr Singleton, requesting clarification as to the nature and location of his alleged appointment.'

This agreed by the meeting, Roberts began feeling more confused than ever about the implications of the documents in front of her. 'Has everybody had enough time to stimulate the papierwork?' She was glad to imply she had understood them, and hoped everyone else really had. David her husband had explained some of the most salient points to her, but it was really all too much to take in, and she didn't know for how long she could sustain her simulated expression of engrossment.

'I think we have read all we need to,' said one of the yes men on the board, much to Roberts's relief.

'Good, well now we have to make a dissertation on what we need to do about it.

'For heaven's sake lass, we wouldn't be acting responsibly if we didn't suspend Laurence with immediate effect,' Richards bawled incredulously.

'I'm afraid I agree. We need a proposal to suspend him and arrange a meeting with him to dissuade the maps percolating to the um...' Suddenly, Roberts was stricken by dread.

Laurence is my election agent!

What might Boyle do to her should he decide to view the minutes, which he undoubtedly would? If they showed that she, Phyllis Roberts had proposed, or even seconded, a motion to suspend him, what terrible forces could he unleash on her?

Had the Board decided to suspend or, horror of horrors, sack Boyle, she could at least have appealed to him that it had done this without any encouragement from her. But not if she had actually put her name to such a proposal. 'Can I check that whomsoever we design, no board members' names are given in the minutes?' she asked, in desperation.

Through the fog of her anguish, Roberts noticed Grit smiling at her.

* * *

'I would have thought that unless a named vote was agreed, I should only name the proposer and seconder.' In spite of the extra burden of making notes for the minutes, this was the first time Grit was thoroughly enjoying taking part in a board meeting.

'I think that is correct,' said Roberts miserably, and began conferring with Cockburn, who was sitting on her right. He looked briefly at a paper in front of him and nodded, 'That's a relief,' she said under her breath.

'What's that she's saying?' Richards asked Grit.

'Mrs Roberts was checking that the names would *not* be given in the minutes of those who vote for and against suspending the principal,' she explained slowly.

'Oh aye, aye.'

'But those of the proposer and seconder will. Are you willing to propose the suspension?'

'Yes.'

'As Chair, I think someone else should soliloquy the movement,' said Roberts, parrying.

'Surely you aren't feeling faint-hearted, Chair!' Grit grinned at Roberts, who looked as if she was working hard to repress the urge to bite back.

'You would only be too happy to, I expect,' she replied, caustically, after a few moments wiping her brow with her handkerchief.

Grit would have had no compunction in proposing or seconding the motion. But she was gripped by a sudden doubt. After all, she was known to have issues with Boyle. Would seconding the motion make it look as if she was exercising a grudge? On the other hand, what about those who wanted to be in The Maestro's good books? How would it look to Boyle if one of their names was on the motion to suspend him? The answer to that question proved quite delicious.

'I don't think I should do it, Chair,' she said, trying to look as earnest as she could.

Roberts tutted, 'Is there anyone else, then?'

No replies.

Richards's hearing aid made a whistle as he fiddled with it, 'Am I getting it right that none of you buggers is prepared to let his name appear in minutes next to a decision we know we have to take?'

'That's the size of it, Mr Richards,' said Grit.

Roberts looked harrowed, protesting, 'BUT I DON'T WANT TO DO IT!'

Cockburn gave his opinion, 'The meeting is obliged to suspend Mr Boyle, given the nature of the offences and contents of his contract of employment, but somebody will need to second the motion for it to be properly carried.'

Now sweating profusely, Roberts tutted and sighed, 'Oh, very well.'

This motion agreed, Grit asked, 'Who is going to run the college in his absence?'

'Oh yes, I was just mowing to that, careering forward,' said Roberts, now apparently withering in angst from a notion of the unfathomed consequences of what she had just done.

'As we have twenty three vice-principals, we cannot be at all sure which to select, even if it will be on a temerarious basis. How should we do this, Mr Cockburn?'

'Normally there would be a deputy in place who could step straight in,' he replied, 'but having studied the college's governing documents, it seems there is no one person so designated.'

'Is there not even an infelicity as to who should take over?'

'None at all, I'm afraid.'

Roberts began flailing for a practical way to proceed, 'Miss Morrell, do you know if Mr Boyle has ever taken leave of absence from his post?'

'The only time he has been absent was one day last year and for very good reason. Believe me, I know. Anyway, if he had needed anyone to take over, I am sure I would been asked to deputise.' The ends of Morrell's mouth twitched upwards. 'At Durham College, I was acting principal on a couple of occasions he was absent, but The Maestro does have an excellent attendance record.' She brushed her hair back indulgently and pouted. 'I probably shouldn't be here while such a decision is taken,' she said, 'but to put the case for myself, I believe I am in a unique position to hit the ground running. I know how Titas College operates and I daresay a better overview of our staff and how best they can be used than anyone.'

A light went on behind Roberts's glasses, 'Are you really willing to do that, Miss Morrell?'

'Absolutely. Believe me, I would have no problems taking over at all. None whatsoever.'

'Perhaps I should tell the meeting about the occasion quite recently when Miss Morrell approached me asking if I would find out about a certain Wilfred Garnier,' said Grit.

Morrell raised a hand, palm facing down towards her, 'Shhhh. I'll explain that later.'

'I'll bet you will, once you've got your feet under the table! What was it you said about plate tectonics?'

A brief but cold silence struck the meeting, as Morrell projected a look of undisguised hatred towards Grit. Cockburn-Bookend muttered something about an independent decision.

Roberts sighed again, the small light of hope behind her glasses well and truly extinguished.

Morrell got up. 'I have to take my leave now, Chair. I'll leave you to discuss it. I apologise for my presumptuousness. Please understand my first duty is to Titas College, and it seemed a practical way forward. Now I have another engagement I really *must* attend.' Her pout ballooning with embarrassment, she departed slowly, closing the door behind her with a very deliberate action.

'What would be the lawful way to procreate?' Roberts asked Cock-End, who paused to allow for the spluttering to subside.

'The college could advertise the job internally and, if there is no HR committee, the board would appoint a panel to assess applications. Similar to making a permanent appointment, in fact. The alternative might be to change the governing documents to appoint a deputy, but that would take even longer.'

'WE CAN'T GO WITHOUT PRINCIPALS FOR THAT LONG!' whined Roberts.

'It looks as if Our Laurence has left us with a right bloody mess to clear up.' commented Richards.

Cockburn nodded, 'While I wouldn't recommend it from a legal perspective, and it is for you to make this decision – I'm certainly not going to – perhaps the best way forward in practice would be to agree now on someone as uncontroversial as possible to be caretaker principal, and invite them to take the roll on.

'That's just what I was cognitizing,' said Roberts, 'How about Myrtle Howard?'

'But Mrs Howard has to be bogged down with running *Novum,'* said Grit.

'You have a very good point, there,' said Donoghue, his heavily lacquered quiff making him look every part the ageing star of a 1980s pop video, 'Can I suggest Mr Scruton?'

This was met with a couple of nods. 'My dad once had the brewery accountant running the company for a short while,' said Richards. 'Sales fell thirty percent on the previous quarter. The man had no appreciation of what makes a good brew.'

Roberts held either end of her pen in each hand. 'I hate to say this,' she said despondently, 'we have twenty three vice principals, and I don't think any one of them has any more ideation than I have how to run Titas College in the abstinence of Maestro.'

Grit was just about to suggest facetiously that Roberts should put herself forward for the position when a heavenly idea struck her. 'Why don't we invite Dr Joan

Fisher to take over the running of Titas College? On a temporary basis, of course.'

A bright ray of sunshine filled the classroom in a way that would never have been possible in the Board Room. Then Boyle burst in.

* * *

'WHAT'S THIS? FREELOADING COLLEGE ACCOMMODATION, ARE WE?'

In collective shock at his gate-crashing their meeting about him, nobody spoke as he scanned the room, eyeballing everyone present, before leaving without closing the door.

Having a hugger-mugger without me, eh? Heads will roll!

Sixty Eight

Dr Fisher had rented a small furnished flat next to Titas College for the time being, unaware that it was in the same block as the one Villiers had rented. Unpacking her necessities, she couldn't help worrying.

Normally she would have expected to turn such an offer down. She knew there wasn't anyone else as well-placed to step in at such short notice, particularly given Boyle's division of power – and information - amongst the Vices. Also, having retired six months before, nothing had filled the gap where her career had been. In short, she was bored, but did not want to commit to anything permanent. Or did she? Was it that what she had actually needed was a long holiday rather than a permanent one?

These worries were dashed aside as her mobile rang. It was Grit.

'Did you know Boyle's been suspended?'

'So I understand, dear, especially given that I am the caretaker principal. It was at very short notice indeed, but then you'll know all about that, won't you?'

'Yes, but I didn't know you would hear so soon.

Dr Fisher surprised Grit with her next suggestion.'I shall finish unpacking before anything else. But why don't I meet you later?

'Are you here in Witton already?'

'Yes dear.'

At two o'clock they met for lunch at Jan's Café. It was not exactly a sumptuous affair. Grit ordered soup with a roll, and Dr Fisher a salad with a pot of tea.

'Were you staying here, or do you have to go back home tonight?'

'No, I've rented a flat in that block next to the college. My plan was to stay here during the week and go home at weekends. I did think of going by rail and doing work on the train, but I'd still have to wait and change and then drive home from Penrith. Besides, it would come to almost twice what I'll be paying in rent here.

* * *

Sitting in the café, Grit looked at Dr Fisher. She was ill at ease about something. Dr Fisher glanced at her and then out of the window, saying eventually, 'It's my little darlings. I don't like having to leave them for so long at a time. Still, Geoff and Alice, my neighbours are very good. I trust them entirely. It's just...'

'Your little darlings?'

'My cats.'

'What is the worst that could happen?'

'Oh Margaret, I hate to think!'

Grit was taken aback. This was the first time she had seen Dr Fisher show anything that looked like vulnerability, and about her cats of all things...

'Sorry, I said that wrong. What is the worst that is likely to happen?'

'One of them gets run over: Genghis is quite wayward, and Cleo isn't the most streetwise.'

'But Geoff and Alice would let you know straight away if anything happened, wouldn't they?'

'Of course.'

'And they haven't, have they?'

'Not as far as I know.'

'So until you hear from them, maybe it's better not to worry?'

One reason Grit liked Dr Fisher was because she cared about people. But finer feelings were not her forte. If something was to be said, Dr Fisher would always say it. One example had been the time when Grit telephoned Dr Fisher about Horace Villiers and Dr Fisher went straight to the metal about Grit's father's demise. But cats are independent creatures: why would Dr Fisher be so anxious about them? She wondered if Dr Fisher's unease might have been about something else, 'You still don't seem too happy if you don't mind my saying so. Boyle's gone. Isn't that something to be celebrated?'

'That is precisely why I am not happy. Not happy at all.'

'I don't understand. I thought you didn't like him either.'

'My opinion of Laurence Boyle is irrelevant to this, though I sincerely hope his departure will be a permanent.' Dr Fisher held her cup of tea to her mouth as her muse became resolute. She put it down and tipped some milk in from the little jug on the tray.

'Had you thought of applying for the job permanently?' Grit was hopeful in her enquiry.

'No dear, I'm retired.' She took a sip of the tea and sucked her teeth, 'and Boyle's case hasn't been heard yet.'

A pause ensued before she continued. 'Gossip.'

'Gossip?'

'I just wondered what you'd heard.'

'I spoke to Marjorie, and looked it up. Her old boyfriend is Boyle. What's more, ...I don't think there is any doubt he was stealing money from the Students' Benevolent Fund.'

'That was what I'd heard,' said Dr Fisher. 'But is it not possible you will be a prosecution witness?'

'It's possible, but I don't see how our talking can prejudice me.'

Dr Fisher was silent for a moment. 'I'm not...'

'Not what?'

Dr Fisher inhaled deeply through her nose. 'I'm not happy because all this shows the system is rotten. Rotten to the core.'

'Phew!' said Grit, taken aback. 'That's my sort of talk, but I never expected to hear it from you.'

'No, well,' said Dr Fisher in a very brief, clipped fashion, as she put her cup back on its saucer.

'Well?'

'Oh, confound it! What troubled me from the start about Boyle was the way he treated the staff. He managed the stage to make himself look good, be it with the Department of Education, Prolapse, or the auditors. The remit in which these bodies operated does not give them incentive to look behind the curtain. Or they didn't want to know. Just the sort of thing that can lead to practices like predatory pricing.

'In my opinion – and this is only my opinion – Boyle should never have been appointed in the first place. But, having said this, I leave myself open to accusations of having a grudge because he got the job and I didn't.'

'I am not browning my nose when I say you would have been a better appointment.'

'Actually, no. Well I didn't really want it. A great big college like Titas. Too impersonal. And I don't want to be its principal permanently. Really I don't. Couldn't keep tabs on the staff. Too much concern with appearances and remote ways of managing. Having to use methods I don't like. Methods Boyle enjoys.'

'So why shouldn't Boyle have been appointed?'

'You're on the Board. I think you can answer that question as well as I can, dear.'

'I don't think I can. After all, he was appointed before I got elected. But what's the problem now he's gone?'

'He hasn't gone yet.'

'As good as.'

'Perhaps. You shouldn't underestimate him.' Dr Fisher sighed. 'All of these bodies failed to make a fair assessment of a creature that was to some extent a product of theirs. Meet targets. Tick boxes. Fiddle to make the books balance. Over-ride any opposition on the grounds that it is all necessary within some market-based model. Parade it as the best practice of how to run a college and expand it as far and as wide as possible. Education is about more than that. – and do you know what Boyle's been arrested for?'

'I heard it was embezzlement.'

'Exactly!' Dr Fisher almost shouted, banging the table with her flat hand, startling Grit in the process. 'It's financial theft, actually. Amounts to the same thing, though.'

'That's enough of that, thank you very much,' called Jan from behind the counter.

'Better to get him on something serious,' said Grit, a little shocked at the closest she had ever seen Dr Fisher to an outburst. 'But do you know what I thought would have been far more satisfying?'

'What?'

'Getting Boyle sent down for Horace's murder. When all's said and done, he might as well have pushed him off that tower himself.'

'I obviously don't know as much about that as you do, dear.' Dr Fisher looked directly at her.

Grit explained, 'I spoke to his wife Marion quite recently. Boyle made Horace's life a misery, apparently.'

'I think I understand, dear. In which case the idea of Boyle going down for murder does seem strangely delightful.' She smiled unexpectedly. 'Of course actual murder is a little far-fetched. After all, I would imagine Boyle barely capable of climbing the last flight of stairs to the roof, let alone do a Michael Caine at Trinity Square.'

'Trinity Square?'

'You know the film, "Get Carter"?'

'Sylvester Stallone?'

'No, dear. Anyway, all of this misses the point. The system failed entirely to get rid of the monstrous carbuncle. It has taken the god of Mammon to do it. And, while I'm sure most of us have broken the law from time to time, the sort of person who does best in the current system tends by incentive to be a chancer. How many people who work in today's education system, like Boyle, are motivated ruthlessly by money and targets but who, unlike Boyle, don't happen to have anything like financial theft hanging over them?'

'I don't know.'

'Rest uneasily, dear, quite a few. I've met them at conferences. And there are several on the staff here that I know of.'

'Alison Morrell.'

'And the rest. I shouldn't accuse them of being overly ambitious because that is how people are encouraged to be these days. The trouble is that those who embrace Mammon are those who grasp their way to the top. We end up with a dysfunctional model reproducing itself for generations.'

Grit considered what Dr Fisher had said. She couldn't help feeling cynical. 'Then how come you got to be Principal at West Durham College? Were you dragged kicking and screaming to the position?

'Margaret, dear, I have never wished you to have any illusions on that front. I wanted a principalship, badly. And I'll admit that I wanted the power that went with it. It was because I was arrogant enough to believe I could do the job very well.

'But do bear in mind this. I was appointed to West Durham College in nineteen ninety. Colleges were still under the control of the local education authorities then. They had the final say, rather than some highfalutin gaggle of waifs and stays on the board of governors. No offence intended.'

'None taken.'

But I do admit it, I was ambitious. Very ambitious.'

'So what is it that makes the difference between you and people like Boyle?'

'QED, dear.'

'Oh, sorry?'

'When I had designs on being the head of a college, I was working with people who weren't interested in targets, at least not to the same extent. And I thought I could help people to improve themselves, to develop their interests, and help to mould them in to something more useful, more fulfilling.

'When tangible ideals are expressed in the form of targets they become divorced from reality. If reality provides a way of doing good, why devise a system that is based on an imperfect understanding of it? Surely you have similar ideas, though, with all you have done, haven't you?'

'I never wanted to rise up particularly - probably because I've never trusted bosses on the whole. Didn't want to be like them.'

'Why did you want to go into teaching?'

'What jobs were there when I left university?' Grit was being obtuse.

Dr Fisher seemed suddenly aghast, 'YOU AREN'T SERIOUS! Teaching should be a vocation. But what about what I observed in your lessons? What about the way you put your heart and soul into starting that crèche at my college? I would expect more from you than, "What other jobs were there?"'

'Do you mean was I idealistic about what I was doing? Perhaps. Well yes, actually. Didn't give it much thought. I still like teaching, but it's all the other shit. Sorry.'

'That's what I mean. It's the intangible aspect of teaching.'

'You mean the power thing?'

'No. Not at all. Though I know some of the best teachers I had at school and university were prone to a touch of the old Napoleon complex. But it's the sense of wanting to communicate something, to have something to *give* - and to help others at the same time. That's what the system wears out of people these days, replacing them with a lot of half-baked mantras. I mean, "SHINE". Good grief!'

Dr Fisher looked hard over her reading glasses at Grit, 'And with things as they are, who - or what - will come next?'

'It can't be anyone as bad as Boyle, surely!'

'Can't it?'

'But surely if you-'

'Rest assured, dear. It isn't going to be me. Not longer term.'

'But we need you. The situation needs you.'

Dr Fisher sighed.

Sixty Nine

Sitting in a sumptuous office in the chambers of Hardman-Lambert and Hoogstraten, Boyle was still railing from the car crash of a meeting he had had with the governors. And he was resolved to teach that Phyllis Roberts a lesson or two about loyalty.

'I make a rule never to ask my clients this, but on this occasion I'm going to make an exception,' said Roger Hardman-Lambert QC, his leading counsel.

'You're going to make an exception for me?' Boyle, somewhat flattered, was distracted briefly. Life had just been one big come down recently. Having had to postpone his holiday to answer a lot of stupid questions about whether he had changed his name was bad enough, but to face charges of financial theft had put the tin hat on things. But he was a fighter, not a quitter, just as whoever the termites behind his persecution would find out. And then they would pay. Oh yes...

The thing was he suspected his wife didn't believe he was innocent. That wouldn't normally have mattered to Boyle in the least, so why should it now?

He had to force himself away from this question, to face a little matter that, considering his recent meeting with the board of governors from Titas College, seemed irrelevant, and which he could have done without.

Hardman-Lambert stared across at him sternly. 'There's the change of name and failing to declare your criminal record when you were William Garnier. Of course this was not a criminal offence, but it does conspire against the upstanding character we want the jury to think you are. They would have had you *in flagrante delicto* there, but as previous convictions are precluded, it's inadmissible in court unless they can demonstrate its relevance to this case.'

This put Boyle's nose out of joint. 'I hired you because my solicitor here said you were the best and I have checked up on you...'

'Oh yes?' As Hardman-Lambert expected his reputation to precede him, he hid his affront, especially as Mr Privet nodded emphatically in agreement.

'...So you'll appreciate my fermentation when you tell me what my name used to be, because you got it wrong.'

Hardman-Lambert scanned his notes, 'Oh yes, sorry, Wil*fred* Garnier. Anyway, that is nothing to worry about.'

'Nothing to worry about, eh? This tawdry little matter has only likely cost me my career. And the chances of my actually receiving my OBE will have lengthened somewhat. You know I changed my name back to Boyle to try and distance myself from what happened to me when I was at university. It has haunted me ever since.'

'So you changed your name *back* to Boyle?' This seemed to answer a question which had been puzzling Hardman-Lambert ever since he had first set eyes on the brief, 'Was that your name when you were born?'

'Of course.'

'I see, but I thought that at the time you changed it back, you'd have been thirty, or was it twenty nine, when you did this, wouldn't you?'

'That's right, well you see um... there was a bit of other trouble I got into, regarding expense accounts when I worked in admin. at Cholmondeleys down near Darlington. I had declared my conviction when I applied for that job and when some money went missing, I was blamed for it. It might've been my responsibility, but I honestly didn't know how it happened. A bastard called Horace Villiers picked up on it.'

'Of course, the prosecution wants to bring the letter he allegedly wrote as evidence of your impropriety.'

'Do they now? Reptiles!'

'Happily, I'm sure the judge will rule it inadmissible.'

'Good. Anyway, I wasn't sacked, but I knew my days there were numbered, so I changed my name and put in for a job at Filch's estates agents in Witton-le-Cone. Because I had a different name, I didn't have to overcome a tarnished reputation. From there, I worked my way up to be area manager. I got the job at Durham College as a senior co-ordinator, and soon got to be principal there. If there was one lesson I learned throughout all this, it's about understanding the zeitgeist. If you can do that, you can make people believe almost anything. There are a few exceptions, but they're generally termites.'

Hardman-Lambert took a few moments to absorb all this, before re-orienting himself. 'So why change it to Wilfred Garnier in the first place, if you don't mind my asking?'

'That happened was when I was nine. My mum left my dad and got me to take the name of the man she dragged me off with for a new life in Carlisle. As for the Wilfred, it's always been my middle name. I don't use it now. All this has ruined my life. I'm afraid my wife has had enough of all this I've been put through, and I'm sure she's thinking of leaving me. Basically I'm a broken man.' Boyle shook his head from side to side as he said this, the flesh of his face lagging slightly behind the movement of his skull.

'Come, come, Mr Boyle. From what you have told me, it seems you have pulled yourself up by your lap straps at least twice.'

Boyle did not appear satisfied with this response, so Hardman-Lambert tried a different tack. 'Of course, should it come to that we can use this in a plea of mitigation to the judge.'

Boyle folded his arms, 'This should all be immaterial as I expect to be found innocent of these completely false charges brought against me.'

'Which brings us back to the question I was going to ask you, a question to which I am now satisfied I know the answer.'

'And that is?'

'Did you embezzle three hundred thousand five hundred and fifty pounds from Titas College's students' benevolent fund?'

'Don't make me laugh. How the hell was I supposed to have done that?'

'How indeed? According to the prosecution, you used your laptop to set up a false website to mimic the fund's own account and mapped it to other sites, emulating the various banks sums were supposed to be made into. They will use your credit card statements. Three payments of six pounds and twenty pence were made in order to purchase alternative Internet domains.

'For Fff's sake!' In what he may have believed to be such august company, Boyle couldn't quite bring himself to articulate the "F" word in its entirety. 'I saw the first payment and thought the wife had bought something with my card. I did go to the bank to question them.'

'That bit's covered. We already have written statements from two of the clerks in your local branch. They state you did question what the payment was. This might help convince the jury, but is not actual proof that you did not make the payments yourself for the purpose alleged by the prosecution. Your appearance at the bank to question it, the prosecution claims, was a ruse to hide what you were doing.

'Load of s-h-one-t!'

"They are saying that either you or an accomplice used the computer at Student Services to connect to the site, which it would do automatically after the first time. You directed the money to another account belonging to the benevolent fund to which you had access, and set up *SWIFT* transfers to deposit it in your *Sparbuch* account.'

'But it's ludicrous! I'm technology agnostic, me, and proud of it.'

'Tell that to the judge.'

'Really?'

'Is there someone who can verify you couldn't have done what the prosecution are claiming?'

'I'd expect twenty two of my vice principals to do that. No. Make that twenty one. Then there's my secretary.'

'I was thinking of just a few highly respected people.'

'Try Myrtle Howard. She is in charge of the college's offender learning programme. I could also ask my friend the county music adviser.

'Good, well we'll see if we can call them. All prosecution has is circumstantial evidence, so if we can provide a more plausible theory of how the whole thing was orchestrated, and by whom, that would be a great help to us.'

'How would I know who did it? I told you already; it's a frame-up. There are plenty of termites in that place would jump at any chance to screw me over.'

'I'm sure there are. The question is-'

Suddenly, Boyle became incensed. '-WHAT DO YOU MEAN YOU'RE SURE THERE ARE? I SAVED DURHAM COLLEGE. I HAVE BEEN OFFERED AN OBE! Did you know there are still over a hundred members of staff from there who now work for Titas? Are you suggesting that employees from the college I saved don't like me?'

'As you said earlier, Mr Boyle, you have had to make tough decisions. Anyone with the burden of high office is likely to have to make those. I would suggest that anybody who emerges from such a role without having made at least a few enemies has been far more fortunate than most - or isn't looking in the right places.'

Boyle stared into middle-distance, squinting slightly, his arms still folded. 'You put that extremely well, if I may say so. But just so you know, I am known as *The Maestro* at college. That's what they call me, and for good reason.'

'Thank you.' Hardman-Lambert really did need to get the meeting on track, or they would be there all day. 'The question is who actually did it? The Police believe there is enough evidence to prosecute, but neither the Internal Auditor nor the Audit Committee has been able to shed any light on it and the external auditors have resigned.'

'Oh aye, the Internal Auditor, Stuart Singleton!' Boyle smirked.

'Stupid Simpleton, more like. I don't have to tell you how useless he is. You realise how much we under-bid for the prison education contracts, just so we could get them - put the other providers out of the running, you know? He didn't notice until we bought our way out of the Sutton Coldfield contract. Soon Titas will profit from taking it back on, now North Berwick College has got the price up for us. But Singleton doesn't understand the reality of business. He's one of these pedantic pen-pushers who never take their blinkers off.'

Boyle seemed to be acting as though his counsel, Hardman-Lambert, had become an Insider. 'Then there were all the *explained* absences in registers. He did notice those. Told us just to be more careful. It never occurred to him that it was because they were "explained" absences, our funding wasn't cut. Or maybe nobody dared tell him. What a cretin! He was quick enough to pick out small discrepancies in the wages account, but never drew our attention to just how much we were spending on legal fees fighting cases against those termites with a grudge to bear.

'Still, we'll get all that back in wages saved under the new contracts eventually, so I would consider it a qualified victory. A couple of years and the termite-solvency ratio will be just fine.' Having unfolded his arms, Boyle removed his handkerchief from his shirt's breast pocket and was twisting it tightly between his hands.

Having listened to Boyle's diatribe, Hardman-Lambert was intrigued for Boyle to explain the exact meaning of the "termite-solvency ratio" but wasn't going to waste time on something only distantly related, so returned swiftly again to the matter in hand. 'Assuming we can't prove how this crime was committed or by whom, we need to establish that there is reasonable doubt.'

Boyle looked suddenly more innocent than he had ever done, almost child-like. 'Do you think we have a chance?'

'A chance? Most certainly! But that doesn't *mean* you will be found innocent, of course.'

A gloominess came over Boyle's face. 'I see. What are we looking at if it's guilty?'

'A maximum of six years.'

Boyle exhaled, 'Bloody hell.' The redness returned quickly to his jowls, 'so how would you rate our chances, er, percentage-wise?'

'Too early to say. I've found in my considerable experience that this sort of thing hinges very much on the presiding judge and the jury. We won't be able to assess those accurately until we are actually in the court room.'

'So are we talking fifty-fifty or eighty-twenty against?'

* * *

Boyle was grasping desperately for reassurance. He had spent the last thirty five years trying to live down being thrown out of teacher training college in Durham. All the cases he had fought against members of staff – in and out of court – had never worried him, not that he actually had much to do with them once they had gone to court. He just felt enraged toward those – all of them – who dared bring cases against his college. He would never admit he took this personally, but sometimes this anger would spill over. When he recognised one in the corridor, he would normally glare furiously in his or her direction. Occasionally he would call them a “loser” or a “fucking termite” when he was sure he wasn’t in earshot of any Outsiders. This had been cited a number of times by staff and ex-staff in employment tribunals, but never corroborated.

But suddenly he felt as if he was that naughty young student again, caught with his fingers in the till. This seemed so unfair, so unjustified; particularly after all he had done for further education. After all, he had been offered an OBE, hadn’t he? And when he was found innocent of these charges, or even if he wasn’t, he would bide his time and revenge against whoever it was who framed him would be the sweetest ever. Oh yes.

His reverie – this time silent – was interrupted by Hardman-Lambert, who had reached a conclusion which displeased him, ‘I really couldn’t rate your chances, Mr Boyle. Similar cases give us very little to go on. But there is one thing I really would recommend.’

‘What?’

‘That you do not give evidence from the witness box.’

Boyle was aghast. ‘Why ever not?’

‘How shall I put it? You come across as a forthright sort of person.’

‘There’s nothing wrong with that, is there?’

‘Not in itself. It’s just that the judge and the jury could interpret this as protesting too much. Then there are the feelings of contempt you have demonstrated towards your colleagues. Should those be brought to light, and I have no doubt prosecuting counsel will attempt to make the jury aware of them somehow, it is unlikely to endear you to them. And that could be fatal as far as your case is concerned.'

'Rubbish. I value my colleagues. Those who are worth their salt appreciate the decisions that have to be made to keep College afloat. It's just that there are always some bastards who prefer to bite the hand that feeds them. Then there's FUCA egging them on.' Boyle spat out the name of the union as if he had just realised he'd accidently taken a mouthful of arsenic. 'I want my day in court. It's the least I'm entitled to, given these despicable charges brought against me.'

'Well we'll decide on the possibility of your giving evidence in court later on then, shall we?'

Unaware that Hardman-Lambert was hoping to God and Cicero he would be able to talk him out of what he was now sure would be a passport to the stripy hole, Boyle muttered, *Six years,* to himself. *We'll see about that!*

Seventy

Summoned to provide a witness statement, Grit felt a sudden surge of adrenaline. She loathed Boyle. There were so many reasons why. She thought about how fear now drove so many members of staff, and that his malign ways probably led to Horace Villiers's death. She hated how he had vice-principals strategically placed at meetings of the board to support his druthers.

She hated the way Titas had forced staff who had worked in other local training centres and prisons across the whole country to work on worse terms than virtually everyone else in further education. It was as if Titas College had become a cancer devouring all the F.E. cells in its path.

Another thing she detested was the way he called her "Margaret" in board meetings, oiling at her superciliously with his polyps. What a disgusting creature he was!

After her meeting in Durham with the irrepressible Marjorie and her check with The Gazette, it was clear, Villiers's 1985 letter stating concerns about his accounting practices really put the tin hat on The Maestro as Grit was concerned.

Who, but someone who had got chucked out for theft could also be responsible for pilfering and embezzling from the Students' Benevolent Fund for his own gain?

He had taken a step too far, thank God. Now was the chance finally to lance the boil, to expunge the disease that had infected so many for so long with a strong dose of radiotherapy. She would provide her written statement, but did that mean she would be called? If she wasn't, did that mean she could attend the trial during her free periods?

* * *

'In my humble opinion, you've done your bit,' replied Inspector Smirthwaite when she telephoned him about the possibility of being called to give evidence. 'Given how you obtained the file on the phishing website, there is the not inconsiderable possibility you might end up incriminating yourself in the witness box. And we don't want that do we?'

Having thanked him, Grit found herself making her way to the public gallery during the afternoon session on the second day of the trial which, fortuitously, was a Thursday. And whom would she find giving evidence in the witness box?

'At what point did you notice the payment had not gone into your bank account?' asked the prosecuting counsel, Ms Ricarda Head.

'I don't know exactly,' said Wesley, 'I got a payment slip that came with the letter telling me I'd got the grant. Then I bought a laptop and it went through. It would've been the next day when I went to do some shopping, my card was refused. I phoned the bank and found out then that my account was empty.'

'What was the balance, exactly?'

'Eighty nine pounds and ninety six pence in the red. The bank charged me a fifteen pound overdraft fee for that.'

'What did you do then?'

'I went to Student Services, and they just told me I'd got the money. Then I went to see my tutor, Miss Bulmer.'

'Let's get this clear. Student Services produced documentation to prove the money was sent to your account and your bank produced a statement from you showing that it wasn't.'

'Yeah. That's right.'

'Thank you, Mr Johnson. Can I refer the jury at this point to Exhibits H and I? If you'll wait there for a moment in case my learned friend wishes to ask you any questions.'

Hardman-Lambert rose to his considerable height and flourished his robes rather like a matador might his muleta. 'Mr Johnson, only two weeks after your determining an issue with your account, did something happen?'

'Did what?'

'Was there an incident at Titas College?'

'Incident? I don't... Oh, yeah, you mean the demonstration. You know one of the lecturers died. I thought it looked like he killed himself. Well, there was a sort of vigil, like, because word had it he'd been bullied by Mr Boyle.'

Annoyed at the inclusion of this, Hardman-Lambert passed on to the line in hand. 'Can you tell the jury what happened at the demonstration?'

'Which bit? Some of us were there all night.'

'Perhaps you could start at the point my client came out to address you?'

'Oh yeah, well he kind of tripped and made a joke about it. Then he called us "dudes and dudettes" and said how he'd come to "touch base" with us. I mean what sort of old codger talks like that?' Wesley looked cautiously towards the dock to see Boyle seething directly towards him.

Hardman-Lambert ignored Wesley's question. 'For the benefit of clarity, to whom are you referring here?'

'Eh?'

'Who are you talking about?'

'Oh, er, Boyle. I mean the pr-, the accu-'

'-So you are talking about my client?'

'Yeah.'

'Thank you. What happened next?'

'He went on about how if he'd made a mistake he'd put it right, but if lecturers weren't up to college standards they couldn't keep them on.' Wesley slumped slightly and began looking slightly puffy around the eyes. 'Someone shouted at him that this was slanderous. I'd guess towards Mr Villiers.'

'Please continue, Mr Johnson.' Hardman-Lambert allowed himself a small smirk.

Wesley started to fidget slightly. 'Well, then, um, something hit him in the face and he gipped a bit, got radged and walked off.'

The learned judge, Leslie "Frank" Butler intervened in his husky echo of a voice, 'I have to confess I am not familiar with some of this vernacular, Mr Johnson.'

'You what, Your Honour?'

'You have used two terms with which I and, I imagine, some members of the jury are unfamiliar. When you say the defendant, and I quote "gipped a bit", can you explain what you mean?'

'I see, Your Honour. What I mean is he puked a bit. Not a full-blown barf, you understand, sir, more like an overflow.'

'If I said you were telling the court that the defendant vomited slightly, would I be describing things accurately.'

'You would, Your Honour.'

The judge looked at the jury knowingly 'And when you said he "got radged", would it be correct to say you were telling the court the defendant became angry?'

'Almost, Your Honour, but radged is more...' Wesley waved his arms about furiously, making a sound from his throat.

'Oh yes, I think I see. You were telling the court that the defendant became angry and flustered.'

'Kind of.'

'Kind. Of? Mr Johnson, I expect people taking the witness stand in my court to answer questions clearly and to the best of their ability. Did the defendant become angry or flustered, both angry and flustered, or neither angry nor flustered?

'Both angry and flustered, Your Honour.'

'I see. Thank you, Mr Johnson. I'm glad we've managed to get to clear that up. Please continue, Mr Hardman-Lambert.'

'I'm sure we are all grateful for Your Honour's most elucidative intervention, Your Honour.'

'Yes, alright. Get on with it.'

'Are you aware of the origin of the projectile which hit my client in the face?'

'The what?'

'Do you know where the object that was thrown or fired at my client came from?'

'Not exactly.'

'Not exactly, eh?

'Is it not true that a clip, widely watched on *Candid* shows beyond question that you are the originator of the projectile?'

'What are you talking about?'

'Did you throw the object that hit the defendant?'

The judge cut in, 'Mr Hardman-Lambert, I have already refused an application to show the said clip to the jury. I fear your little stunt may be an attempt to discredit the witness. The jury will disregard the question.'

'Of course, Your Honour.'

Wesley clearly knew where things were going. Grit was unaware he had already been arrested and charged with aggravated assault for his offence in the magistrate's court. 'Alright then,' he said. 'I threw it. I might have got thrown out of College for yeeting it at him, but it was worth it!' Wesley said this with a degree of relief.

'Order in the court,' echoed the judge, 'The jury will also disregard the answer the witness has given.'

So that was why Wesley got kicked out! thought Grit. *I was sure it was part of a cover-up. Why in God's name did you have to give them that excuse, Wesley?*

As he sat, Hardman-Lambert swooped his robes at the jury as if to intimate some sort of victory.

'For the Court's information, this little display by the defence was clearly an attempt to entrap and discredit a witness. That is why I have instructed the jury to disregard it. Mr Hardman-Lambert, you are *in tenues glacies,* and shall be raising the matter with you in my chambers.'

'As Your Honour pleases.'

Seventy One

Having continued to insist he must be allowed to give evidence, Boyle had finally beaten down Hardman-Lambert's appeals to him that it would be an unwise course. He felt a surge of confidence as he made his way into the witness box. There were several ghosts he intended to lay to rest, as well as a few scores to settle. His counsel was suffering from the unfortunate misapprehension that he would appear to the jury as something other than the honest, conscientious, hard-working humanitarian he was. He had been selected to receive an OBE, after all.

Boyle stood waiting for some time for Ms Ricarda Head to fire a question, wondering if this apparent pause in proceedings were some sort of ploy to catch him off guard. No chance.

'May it please Your Honour, members of the jury; are you Laurence Wilfred Boyle, principal of Titas College?'

'I am.'

'Are you currently under suspension from your position pending the outcome of this case?'

'Yes, er. No.' Boyle was flummoxed already. Understandably concerned with the charges of which he was innocent, he had preferred lately to forget the other reason for his suspension from work. This was the fact that he had committed a criminal offence under a different name in nineteen seventy six and failed to declare it to either Durham or Titas colleges. But he should have been safe. After all, he couldn't discuss his previous convictions in front of the jury, could he?

To his enormous relief, Boyle's counsel swept to his feet, like a giant raven, 'Objection!'

'Yeees, Mr Hardman-Lambert?'

'My client is not here to discuss his current employment situation, Your Honour. May I respectfully insist my learned friend concentrates on the matter given on the charge sheet?'

'Quite so. Restrict the line of questioning to the matter of theft from Titas College's Students' Benevolent Fund.'

'Of course, Your Honour. Mr Boyle, do you accept that some three hundred and fifty thousand five hundred and fifty pounds have been accounted as debited from a bank account held by Titas College's students' benevolent fund that should have been paid into bank accounts of the beneficiaries, like Mr Wesley Johnson here. But no corresponding credits materialised in their own bank accounts?'

The exchange by various parties in the court gave Boyle the impression that he would be spared questioning on that matter of some discomfort which, for the life of him, he couldn't remember. 'So it would seem. I'd like to get to the bottom of it. But it had nothing to do with me. Perhaps I should point out to the court that, as principal of Titas College, I am well rewarded for my considerable expertise. I was in fact the first college principal in the United Kingdom to be paid an annual salary of more than three hundred thousand pounds.

'As my counsel has advised me, an article in the Draguian Educational Journal to this effect has been submitted as Exhibit K.'

As Boyle stood proudly in the witness box, Hardman-Lambert cast a glance towards the jury. What he saw made his silk robe wilt.

'Yes, well, er...' Boyle continued. '...the point I'm making, Your Honour, is that I have *absolutely* no need to go pilfering funds from the Students' Society.'

'The Students' Society?' Ms Head repeated back to Boyle.

SHIT, SHIT, SHIT!

As he did his best to pass on from this mistake, Boyle did not want anyone to know just how mortified he felt, 'I mean the Students' Benevolent Fund,' he corrected quickly. 'And while we're on the subject, I would like to say just how proud I am that Titas College has established such a fund for the benefit of its disadvantaged students.'

Hardman-Lambert cast another glance. Some of the jurors looked more sympathetic. Not enough to acquit, though.

At this point prosecuting counsel decided to begin a new march from a different angle. 'Do you like Austria, Mr Boyle?'

'The country or the tune?'

Boyle's counsel came suddenly to from evaluating the jury's reactions to his performance in the witness box, 'Objection! My client's preference, or otherwise, for a particular nation, is totally irrelevant.'

'Indeed Ms Head. You will confine your questions to the accused's understanding of the facts of the case.'

'The relevance of the question will become plain shortly, Your Honour. Mr Boyle, do you own a chalet in the Austrian Alps?'

'No I do not.'

'I see. That is a slightly strange answer, given that we will be providing evidence that you occupied a property in Rührseligestadt durin-'

'-That's right. It belongs to my wife.' Annoyed, Boyle reverted to type, 'YOU CLEARLY HAVEN'T DONE YOUR HOMEWORK, PET!' He projected a sneer throughout the court room. Hoping for an intervention from the judge, Ms Head braced herself at Boyle's term of address.

The judge remained silent, so with some fortitude she continued, 'Do you hold an account known as a "Sparbuch" or "Passbook" account?'

'No I certainly do not. I don't even hold Austrian citizenship.'

'As has been presented to the jury, Exhibit B is of a Sparbuch account book which on the thirty first of December in the year two thousand and thirteen held the grand total of three hundred and ninety seven thousand six hundred and sixty three Euros and ninety two Euro Cents. Do you know how much that converted to in Pounds sterling at the time of the last entry?'

'I didn't until it was explained to me, first by the police and then by my counsel. Apparently it is the same as the amount missing from the Students' Soc-Benevolent Fund. I didn't know that. but I accept it.' *Fuck, I almost slipped up again!*

'I'm glad you accept it, Mr Boyle, because that is undoubtedly the case. Can you explain for the benefit of the Jury exactly how Exhibit B came to be found in your office?'

'NO I CAN NOT!'

'Mr Boyle, you must control yourself.' The intervention by the judge proved two-sided. 'Prosecuting counsel will refrain from antagonising the defendant. Shall we have a brief recess so that everyone can regain their composure?' In spite of the fact that it was aimed ostensibly at him, Boyle was glad of the judge's intervention.

'No, er, thank you Your Honour. I'm happy to go on.'

'If you insist, Mr Boyle. But should you demonstrate any repeat of your outburst you must remember that I have the power to find you in contempt of court.'

The following question made Boyle wish he had not made such a valiant gesture. 'Have you ever been known by any names other than Laurence Boyle?'

A quick swoop of the now drooping silk robe came to his rescue, 'Objection, admissibility.'

Ms Head was on the ball, 'Your Honour the previous conduct of the accused is relevant to this case.'

Lord Justice Butler nodded knowingly, 'The relevance has not been proven in law, Ms Head. You will confine yourself to questions relating to the theft of monies from the Students' Benevolent Fund.'

'Thank you Your Honour- My apologies.' The obsequiousness in her voice showed this young, dark beauty was already adept at toadying to the bench, even in the face of male chauvinist adversity, but this evidently did not stop her from pushing the point. 'If found innocent in this court, do you expect to be reinstated to your position as principal of Titas College?'

'Of course.'

'Are you quite sure of that?'

'Absolutely!' As he said this, Boyle began to remember, through the fog of the court room, the ugly truth.

'Thank you, Mr Boyle. Do you have a criminal record under the name Laurence Boyle?'

'No I most certainly do not. Ever since my unfortunate, youthful indiscretion I have led a completely law-abiding life. Completely!' Then he realised he might be able to play a small omission to his advantage, 'Sorry, Your Honour. I tell a lie. At the risk of perjuring myself, I have had three, sorry, four, convictions for speeding and all but one of them are spent.' He peered towards the jury hoping to raise a giggle, but had to make do with a smile from a grey-haired man on the back row.

'Is that right, Mr Boyle? And what youthful indiscretion might that be?'

Boyle's counsel rose, but the judge was on the case. 'Ms Head, this really is unacceptable. You are leading the accused to discuss a matter I have already ruled as inadmissible. The jury will disregard any reference to it.'

'As Your Honour pleases,' Ms Head looked across to the jury. The expressions on their faces, ranged from curious to accusatory. 'So to bring us back to the reason for your suspension, are you still certain that, should you be found innocent of the charges relating to the theft of three hundred and fifty thousand five hundred and fifty pounds, you will be re-instated.'

Boyle equivocated for a moment, '...Of course one can never be certain of these things. After all, mud sticks and all that, BUT TO BE HONEST, I see no reason why not.' He was keeping from the court the matter of the conviction under another name, but as the judge had ruled anything on those lines inadmissible, he thought himself unassailable, at least as far as that accusation was concerned. But this did not make him feel better: in fact he felt like he was back at the demonstration when he puked slightly from the stinking projectile lobbed by the termite Wesley Johnson. That time he had the luxury of being able to withdraw from the scene. On this occasion it would not be so straightforward to do so. His temper was starting to get the better of him and he began to shake, adding, 'I can't be expected to read the minds of my college's board of governors. Have you any more questions for me?'

'Yes. Laurence Boyle, I put it to you that you, or someone working under your direction, set up a phishing website on your computer with the aim of stealing funds from the Students' Benevolent Fund.'

'Absolutely not.'

'Having taken control of an unused bank account held by the Students' Benevolent Fund with you copied its "skin" to your phishing website and proceeded to withdraw the monies paid into it in cash, depositing them initially in this account.'

'What would I want with a fishing website? I hate the smell of fish!'

'You don't seriously expect the jury to believe you don't know what I'm talking about do you?'

'Yes.'

'Having withdrawn those funds, you used an international SWIFT transfer to move them into your "Sparbuch" account – an account the passbook for which was found in your office. An account opened for that very purpose – to hide the stolen funds from the reach of the authorities.'

'I certainly did not. I know nothing about that. It's a frame-up I tell you, a frame up.'

'No more questions, Your Honour.'

At this, Hardman-Lambert swept to his feet, 'Mr Boyle, if all this is true, can you tell the court why you were using an account in the name of the Students' Benevolent Fund?

'I wasn't using it. I never even knew such an account existed.'

'Would you consider it a hypothetical question?'

'Well I'd have to, wouldn't I?'

'Why would you have to? Please, tell the jury.'

Boyle struggled to find an adjective that was not an expletive, 'Because I never took the *confounded* money in the first place.'

'Precisely! No more questions, Your Honour.'

This is my chance, thought Boyle. 'I've a couple of home truths to make the court aware of.

'Silence!' shouted the usher, but Boyle would not be shut up so easily,

'I am the highly respected principal of a very large educational establishment. I got where I am by making tough decisions.'

'Silence in court!' bellowed the usher, but Boyle continued,

'Not all of these have been popular with everyone. Some of the termites, people, sorry, who come into my office every day would gladly see me up the road and-'

'-The witness will contain himself.' Engaged in taking notes at the beginning of the outburst, His Honour had been dazed for a few moments before jumping in with what sounded like a scream resonating from the cells below. 'I'm sure your counsel will make the points necessary to your defence in his summing up.'

'But it's clear to the biggest idiot that some ba- - person, or persons stitched me up, and I just hope the ju-'

'-If the witness chooses to speak out of turn in my court I will find him in contempt. Is that clear to you, Mr Hardman-Lambert?' The echo emanating from the judge sounded closer now, as if it had reached the outside of the courtroom doors.

'Eminently, Your Honour.' Boyle's defence counsel supplicated with considerable grace. So much so in fact that Boyle was impressed that, rather than placing himself in contempt, something over which the judge had already granted exceptional latitude, he was just about able to contain himself within his glowing red face.

'Have you any further questions for the witness, Mr Hardman-Lambert?'

'No questions, Your Honour.'

Boyle was dismayed, 'I thought you were going to give me the opportunity to tell my side of the story!' Suddenly, he felt the tightening of his chest, like the one when he drove into College to find the protest going on, but this time it was accompanied by a shooting pain down his left arm.

Hardman-Lambert made a parrying gesture in Boyle's direction, and Boyle stood down pressing his lips together hard. As he climbed from the witness box, he bent slightly forward, clutching his chest, but as soon as he was clear of the box, the pain left and, while not satisfied with what had happened, he thought he had given a decent account of himself and would soon be speaking to his counsel about why he was not allowed to say a great deal more.

* * *

In summing up, Ms Ricarda Head stated that the evidence indicated very strongly that Boyle had to have taken the money from the Students' Benevolent Fund. Further, there was the fact that the "Sparbuch" account book was found in his office. The second Students' Benevolent Fund account had been operated by someone able to pass all its security checks using Boyle's identity. 'Members of the jury, you have been invited by the defence to believe that someone was impersonating him. But who could this be? In his defence, the accused has given us no candidates for this alleged impersonation. The idea that the defendant has been subject to some vicious frame-up is, like the rest of the defence, a fabric of fantasy.'

Boyle's counsel made great play of the fact that, in spite of what looked like a smoking gun, there was absolutely no proof the Sparbuch was his and, moreover, as successful and canny a manager as Boyle would never have made the mistake of leaving the passbook in his office had it been his. The lack of *prima-facae* evidence to indicate a frame-up was most unfortunate, but there indeed remained a reasonable doubt. The presumption of innocence was indeed sufficient that they should find Boyle innocent. Further, the evidence given showed that Boyle had been an upstanding citizen for many years, and that because of the cuts he had made of staff wages in order to avoid the financial collapse of Durham College, he was bound to have enemies. The theft was therefore committed by persons unknown in order to frame Boyle and no doubt the prosecution service would bring about charges if they were able to uncover sufficient evidence.

'Sadly, members of the jury, in spite of the prosecution's protestations, this is indeed a case of the elusive Mr or, indeed, Mrs X. Whether his name is Laurence Boyle, Wilfred Garnier, or Joe Bloggs, to convict my client would be to take the easy route. Call him guilty and allow to walk free Person or Persons X.'

Following the departure of the jury to consider its verdict, an electric atmosphere prevailed inside and outside the court.

Seventy Two

As soon as she had left the court building, Grit checked her phone. It showed that Marion Villiers had tried to telephone her whilst she was inside. Then she bumped into Wesley.

'Hello Miss. Come to see that bastard get his comeuppance, then?' Wesley's voice caught her from behind.

She turned. 'I wouldn't have put it quite that way.'

He smiled wryly, 'I know you wouldn't.'

'Can I ask you something?'

'Sure.'

'Is it because you threw the stinking orchid or whatever it was at the principal the reason you got thrown out?'

'Yeah, I guess. I thought you'd have known.'

'No, nobody told me. It's funny because teachers tend to share that sort of thing, but my boss told me nothing more than that you had been excluded. I thought it was because of the fuss I helped you make over the grant for your laptop. I reported it to the auditor, you know.'

'Thanks for doing that, Miss, but no.'

'Why, for God's sake?'

'Why what?'

'Why give the college a good reason to throw you out?'

'I hated that bastard. Everything he was doing.'

'That shouldn't have been your worry. Not as long as you were getting your education.'

'I know, but you know what I'm like. Besides, I've got a job,'

'Doing what?'

'Looking after greenhouses, growing tomatoes... mostly.' Wesley winked disconcertingly.

'I didn't think that was your thing.'

'The power of plants made Boyle look like the prat he is.'

Grit couldn't disagree, 'As long as you are doing alright.'

'Yeah, I'm fine, Miss. Anyway, I'm going in to wait for the verdict now. See you around.'

'I hope so.'

Back at her phone, she returned the call to hear a tearful-sounding Mrs Villiers at the other end. 'I wondered if you could come round now. I've got something I think you should see.'

Grit was torn. She really wanted to be there for the verdict, but on reflection she didn't have to be and would find out anyway in due course. Now she was needed elsewhere.

'I'm in town at the moment. Can you give it half an hour?'

She walked back to her car. Two hours' parking wasted, she thought, looking around vainly for someone who might be able to use the ticket. Oh well. The car took several attempts to start, limping its way to Mrs Villiers's house.

The front door was open so Grit knocked and made her way in, 'Hello?'

'I'm in here,' said Mrs Villiers from Horace's room.

'What's wrong?' asked Grit,

Mrs Villiers handed her an open envelope, with writing on it, '*To be opened in the event of my death.*'

'My son found it this morning when he was clearing out Horace's flat. He'd left it locked in the top drawer of the desk he used there.'

'Can I read it?'

'That was why I asked you to come.'

Grit took out the hand-written note and read it. It began,

'*To my dear wife, Marion and children, Christopher, and Samantha. I hope one of you is the first to read this, and trust you will show it to the other two.*

I hate to leave you in this way, but have decided I cannot live by myself without the kind help and tolerance you have all given me over the years. Marion, I know, darling, that if I come back to live with you, the stress will probably kill you, so have decided to end things for myself. This decision is entirely mine. You have done nothing to drive me to it, so I am telling you now; you must not feel any fault lies with you. It doesn't.

Please don't be too alarmed about my likely manner of departure. There is so much wrong at that college and a lot of it is certainly the principal's fault. He behaves as if he knows me from somewhere and has a grudge. I was sure I recognised him, but the corrupt employee we had at Cholmondeleys I took him for had a different name.

I made a professional mistake referring the hand dryer for testing in his office before it was ready, but if it is installed after I am dead, any "accident" that could happen subsequently would be his fault: a shame I won't be there to see it.

Do I really care about my memory being tarnished? Well if you can live with it, so can I (no pun intended). Anyway, if I can raise any alarm bells by creating a significant event at that place, then it will have been worthwhile.

Please go on with your lives, make of them what you can and be happy. I hope this will be easier for you all with me out of the way.

My undying love to you all,

Horace.'

Grit did not know what to say. In spite of her previous meeting with Mrs Villiers, she still harboured the notion that Boyle was behind Villiers's death. Did this note show otherwise? She wasn't sure. After all, people can be driven to do things by factors they would never cite themselves.

Some time passed. Grit said eventually, 'Thank you for showing this to me. Is there anything I can do?'

Mrs Villiers rocked forwards and backwards in the armchair, holding a tissue to her nose. Eventually she gained enough composure to speak. 'Dear Horace certainly put one over on Boyle, didn't he?' She began to giggle. The giggle became a laugh.

On reflection, Grit could see that the situation did have its funny side, but was surprised that Mrs Villiers was able to see it in the circumstances. It was the first time she had really appreciated the humour that Villiers had subjected her to a number of times and nearly always received irritation or anger in response.

As Mrs Villiers's laugh became hysterical, Grit couldn't help laughing too. Horace had had his revenge in his own way and, even if he had made sure he was not present to appreciate it, she, Mrs Villiers and, no doubt in time, quite a few others would come to see a certain deliciousness to the way Villiers had enacted his revenge.

'Can I get you some tea?' Grit asked when their laughter had eventually subsided.

'I've been drinking tea all day. Do you think you could get me a coffee?'

Grit did as she was asked, although it did take a while to find everything without resorting to asking Mrs Villiers where it was. Maybe tiny kitchens did have their advantages. She found the dreaded jar and hacked a few more of the congealed granules from near the bottom, making one for herself out of politeness.

When Grit returned with the coffee, she handed Mrs Villiers one of the mugs. One sip was enough to shock her partly from her miserable state, 'That's awful,' she said quietly through a grimace.

Grit didn't know whether to take this as an insult. She knew it WAS awful, 'Have I made it too strong, or...?'

'Oh no, no, you've made it just fine. When you came before, did the coffee I made you taste like this?'

'It did a bit, I'm afraid,'

'Dear me, you should have said something. To think I've been serving this bilge-water to everyone. I don't normally like coffee, but I do know how it should taste and this definitely isn't it. No wonder the Women's Institute cut me out of their rota.'

'I'll get you a new jar next time I come,'

'That's a very kind thought, but I think it's something I need to do straight away. And I'm chucking this out.' She got up and went into the kitchen. Grit heard the distant sound of a pedal bin opening. The clang of something fairly substantial dropping into it had a cathartic quality.

Grit did not want to leave Mrs Villiers on her own, but had to go and pick George up from school, so she was glad that a man in his early twenties, presumably Christopher, arrived.

Seventy Three

When, finally, everyone in the court room was ready, distant coughing presaged Mr Justice Butler's entrance. This sound was all too familiar to the regulars in his court. Indeed, the consumption of some eighteen full-strength cigarettes while the jury was out meant that His Honour was probably about the only person in a reasonably relaxed state.

'Will the foreperson of the jury please stand?'

A short, but fearsome, female in her thirties stood up. She looked so serious that her brow seemed as if contorted much further it might have been persuaded to touch her bottom lip.

'Have you all reached a verdict on which you are agreed?'

'We have, Your Honour,' she nodded earnestly.

'On the charge of financial theft, do you find the defendant, Laurence Boyle, guilty or not guilty?'

'Guilty, Your Honour.'

'Is that the verdict of you all?'

'It is, Your Honour.'

For a few moments, an incredulous silence fell upon the court. Nobody, it seemed, could quite believe The Boil had been lanced. Then a burst of applause from the public gallery took several attempts by the usher to silence.

'Very well. I must confess to being a little surprised at your verdict,' said the judge, 'This being the case, I shall take a ten minute recess to consider what would be a suitable sentence to pass.'

At this, His Honour withdrew to smoke another couple of cigarettes. Boyle looked about to explode again, 'YOU'RE WRONG!' he shouted out, 'YOU'VE GOT IT TOTALLY BACKWARDS, YOU USELESS BUNCH OF IMBECILES.'

He was about to be apprehended by an orderly, but this time he grasped his left arm, clearly in some pain. Hardman-Lambert sent his junior to attend to Boyle, saying that in the circumstances an appeal would almost certainly be heard. The junior went across to find Boyle keeled forward and attended to by a court orderly. From this position, he called out, 'I'LL HUNT DOWN EVERY SINGLE TERMITE ON THE JURY OF THIS MARSUPIAL COURT AND KANGAROO-KICK THEM SO THE NORTHERN TIP OF QUEENSLAND WILL BE POKING OUT OF YOUR POISONOUS LITTLE MOUTH.'

Through his pain, Boyle felt he had delivered a suitable dressing-down. Perhaps fortunately for him, the strain in attempting to shout this left his concluding words barely possible to determine, 'AND I'LL RIP THAT BASTARD JUDGE'S KIPPER FACTORY OF A THROAT STRAIGHT OFF HIS SCRAWNY SPINE.'

Hardman-Lambert's junior called for an ambulance.

Later, having received news that Boyle was stable in hospital, having suffered a major heart attack, Mr Justice Butler re-convened the court to tell them that sentencing would be deferred until Boyle was well enough to face it. But he warned that the severity of the charges indicated a custodial sentence.

* * *

Later that day, Hardman-Lambert decided to take the unusual step of visiting his client in hospital. The notion of grounds for an appeal would, he hoped, prove a tonic to the ailing Boyle.

Seventy Four

For all the things that had happened since she was in charge of West Durham College, Dr Fisher felt content to be sitting behind the principal's desk, even if the position was temporary. As a caretaker principal, there wasn't a great deal to do, although there would be much to be attended to if it was decided by all relevant parties she should remain in the role permanently. All things considered, this was an unlikely scenario, and she knew it, not that it bothered her in the least.

There was a quiet knock at the door. It was Cyril Richards.

'Sid, my dear! It's been such a long time. Sit down, sit down. Was this a social call, or...?

'No lass... Alright, yes it is!' He hugged her, a little unsteady on his feet as this caused his walking stick to be too far away from his body to provide much support. 'I'm just over the moon to see you back in charge. I always thought that Laurence were a bad yin.'

'Would you like some tea?'

'Aye, that'd be grand.'

She pressed the buzzer on the intercom, forgetting Lisa had gone.

'Of course, she's left for the day.' Dr Fisher got up, took a kettle into the en-suite, and filled it, 'You know she's leaving; got a new job as a computer programmer. Of course I shouldn't tell you her business, but I thought more power to her elbow.'

'That's alright. I knew already. She's my niece, you know. A very bright lass. Just finished a degree in computing. Got a first from the Open University. She's been a great help to me, I can tell you.'

'Really? I had no idea she was your niece.'

'Aye, aye.'

They paused as the kettle came to the boil. Dr Fisher warmed a tea pot, put a couple of bags in and filled it. Then she looked out of the window, 'You know, in spite of all you've said about him, when Laurence Boyle took the stand and denied all knowledge of fraud, I could have sworn he was telling the truth.'

Richards chuckled, 'I never knew you were there.'

'I did pop in for the verdict. I didn't see you.'

'I wasn't there. But you thought he were telling the truth, then?'

'Either that or the man was dreadfully deluded. Of course that's another possibility.'

'No, I reckon you were right about that, pet.' Richards looked sheepish, something Dr Fisher took this as an indication he *knew* that Boyle was indeed telling the truth.

'Sid, is there something I should know?'

'No, but there's plenty you shouldn't.'

'Is one of these things that you know my instinct to have been right.'

'I'm sayin' no more on the matter.'

'Surely ***you*** wouldn't have had a hand in all this?'

Richards paused, but did not reply, instead changing the subject. 'If you're just staying here temporarily, like, what've you done with all your cats?'

'I have some very dear neighbours looking after them for me. Of course I'll pop back and see the little darlings at the weekend.'

As Dr Fisher poured the tea, Richards got his pipe out and filled it. Noticing, she climbed up onto the executive, leather office chair and from that onto the desk, before fiddling with her glasses and chain. She tried them on and then off, finally pushing what appeared to be the button on the smoke alarm that was on the ceiling above, 'You're not allowed to smoke in here, but today I'm prepared to make an exception.' *Blast all this Health and Safety!*

'Sorry lass, I'd forgotten. And I'm grateful you're prepared to make an exception tonight,' he said, as he lit it with a flame-thrower lighter. As Dr Fisher clambered back down, Richards puffed away to create a formidable smokescreen.

A sinister sounding voice emerged through the smokescreen, 'You want to watch what you're saying. Pfrrrt. You want to watch what you're saying. Pfrrrt.'

'It's me bloody mobile,' said Richards and after a few more seconds the voice stopped as the device dropped to the floor. 'Bugger it, they can wait!' he said, chuckling again, still unseen through all the smoke. Then there was a pause.

'A curious ringtone,' Dr Fisher observed.

'Aye, our Lisa got it off "freeringtones dot com" Apparently it's Boyle relieving himself in that bathroom.' Through the fog, Dr Fisher could just about see the bottom end of a walking stick pointing to the relevant door.

'Yes, I thought it sounded like him. How on earth could that have got on there, I wonder?'

'I'll look it up. Richards fiddled about on the floor with the handle-end of his stick, attempting to pull the phone towards himself. Dr Fisher was about to offer to pick the thing up for him, but eventually he retrieved it and wafted much of the smokescreen away so he could see the screen of the phone. Dr Fisher poured the tea as he fiddled with the device.

'The ring tone I used was uploaded by someone called Toby Smith and he wrote, "Stinky principal, Lorrance Boil threatening my dad. Sounds like he's having a poop (principal, not Dad). Dad is a total pajero with tech, so probably didn't even know he had recorded it."'

Impressed by the old man's deftness with a smart phone as much as amused and repelled by the image conjuring itself in her mind, Dr Fisher tried to keep a straight face, but couldn't help smirking just a little. 'Bob Smith was trying to contact me a few weeks ago. When I finally got back to him, he said he'd lost his phone. Now we know who had it! I suppose I'll have to tell him. A shame, though.'

Richards laughed out loud, 'Aye, it is that!'

'Fascinated as I am by this, I am still waiting for an explanation of something far more important.'

There was another, longer, pause, while Richards worked hard at replacing the smokescreen. She continued, 'Boyle has been convicted of financial theft. It was alleged he did it by using his own laptop to guide the college's internal system towards a fake website, which diverted funds to his deposit account.'

'Something like that, aye.' The smokescreen was beginning to clear again.

'But Boyle was never that great with technology. I mean he could manage it, but I never took him to be an expert. I could always be wrong, of course...'

'I never thought he was much cop with it either. Being a right prat's about the only thing he's good at, come to think of it.'

'But as I've just found out, there was an expert who probably had access to his laptop. An expert you have just told me is your niece.'

Dr Fisher could now see Richards quite clearly. He did not look as if he had been having a chuckle. In fact he looked sad. 'I wouldn't know anything about that.'

This was too important for Dr Fisher to be diverted. 'Let's get this straight, Sid; Boyle was the rotten head of the largest college in the region. On that we are agreed?'

Richards chewed the stem of his pipe and then nodded his head sideways, 'Aye.'

'One thing that escapes me is how the money turned up in the Austrian bank account. You wouldn't have any idea, would you?'

'There are ways it could be done. You know Witton-le-Cone is twinned with a little town in Austria, called Rührseligestadt?'

'Yes.'

'When I was on Witton-le-Cone District Council, we visited it. That was when I found out Laurence had a place there. I even bumped into him once or twice. And do you know what? I spent last summer there. Had a grand time, I did. There's a couple of little shops with a fine range of pipe tobaccos, you know. Lovely scenery, and those Austrians know how to run a local council, if you follow me.'

Dr Fisher was not sure whether Richards was deliberately hinting to her his involvement in a frame-up of Boyle. Normally she would have asked the question outright. But it was such an outrageous suggestion that maybe he was winding her up about the possibility. Given the far-fetched nature of the scenario, even she skirted around it by pointing out the harm that such an act caused elsewhere. 'But does the end really justify the means?'

'The end is justified if it leads to increasing the power of humanity over nature and to the abolition of the power of one person over another'

'That's what Marx said, but it hardly did that, did it?'

'Did what?'

'Increase the power of humanity over nature or of one person over another.'

'Aye it did. We're rid of that Monstrous Carbuncle now, aren't we?'

'What about all those students who needed help from the benevolent fund? They were punished because they bought things they couldn't afford?'

'Aye, that was unfortunate. I reckon, if it were done in war time, it'd be called "collateral damage".'

'Fine, Sid, I get that. I don't agree with it, but I'd understand, I think, were it not for the fact that Boyle was found to have done something already for which he could have been dismissed.'

Neither spoke for several moments. 'I suppose it's too much to ask you to keep quiet about all this,' said Richards eventually, 'Careless talk and all that?'

'About what?'

'You were always a good girl.' Richards rose to leave, stumbling and grabbing onto the back of the chair before correcting himself. 'Fare thee well, lass.' He knew had said too much.

'Goodbye Cyril.' Dr Fisher was dismayed but not at all surprised by the haste of Richards's departure.

As she left Titas College for the day, and for some time afterwards, Dr Fisher couldn't really fathom out exactly what had gone on. The idea that Boyle had been framed for the theft from the benevolent fund was not an attractive one. Should he be pardoned subsequently, that meant there was always a chance he could return to the fray. Dr Fisher shuddered.

Before that, if it happened, would be her tenure. There was so much wrong with Titas College: the fiddling of the offender learning contracts and attendance records, the cheating on with Entry Level Literacy and Numeracy, the on-going cases brought to tribunal by so many members – and ex-members – of staff. Then there was the fact that, with the new staff contracts, Titas was running at a profit. Or at least it would have been, had it not been faced with such enormous legal bills. Good business, eh? On the subject of good business, was this what Titas, in the guise of Boyle and Howard, had been up to, when they had been engaging in a policy of predatory pricing over the contracts to run the prison education services? Dr Fisher had little doubt, but as the matter was still under investigation by the AFT, perhaps it wasn't something she would have to address.

Further, what she knew about was no doubt only the tip of the iceberg. Was it realistic to address any of these issues in the short-term? Perhaps not: she wasn't sure, but thought the best she could do would be to investigate and keep records of everything that in her view seemed amiss, and report it if it seemed dubious or illegal in any way. The trouble was that the first of these suspicions centred on the Students' Benevolent Fund...

She would have loved to review the staff contracts to give more generous terms and conditions, to put a stop to the falsifying of registers and cheating at exams, but that didn't make business sense, did it? On the other hand, speaking of business sense, did the college really need twenty three vice-principals? And what were they? Generic managers as far as she knew. Dr Fisher had always thought of herself as an academic, but it seemed academics were no longer what were wanted in colleges. Was this merely self-serving snobbery?

And was she just trying to garden in a storm? Dr Fisher baulked at the thought of the magnitude of a task should her position ever be made permanent.

Seventy Five

Cyril Richards knew precisely why, with the assistance of his computer-scientist niece, Lisa, he had framed Boyle for the theft of funds from the Students' Benevolent Fund. Indeed, the framing of Boyle was Richards' main reason for proposing and endowing the fund in the first place. As long as he was still alive, there could be only one big cheese in Witton-le-Cone, and that was Cyril Richards. Why else would they have made him President of the Worshipful Order of Brewers? That, and the fact that prior to the inception of Titas College, he had been in charge of the biggest employer in Witton was why he was the most respected local person.

But he was old and tired and not very well. Once people finally lose their grip, they have to bear in mind who would succeed them in their esteemed local role. Richards was going to make damned sure that person would be anyone but Boyle. The man came from Carlisle and, besides, wouldn't have known the difference between a good brewer's yeast from a packet of couscous.

Boyle inherit Richards's mantle? Urgh! Richards's jowls shuddered at the thought. Besides, nobody was going to replace Richards in his esteemed role as long as he had anything to do with it and, as such, the duty to stop this happening had therefore lain on Cyril Richards' shoulders. And if the cost was the wrongful conviction of Laurence Boyle, not to mention a few students having their grants postponed then, in his view, it was a price well worth paying. Apart from that, one also had to think of the welfare of the students. After all, had it not been for

Richards and the half a million he had donated to it to get things started, the Benevolent Fund would probably never have existed. As Dwight D. Eisenhower once said, there is no victory at bargain basement prices.

Seventy Six

Grit had missed the verdict and Boyle's health scare, but no matter. She would hear of them soon enough. And with Boyle apparently out of the way and Dr Fisher in temporary charge, she was walking on air.

But of course she knew nothing of the revelations now suspected by Dr Fisher. Heading back from Marion Villiers's house to pick George up from school, Grit wondered about whether Villiers's reasons for ending his life had any consequences of note. Were all her efforts to find out about his death for nothing? Would she have been involved with Smith if it hadn't been for her dogged curiosity to find out about Villiers? Had being found in Human Resources actually saved her job because Morrell had been afraid of what Grit found in her file? If it hadn't been for her asking about Villiers, would she have made herself just as unpopular with the other governors? Probably. Thinking that, what had looked like a shot in the dark by Villiers seemed to land so accurately on its target, Grit couldn't help smiling. It seemed his wife appreciated his sense of humour - and what a sense of humour it had turned out to be.

Pulling up near the school gates a few minutes early, she turned the engine off while continuing to muse on these thoughts, which ended up being about Smith. In spite of all she loved about him, the cozen way he seemed to act on occasion made her altogether uneasy. And that was before Helen was included in the equation. Just how might Smith have explained his "promotion" to Helen,

Grit wondered? No, there was no future for them: a shame, perhaps, but that's life.

Just as she was becoming resolute in her conclusions, her mobile rang.

'Hello Bob.'

'Is it alright to talk for a minute?'

'I'm waiting for George to come out of school, but I suppose I can give you a few moments. What is it?'

'I thought you should know. Helen's thrown me out.'

'Is it because...?'

'...She got to know about us. Yes.'

'How?'

'I'm surmising Boyle will have let the county music advisor know. I'm guessing it was because I sent an anonymous tip off about the predatory pricing to Charles Byford. He's the principal of Jaywick College. Had you heard they reported Titas to the AFT?'

'Yes, but I know you warned me something like that might happen.'

'Anyway, I'm guessing Maestro put two and two together.'

'Thank you for letting me know, Bob. If it's a question of a gaff for the night, I'm not sure...'

'Oh no, not at all. But now you come to mention it...'

'Don't know if it's a good idea; especially if I'm the reason Helen threw you out.'

'Fair enough.'

'Here comes George. I'll talk to you later.'

'Okay.'

As she hung up, Grit noticed George seemed to have more energy than usual as he ran out through the school gates, with the hood of his coat on his head and the rest of it flailing behind as ever. 'Hi Mam.' he said happily as he got into the car.

'Are you alright?'

'Yeah, I've got a new teacher. She's much nicer than Miss Roberts,'

'Have you really? I'm so happy for you.' She kissed him on the cheek. 'Now put your seatbelt on. What's her name?'

'Mrs West.'

Blimey! Grit thought.

'Mam, can I have the new DeltaTerminus for my birthday?'

'But your GammaTerminus is only a year old,'

'I know, but Zombie Expunger Three is coming out next month and it's only going to be compatible with DeltaTerminus,'

As they spoke, Grit had tried several times to start the car, but it was having none of it. She called the breakdown service with the feeling it was probably the end of the road for her old Suzuki.'

'Can I get back to you on that one?' she said, 'I think *I'll need to get myself a new car for a st...* first.

>>THE END<<

Boyle and Grit will return in "Parking by Gaslight"

Printed in Great Britain
by Amazon

42022338R00225